The
Review of
Contemporary
Fiction

o. 2
Summer 1996

ISSN: 0276-0045
ISBN: 1-56478-098-8

Editor

JOHN O'BRIEN
Illinois State University

Managing Editor

STEVEN MOORE

Senior Editor

ROBERT L. MCLAUGHLIN
Illinois State University

Associate Editors

BROOKE HORVATH
IRVING MALIN
DAVID FOSTER WALLACE

Guest Editor

PHILIP LANDON

Typesetter & Designer

SHIRLEY GEEVER

Editorial Assistants

LISA ALBAUGH
RICHARD BLANKENSHIP
CARISSA BRUSCA
REBECCA COOPER

Cover art: Nils-Aslak Valkeapää, from the jacket of his book, *Aurinko, isäni*

The Review of Contemporary Fiction is published three times a year (February, June, October) by The Review of Contemporary Fiction, Inc., a non-profit organization located at Fairchild Hall, Campus Box 4241, Illinois State University, Normal, IL 61790-4241. ISSN 0276-0045. Subscription prices are as follows:

Single volume (three issues):
  Individuals: $17.00; foreign, add $3.50;
  Institutions: $26.00; foreign, add $3.50.

DISTRIBUTION. Bookstores should send orders to:

University of Chicago Press Distribution Center, 11030 S. Langley Ave., Chicago, IL 60628. Phone 1-800-621-2736; fax (312) 660-2235.

This issue is partially supported by grants from the Finlandia Foundation Trust and the Finnish Literature Information Center.

Indexed in *American Humanities Index, International Bibliography of Periodical Literature, International Bibliography of Book Reviews, MLA Bibliography,* and *Book Review Index.* Abstracted in *Abstracts of English Studies.*

The Review of Contemporary Fiction is also available in 16mm microfilm, 35mm microfilm, and 105mm microfiche from University Microfilms International, 300 North Zeeb Road, Ann Arbor, MI 48106-1346.

THE REVIEW OF CONTEMPORARY FICTION

Future issues devoted to: Edmund White, Samuel R. Delany, Rikki Ducornet, Raymond Queneau, Josef Skvorecky, Carole Maso, Mario Vargas Llosa, Wilson Harris, Alan Burns, Curtis White, Milorad Pavić, Richard Powers, Alexander Trocchi, Ed Sanders, and postmodern Japanese fiction.

Back Issues

Back issues are still available for the following numbers of the *Review of Contemporary Fiction* ($8 each unless otherwise noted):

Individuals receive a 10% discount on orders of one issue and a 20% discount on any order of two or more issues. Postage for domestic shipments is $3.50 for the first issue and 75¢ for each additional issue. For foreign shipments, postage is $4.50 for the first issue and $1.00 for each additional issue. All orders must be paid in U.S. dollars. Send payment to:

Review of Contemporary Fiction, Chicago Distribution Center, 11030 S. Langley Avenue, Chicago, IL 60628, phone: 1-800-621-2736.

A poignant story of self-discovery from a talented new voice in fiction.

MY SISTER'S BONES explores the shifting landscape of family, friendship, and love through the eyes of a young girl possessed of a wisdom far beyond her years. Cathi Hanauer writes with the voice of a natural storyteller, capturing perfectly the pain, joy, and pressures of moving toward adulthood, and reminds us of how hurtful — and astonishing — this process can be.

Delacorte Press

Contents

Introduction

Philip Landon

This issue contains work by ten authors representing three distinct cultures that coexist in Finland: Finnish, Sámi, and Finland-Swedish. Most of the contributors are young, avant-garde writers who have not yet been introduced to English-speaking readers. The contents of the issue are drawn from works originally published between 1985 and 1992 and include short stories, excerpts from novels, and a selection from a book-length poem. Each author also kindly agreed to a short interview by mail.

It may be valuable to provide readers with a brief historical sketch of the background from which Finnish literature has emerged. The following synopsis relates primarily to literature written in the Finnish language; the Sámi and Swedish-speaking minorities would tell a different story, as will appear from the interviews with Kirsti Paltto, Lars Sund, and Nils-Aslak Valkeapää.

Historical Background

A European republic located northeast of the Baltic Sea, between Sweden and Russia, Finland was ruled for centuries by its powerful eastern and western neighbors. The country became a province of Sweden in 1155 and remained under Swedish jurisdiction until 1809, when it was ceded to Imperial Russia. After more than a hundred years as a grand duchy of the czar, Finland gained formal independence as a sovereign state in 1917.

Early Finnish independence was blighted by armed conflict: the Civil War (1917-18), the Winter War (to stop an attempted invasion by the Soviet Union, 1939-40), the Continuation War (fought in coalition with Nazi Germany, once more against the Soviet Union, 1941-44), and the Lapland War (to expel the German troops there, 1944-45).

Although Finland survived the ravages of the Second World War as an independent country, the peace terms decreed by the Allies at Yalta did little to allay the devastation of the war. Finland was ordered to pay substantial reparations and to cede extensive territories, including the populous region of eastern Karelia, to the Soviet Union. Refugees numbering 420,000, or 12 percent of the population, had to be resettled, and, without access to the reconstruction funds of the Marshall Plan, it took Finland until 1952 to pay the "war debt" in full.

This economic ordeal was followed by the formidable challenge of trying to project a credible image of neutrality during the Cold War. In accordance with a bilateral friendship treaty signed in 1948, Finland pursued a policy of cautious and principled diplomacy in all its dealings with the neighboring Soviet superstate, while simultaneously taking a separate road in domestic matters, with a commitment to democracy, free market principles, and a Swedish-style social welfare system.

Despite official assertions of nonalignment, postwar Finland was widely regarded as a semi-satellite of the Soviet Union. The country's status became particularly confusing and paradoxical in the seventies and eighties, when the embarrassment of alleged "Finlandization," or forced conciliation by the Soviet superpower, was accompanied by Finland's spectacular if short-lived "Japanization," as the one-time agrarian backwater attained unprecedented economic success. After 1989, the global recession and the collapse of lucrative trade arrangements with the Soviet Union temporarily reversed Finland's economic progress. The resulting mass unemployment and financial problems played an important part in prompting the Finns to join the European Union in 1994.

Literary Origins: The *Kalevala*

Finland's struggle for national independence was empowered by the gradual assertion of Finnish culture during the nineteenth century, which was manifested in the enhanced status of the Finnish language, initially encouraged by Russia as a means of distancing the Finns from Sweden. National institutions sprang up, including the Finnish Literature Society, founded in 1831. The emergence of a Finnish identity took place in the context of European romanticism, with its enthusiasm for indigenous national traditions, epitomized in Finland by its national epic, the *Kalevala,* compiled from the oral poetry of eastern Finnish peasants by the physician Elias Lönnrot and published in its final version in 1849. Lönnrot's sources were ancient songs passed down by generations of Finnish bardic singers; some of the material in the *Kalevala* is over a thousand years old. The verse is alliterative, incantatory, and essentially formulaic. The subjects are highly archaic, the most primitive components being pre-Christian descriptions of animistic rituals and magic. Famous passages include a Finnish creation myth, heroic military episodes, a pragmatic litany of premarital advice to young women, the tragic story of the incestuous misfit Kullervo, and sensitive, respectful apostrophes to nature and the elements. The most heroic and dramatic scenes of the *Kalevala* have inspired the Finnish arts, from the national-romantic oils and frescoes of Akseli Gallen-Kallela and the music of Sibelius to the contemporary operas of Aulis Sallinen and the verse and television scripts of the Neustadt-laureate Paavo Haavikko, one of Finland's leading poets. Following the publication of a new English translation by Keith Bosley (Oxford

Univ. Press, 1989), a British theater company has recently produced a successful dramatization of parts of the *Kalevala* as *The Singing Bones Festival*. The *Kalevala* and the massive archives of related vernacular poetry in Finnish are a key resource for scholars of the epic and of oral tradition generally.

Although the *Kalevala* almost literally spawned Finnish culture, stocking the arts with indigenous heroes and myths, and although the epic thus served as the bedrock of an entire nation's artistic tradition, its contents, of course, antedate the very notion of a nation-state. Together with its lyrical companion collection, the *Kanteletar* (1840-41), only recently available in English translation—also by Keith Bosley (Oxford Univ. Press, 1992)—the *Kalevala* provides a unique record of the rigors and charms of daily life in a premodern, preliterate setting.

Folk versus State: Aleksis Kivi's *Seven Brothers*

Another landmark in nineteenth-century Finnish literature is Aleksis Kivi's (1834-72) novel *Seitsemän veljestä* (*Seven Brothers*, 1870; English trans., 1929), a comic account of the gradual enculturation of seven young men who try to resist the prevailing civilization and indeed all manifestations of cultural discipline: literacy, religious authority, courtship rituals, and the demands of married life. In keeping with the picaresque tradition, the men, of course, ultimately renounce their carefree existence as unattached hunters and trappers and achieve respectability by accepting the morals and manners of society. What is striking about *Seven Brothers* is its informal oral idiom, with most of the text rendered in dialogue. (In fact, the novel was partly inspired by a play—Schiller's *The Robbers*.) The narrator eschews the third person and employs his gift for powerful lyrical descriptions very sparingly, effacing himself so as to give free rein to the spoken word. The boisterous exchanges serve vividly to differentiate the brothers from one another and to dramatize the conflicts among them. Together with Kivi's plays, stage adaptations of *Seven Brothers* have long been part of the repertory of the Finnish theater.

The elements of escapism and romantic nonconformism in Kivi's novel are reminiscent of both the Newgate tradition in British fiction and the scapegrace novels of Mark Twain. As in *Huckleberry Finn*, it is not the reconciliatory "social" conclusion but the transgressive element that now seems interesting in *Seven Brothers*. A Bakhtinian reading might stress the brothers' irreverent treatment of the biblical texts that the parish clerk drums into the heads of his reluctant pupils. Misapplied in the most absurd contexts by the wanton brothers, the language of social and religious authority stands fully revealed in its conventionality. While the anarchic element in his work was widely condemned in his lifetime, Kivi initiated a whole tradition of irreverent, demotic fiction in Finland.

Toward the end of the nineteenth century, social realism devoted to contemporary issues gained increasing importance in Finnish literature. The reformist playwright Minna Canth (1844-97) used the ideas of Ibsen and Darwin for political ends, defending freedom of thought and advocating social justice and the emancipation of women. Juhani Aho (1861-1921) cast a wry, affectionate eye on vernacular culture with his comic novella *Rautatie* (The Railway, 1884), a classic study of the bafflement caused by technological change.

Volter Kilpi: The Forgotten Modernist

In the early twentieth century Finnish literature developed its own idiosyncratic brand of modernism, as writers increasingly emphasized the autonomy and artistry of their craft, experimenting with new forms and stressing philosophical self-awareness. In Finland, however, formal innovation was at first more prominent in poetry than fiction. Whereas the Swedish-speaking imagist poet Edith Södergran (1892-1923), for example, is now recognized as an early modernist of international stature, leading Finnish prose writers of the same period—Joel Lehtonen (1881-1934) and F. E. Sillanpää (1888-1964; Nobel Prize, 1939)—restricted themselves to relatively conventional techniques, exploring social and historical themes.

An important exception is *Alastalon salissa* (In the Parlor of Alastalo, 1933) by Volter Kilpi (1874-1939). His monumental narrative experiment recalls the flamboyance of Joycean modernism with its exploration—and extension—of narrative possibilities. Proceeding in an unhurried, jovial manner, *Alastalon salissa* builds a minutely detailed historical portrait of the coastal community of Kustavi in the southwest of Finland during the 1860s. Originally printed in two volumes totaling over nine hundred pages, the book describes a six-hour parochial conference that culminates in the signing of an agreement to build a bark—the first three-master in the region—and an ambitious bid by the parishioners to compete for the profitable maritime trade in and beyond the Baltic. Kilpi's technical innovations reflect the growing cosmopolitanism of Finnish literature in the period between the wars. Abandoning the linear thrust of traditional narrative, Kilpi allows the story to expand freely sideways, exploring the mindscapes of the individual characters through surging interior monologues, dwelling at length on vernacular and nautical similes, then lurching off on non-naturalistic tangents to recount seafaring yarns and anecdotes. The author uses neologisms, sprawling sentences, and eccentric grammar, testing the very limits of Finnish syntax. Kilpi's language is peppered with idioms of the southwestern coastal milieu, with its Swedish families, place names, and loanwords, and its maritime tradition.

The text gradually reveals the submerged tensions between the individual characters: the resentment that the jaundiced Petter Pihlman feels toward the

men above him in the parochial pecking order and the subtle signs of defer-
ence or condescension that Herman Matsson—host and initiator of the day's
proceedings—shows toward his guests as he carefully calibrates his de-
meanor according to each man's financial clout and corresponding share in
the investment. In keeping with the extravagance of the language, epistemological verities are questioned throughout the novel: the human mind and
sensory apparatus are evoked in quirky, physical images, and the novel insists that neither the emotions nor the cerebral system is fully subject to
rational control. A maverick not fully appreciated in his day, Kilpi received
posthumous vindication in 1992, when *Alastalon salissa* was voted the most
important Finnish novel since independence in 1917.

The Hegemony of Realism

The formal rejuvenation of Finnish poetry in the postwar era, spearheaded
by the acclaimed modernists Paavo Haavikko (b. 1931) and Pentti
Saarikoski (1937-83), was never widely replicated in Finnish fiction, where
comparatively conventional narrative techniques retained their dominance.
Much of postwar Finnish literature has been preoccupied with social justice
and the question of historical destiny, and scores of books have been devoted to Finland's war-ridden past. Women writers have been perhaps less
directly concerned with military themes, although such prominent figures
as Eila Pennanen (b. 1916), Eeva Joenpelto (b. 1921), and Anu Kaipainen
(b. 1933) have also explored political conflict and won a large following in
the historical genre. Mainstream male prose writers, such as Väinö Linna
(1920-92), Paavo Rintala (b. 1930), Veijo Meri (b. 1928), and Hannu
Salama (b. 1936), have achieved some of their greatest public successes
with historical novels composed in an accessible realistic idiom.
    Tuntematon sotilas (*The Unknown Soldier*, 1954; English trans., 1957),
Väinö Linna's chronicle of the 1941-44 Continuation War between Finland and the Soviet Union, became a best-seller and an instant classic. The
book traces the fates of a few ordinary recruits, soldiers whose experience,
of course, bears little resemblance to the sanitized and ideologically tinted
accounts of the propagandist or the politician. The men's familial and re-
gional loyalties by no means fully coincide with the abstract ideas of citi-
zenship and duty to the fatherland. Each of the main characters speaks a local dialect completely different from the standard Finnish of official
communications, and nationalist propaganda and war rhetoric are openly
satirized. For the moral realist Linna, the individual soldier is more than a
mere function of his national identity or a limb on some abstract body poli-
tic. Linna developed his informal, counterofficial historical realism further
in the trilogy *Täällä Pohjantähden alla* (Here, under the Northern Star,
1959-62), which concerns the bitter Finnish Civil War and its repercussions
in the minds of later generations. Linna's habit of viewing ordinary people

in contrast and conflict with formal communities and official discourse is pivotal to Finnish fiction. It has roots in the nineteenth-century picaresque of Kivi and in the folk novel of Aho, and it set the standard for Finland's literary self-portraiture.

A major successor to Linna is Hannu Salama, whose novels explore working-class history, particularly life in the radical communities of the industrial city of Tampere. Like Linna, Salama highlights the frailty of abstract ideals in the face of social hardship and violence, enlivening the historical scene with full-blooded characters and the harsh but warm music of the blue-collar vernacular. His controversial novel *Juhannustanssit* (The Midsummer Dance, 1964) outraged religious sensibilities and led to the bizarre and anachronistic spectacle of his criminal prosecution for blasphemy. Salama was convicted but eventually pardoned by presidential decree. *Siinä näkijä missä tekijä* (Where There's a Crime There's a Witness, 1972) provoked outrage in a different quarter with its raw, inglorious account of the Communist resistance movement in Tampere during the Second World War.

Historical themes, particularly the events of the Winter War of 1939, have remained prominent in Finnish culture during the final decades of the century. The eighties saw a number of high-profile reenactments of World War II—a blockbuster film in 1989 by Pekka Parikka, based on a best-selling novel by Antti Tuuri (b. 1944), and *The Road to the Winter War* (1989), a successful play by the legal scholar and historian Heikki Ylikangas—all in addition to frequent dramatizations of *The Unknown Soldier,* regular television screenings of Edwin Laine's classic 1955 film based on Linna's novel, and a popular remake of the same film, directed by Rauni Mollberg in 1985.

Aside from the collective trauma of war and civil war, a second enduring concern of recent Finnish fiction is the upheaval caused by urbanization and industrialization. Here too literature has simultaneously mirrored historical events and has served as a kind of mechanism of self-orientation. In Finland the transformation into an industrial and urban society occurred later and more quickly than in many other European countries. The urban population has grown at breakneck pace during the past few decades, from a mere 10 percent in 1900 to 32 percent in 1950 and 64 percent in 1993. This migration to the cities caused massive cultural disruption. Modern Finland is still a country of half-built suburbs and urban alienation. However self-consciously, many Finns feel a nostalgic yearning for life close to nature, and the literary historian Kai Laitinen's description of Finnish novels in the nineteenth century and early twentieth century applies equally to the bulk of postwar fiction: "The traditional Finnish novel is close to nature. Nature features in the role of a friend or an enemy or both." (All of the authors in this issue were asked to respond to this statement.) Meditative rural isolation and agrarian values are treasured in a country where most people's grandparents once lived off the land—witness the enormous popularity of the deliberately unsophisticated ruralism of such comic authors as Veikko

Huovinen (b. 1927) and, more recently, Arto Paasilinna (b. 1942).

Both military prose and rural fiction have achieved broad popular appeal through loyalty to an unpretentious vernacular aesthetic. The prize-winning novelist Antti Tuuri has continued to mine the accessible, realist model with his vigorous, graphic novels set in contemporary Ostrobothnia and at the eastern front.

New Finnish Fiction

A collective need for stability and coherence, connected with the protracted process of national healing, may help explain the comparative shortage of experimentation in Finnish fiction, as well as the neglect suffered by innovators like Kilpi. On the other hand, the overwhelming commitment to authenticity has itself spawned innovation, and it would be inaccurate to characterize Finnish literature as completely insular and ingrown. Beckett was discovered early on by the Helsinki stage, and the poet Pentti Saarikoski's acclaimed translations of *Ulysses* and *The Catcher in the Rye* are monuments of cultural receptiveness. Even more important may have been the 1962 translation of Henry Miller's *Tropic of Cancer,* which inspired Saarikoski's own works of free-associative confession. Miller's profane lyricism and self-consciously American ethos of "telling it like it is" had affinities with the anti-aesthetic agenda of the Finnish realists, with their suspicion of elitist culture and literariness. Miller's influence was huge in the 1960s and beyond: in the 1970s the Finnish-Swedish Henrik Tikkanen (1924-84) continued the tradition, pushing authenticity to the limit with his visceral autobiographies. The confessional format could easily have degenerated into a mannerism, but it has helped to overturn conventions and has inspired interesting work. In the 1980s the controversial theater director and author Jouko Turkka (b. 1942) ventured into the realms of pure anxiety with his obsessive, grimly humorous tales of urban mishap and with autobiographical pieces where masochistic self-scrutiny blends with iconoclastic fury. Anja Kauranen (b. 1954) and others have also continued to exploit the spontaneous autobiographical mode, violating taboos in a continuing quest for unflinching authenticity.

The authors represented in this issue have in many ways departed from the above-described traditions. In a sense the eighties and early nineties saw the emergence of the first genuine postwar generation of authors whose works are neither overtly sociopolitical nor curbed by the egalitarian ideal of writing for the people. The autobiographical mode persists, but the aesthetic of relentless candor appears to be on the wane, as self-consciousness and parody dislodge the traditional strictures of realism and confession. What has emerged is a diverse generation of highly original writers preoccupied with the present moment and perhaps more interested in global and scientific issues than in national history. This is not to say that an absolute break has occurred, or that, say, the realist tradition has been surpassed by more sophisticated current writers. On the contrary, the present generation is conscious of its good fortune in having inherited a broad canon of important fiction, rich in peculiarly Finnish virtues: a healthy distrust of domestic and foreign authority and an informed, unromanticized attitude toward nature and political reality. In the hands of today's well-traveled, multilingual generation, which is grappling with a new set of concerns, the inherited principles have been transformed, but not beyond recognition.

Petter Sairanen (b. 1958), one of the youngest contributors, is in some ways also the most old-fashioned. He continues the conventional descriptive tradition, marveling at nature, observing human foibles, and lamenting the rootlessness of urban culture. He combines poetry and narrative and brings to his ecological crusade a comic warmth and light touch. Sairanen's style harkens back to Kivi and Aho and is entirely free of the guilty earnestness that occasionally mars the political classics of postwar realism. Kari Kontio (b. 1956) shares Sairanen's respect for Finnish tradition but is also perfectly at home in the urban jungle. In the novel excerpted here nature figures as a nostalgic, temporary retreat, not as a viable repository of value. Kontio's outrageous narrator is more of a Baron Münchhausen than a Henry Miller, and his sulphurously explicit self-assessments both extend and parody the Finnish ethos of authenticity.

The critical recognition won by Kirsti Paltto (b. 1947) reflects the vigor of Sámi culture and the renewed respect for diversity in the Finnish literary landscape. Original in form and ambitious in scope, her fiction has no need for provocative effects. It explores the sense of community among the Sámi people, who view the world rather differently than their urbanized peers. Local instead of national history is also the subject of Lars Sund's (b. 1953) quirky *Colorado Avenue,* a novel about Swedish-speaking Ostrobothnian immigrants to the United States at the turn of the century. Sund carries no political baggage, and he makes light of narrative conventions, using a deliberate playfulness in reconstructing the lives of his own ancestors. He acknowledges the influence of Rushdie and the South American magic realists and continues the cosmopolitan tradition in Finland-Swedish writing.

Raija Siekkinen (b. 1953) is another writer who has absorbed foreign influences and who uses international settings. She translates from the French and her polished short stories pay homage to Maupassant and Chekhov. Siekkinen has recently been moving toward more oblique forms, but her innovations are tactful and unobtrusive; experiment is never an end in itself. The same applies to Leena Krohn (b. 1947), who also explores the short story form without deviating from an ideal of clarity. Krohn cites the influence of Italo Calvino and Don DeLillo, for example, and has a deep interest in science, which she approaches as an agnostic humanist. Erudition and intelligence are apparent in all her work, but she wears her learning lightly. She has also written successfully for children.

Hans Selo (b. 1945), Mariaana Jäntti (b. 1953), and Markku Eskelinen (b. 1959) have engaged in much more daring experiments. Selo's swirling, baroque prose, which first appeared in 1970, has prompted comparisons with the French nouveau roman. The author himself claims kinship with Kilpi and Joyce. Such comparisons may obscure as much as they reveal. To his credit, Selo is self-taught in more than one sense of the term. His courage to go it alone has produced two freshly inventive books where an idiosyncratic religious philosophy is energized by a delight in the visible world and the Finnish language. His most important mentors are the classical and Enlightenment philosophers. Selo views human existence as part of an evolving cosmic process, and his writing reflects this sense of immersion without surrendering precision or the pleasure of description. Jäntti also has an international pedigree and writes in an epistemologically self-conscious idiom. Her only novel to date, *Amorfiaana* (1986), is freewheeling, sensual, porridgy—and amorphously different. Not always sympathetic to experimental newcomers, Finnish critics rose to the occasion, welcoming her break with mimetic tradition. Indeed, Jäntti makes language visible, detaching it from conventional referential functions and using it instead to celebrate the body, the unconscious, and atavistic drives. Jäntti is one of very few Finnish writers whose work has affinities with poststructuralism, particularly the feminist project of dismantling binary oppositions. Eskelinen has more openly nailed his colors to the mast of postmodernism and is perhaps the only author in this issue who is in complete revolt against Finnish traditions. He is clearly influenced by Borges and Coover, although he takes his narrative experiments in a more explicitly political direction, exploring the postindustrial and postlocal universe of information technology, drugs, crossfrontier pollution, and screen entertainment. His fiction is a jump cut medley of film clips, computer files, and antiauthoritarian desecration, all patched together out of bite-sized fragments carefully desynchronized to short-circuit unself-conscious interpretation.

The musician, poet, and artist Nils-Aslak Valkeapää (b. 1943) has reached a wider audience than any of the above, most spectacularly in 1994, when he performed a Sámi chant at the opening ceremony of the Winter Olympics in Lillehammer, Norway. He travels extensively, from the United States to Japan, and has become a cultural emissary for his people. His work builds on ancient animistic and shamanic traditions but also makes use of modern techniques. For example, his acclaimed *Bird Symphony* is composed entirely of recorded natural sounds, and his chants have been sampled for the latest Mike Oldfield CD. His contributions to this issue are the cover art and selections from *Beaivi, áhčážan* (The Sun, My Father), a visual-verbal epic that won the Literature Prize of the Nordic Council. With great flair, Valkeapää bears witness to the history of his people as he makes his own lyrical journey, triumphantly perpetuating the language of the northernmost people of Europe.

It goes without saying that the present selection is subjective and limited in scope. The cost of concentrating on a fresh group of writers hitherto unknown in America has been the exclusion of internationally recognized figures, such as the award-winning Finland-Swedish novelist and poet Bo Carpelan (*Axel,* trans. David McDuff [Carcanet, 1989]) and the people's humorist Arto Paasilinna (*The Year of the Hare,* trans. Herbert Lomas [Peter Owen, 1995]), who has a following in France. Absent also is the talented young artist and short story writer Rosa Liksom, whose *One Night Stands* (trans. Anselm Hollo [Serpent's Tail, 1993]) was enthusiastically reviewed in Britain and America (see *RCF,* fall 1994, 217). The regret I feel at not being able to include more writers in this issue testifies to the diversity and vigor of contemporary Finnish writing. At the tail end of a century in which the country endured more than its fair share of conflict and tension, accompanied by accelerated social and technological change, contemporary Finland faces the future with an economy on the mend, a culture in turmoil, and a literature in full bloom.

Acknowledgments

Thanks are due to the Finlandia Foundation Trust for its generous support and to the Finnish Literature Information Center and its staff for their assistance and support. The authors graciously agreed to participate without a fee, and I am especially grateful for their inspiring cooperation at the interview stage. John Acher, Markku Eskelinen, Michael Garner, Antti Kähärä, Angela Landon, Jussi Lehtonen, Outi Mäkinen, and Ilmo Massa supplied invaluable information and sources, and Antony Landon made many improvements to the introduction. Marina Luttrell helped me enormously at all stages and read the entire manuscript several times. Very special thanks go to the translators—Ritva Poom, David McDuff, Lars Nordström, Harald Gaski, Ralph Salisbury—and particularly Richard Impola, who stepped into the breach at a critical time and supplied excellent translations on very short notice.

The works included here originally appeared in Finnish, Sámi, and Swedish as follows:

Markku Eskelinen. Excerpt from *Nonstop*. Helsinki: WSOY, 1988.

Mariaana Jäntti. Excerpt from *Amorfiaana*. Jyväskylä: Gummerus, 1986.

Kari Kontio. Excerpt from *Lajinsa viimeinen*. Helsinki: Tammi, 1992.

Leena Krohn. "Lucilia illustris," from *Matemaattisia olioita*. Helsinki: WSOY, 1992.

Kirsti Paltto. Excerpt from *Guhtoset Dearvan min bohccot*. Guovdageaidnu: Dat Os, 1987. Published in Finnish as *Voijaa minum poroni* (trans. Eino Kuokkanen, Oulu: Pohjoinen, 1986); the excerpt published here was translated from the Finnish.

Petter Sairanen. Excerpt from *Sähköllä valaistu talo*. Helsinki: Art House, 1989.

Hans Selo. Excerpt from *Pilvihipiäinen*. Helsinki: Odessa, 1985.

Raija Siekkinen. "Musta aurinko," from *Kuinka rakkaus syntyy*. Helsinki: Otava, 1991.

Lars Sund. Excerpt from *Colorado Avenue*. Helsinki: Söderström, 1991.

Nils-Aslak Valkeapää. Poem 558 from *Beaivi, áhčážan*. Vaasa: Dat Os, 1989.

OUTI ESKELINEN

Markku Eskelinen

Markku Eskelinen (b. 1959) has published experimental novels, journalism, horror stories, and critical essays. Easily the most iconoclastic figure on the Finnish literary scene, he moves effortlessly between the TV studio, the theater, and the visual arts and has campaigned to bring Finnish culture into the postmodern era. Eskelinen's aggressive novels, no less than his brutal pronouncements on Finnish literature, have provoked some hostile responses. More sympathetic critics have welcomed Eskelinen's thematic seriousness and technical originality. The philosopher Esa Saarinen compared Eskelinen's first novel, *Nonstop* (from which the following extract is taken) to the apocalyptic fiction of George Orwell and Martin Amis and praised its evocation of a collapsing consumer society where the coercive powers of the state and the electronic media verge on the totalitarian. Eskelinen's settings are deliberately unspecified, and his concerns are global. The spare style and the chilling social prophecy recall Paul Auster's dystopian novel *In the Country of Last Things,* while the scrambled, distantly Cooverian structure replicates the screens and networks that control contemporary minds. Eskelinen bravely takes on a whole catalogue of unmanageable contemporary conundrums: terrorism, gender roles, the status of art and literature, environmental crisis, and the possibility of subversion. The material seems shallow and easy to digest, and any depth lies in the problematic relationship between the individual elements. Unlike the theory-spinning postmodern intelligentsia, Eskelinen lays no claim to revisionary leverage. Nihilism is rife among the stereotypical personae in his novels, from fashionable intellectuals, outrageous artists, and ruthless terrorists to the obligatory nasties of the secret police. Meanwhile, the impending social and environmental nightmare remains simultaneously unreal and imminent. The studied flippancy of Eskelinen's work belies the depth of his moral commitment. He is more than just a clever entertainer; he responds bravely to the intimidating complexity of the modern world.

Essays: *Jälkisanat: Sianhoito-opas* (Afterwords: A Guide to Pig-Keeping, with Jyrki Lehtola, 1987). Novels: *Nonstop* (1988), *Semtext* (1990). Forthcoming: *Interface* (1996).

Interview

PHILIP LANDON: Can you name any shared characteristics of contemporary Finnish fiction? Do you identify with any of your international or domestic contemporaries?

MARKKU ESKELINEN: Unfortunately, I am able to describe contemporary Finnish literature because I began my career by ridiculing and analyzing it, that is, by investigating the reasons behind the chronic shortage of innovation, the lack of heterogeneity and erudition, the hegemony of realism and homespun modernism, the dominance of an ossified national tradition, and the refusal to engage in dialogue with other forms of art. So, in Finland, I have only domesticated contemporaries. As for the international scene and the anxiety of influence, I will continue to follow my basic instinct: edify, don't identify. Name-dropping would have been fun, though.

PL: How would you situate fiction in general and your own work in particular in relation to mass culture and the mass media?

ME: My relationship with mass culture and the mass media is a simple one: I use what I need. I am convinced that the different military, information, and entertainment technologies that already exist or are presently under development will transform both audiences' literary expectations and the very concept of literature. For example, I believe that the asymmetrically forking paths of Borges and Coover can hardly seem contrived if you happen to be computer literate. In the context of Finnish literature my own output to date (the trilogy *Nonstop*, *Semtext*, and *Interface*) represents the transition from Gutenbergian bookbinding to digital text networks. I sometimes find myself contemplating media centers: Babelsberg, Hollywood, the virtual entertainment arcades of Tokyo. This also gives me cause to consider the nationalities of mass culture.

PL: Kai Laitinen has written, "The traditional Finnish novel is close to nature. Nature features in the role of a friend or an enemy or both." Can we read your work as part of this tradition? Does nature require a new approach from writers?

ME: To the first question: maybe you can, but I think you should not. To the second one: maybe it does, but writers will be writers.

PL: From the *Kalevala* to postwar fiction, much of Finnish literature has been intimately bound up with the question of national identity. Do you see yourself as a member of a more international generation?

ME: We should rather be talking about my *de*generation. Everything you say can be used as identity against you. I don't really believe in identities, be they "national" or "international" or social or sexual; they're all just as trite, ludicrous, limited, and harmful as the notion of two genders. This, of course, is a perspective, a simplification, and a privilege, nurtured by the partially attained ideals of the Scandinavian welfare state.

PL: Contemporary Finnish writers frequently use autobiographical and mock-autobiographical forms. Why?

ME: Packaged in a form favored by the publishers, such fiction combines the infantile ideas about truth, authenticity, and honesty that are shared by untalented writers and a voyeuristic audience. We are not seeing reassessments of genre, skillful parodies, nor autobioheterothanatographies, and I can conclude only that writers are still trying to (re)invent some sort of a new journalism. But they end up producing basket case histories.

PL: Specific local references are scarce in your work. Do you consciously write postlocal fiction?

ME: Yes. I am more interested in places that are not places than in places that are. Similarly, I am more curious about the connections, relative speeds, networks, and overlaps between places than I am about homogeneous places. Vanishing points and heterogeneous, mnemonic, and bodily places are a different matter altogether.

PL: Your novels recycle various elements of popular culture, including images of screen violence. What is your response to the debate surrounding the American film industry's obsession with violence?

ME: Utter boredom. Because my first memories are screen memories. I am hysterically opposed to all obsessions. In my texts violence is layered very differently indeed from the way it is in most mass entertainment. Moreover, violence that has been made invisible also circulates in my books. We are not in Dallas anymore. We are in Panama or Bosnia.

PL: The technology of power is a prominent concern in your work. Your books can seem rather dystopian. When it comes to the possibility of political freedom, are you a nihilist?

ME: I am as far from a nihilist as a samurai is from a sadomasochist. My novels inhabit a space between George and Henry Lee Lucas, between star wars and serial murders. In this gray area certain phenomena are developing and are being developed that may turn out to have fatal consequences for any system that swears in the name of political freedom. Gene technology, anonymous environmental catastrophes, affordable weapons of mass destruction, and the virtual reality that is wrapping itself around the senses will destroy the notion of the (political) subject far more radically, rapidly, and irreversibly than any philosophical skepticism—to name one of the historical contexts that interest me.

PL: As part of your campaign to transform Finnish fiction, you have discarded linear narrative in favor of a fragmentary, "unmasterable" form. Do you see no strengths in the traditional realist method, which can be used, for instance, to develop broad historical contexts?

ME: I have left traditional realism to those who are incapable of anything else. Your sense of "unmasterability" probably results from the fact that my texts constitute an interlaced series of gender- and technology-related supplements. Each fragment is its own unidentical twin, not just a piece in some boring jigsaw puzzle.

From Nonstop, or Missing in Fiction
A Synoptic Margin to a Trilogy

I

2

Obviously, everything is fiction. But you believe some stories and not others. That is why you are here, and that is where we can begin. We have to start from what we have in fact already done. Does that require a comma? Let's leave it open then. Of course a story can be altered as it unfolds. You can generate random numbers mechanically, if you wish. No, I don't believe in coincidences; I believe in accidents. Let's wipe this out. Trust me, this no longer exists. They won't see this. And even if they did, it would not affect the way they'll read the rest. I don't like them either. No, I don't think so.

II

3

I was being shown around.

"Top floor. Sea view. Water bed in the bedroom, Dali reproductions, and state-of-the-art audiovisual equipment in the living room; dehydrated food for six months in the kitchen, in case there's a catastrophe."

"I guess you planned all this for yourself."

"Maybe I did. These days I can afford to prepare for all sorts of surprises and coincidences and accidents. Freedom is a great place. You should visit sometime."

Ruffling my pubic hair for good-bye: "Don't forget what we said. They're prepared to do anything."

The moment the door slammed shut I fell asleep.

4

"Once more. At least."

"Fuck. I'm too tired."

"OK, OK. Let's take a break. With you guys this is like doing brain surgery with a wooden knife."

"You didn't have to come back."

"It was because of amateurs like you that I quit in the first place. You're too stupid even to be simple, every one of you. You don't have the slightest grasp of your roles even."

"Maybe the director's to blame. Let's hire someone else."

"New actors rather. I've got a perfect right to use outsiders if I prefer. You have to get yourselves new roles if you want to go on with this. Let's say an avant-garde artist turned businessman, a burned-out police officer responsible for internal security, a writer for whom literature is an abused orphan, an outlaw immersed in videos, and an interviewer whose strength lies in mediocrity. Any questions?"

"But these have nothing to do with the whole thing!"

"From now on they do. You're allowed to improvise. And by all means keep changing the mannerisms. They're as arbitrary as everything else."

"Excuse me, there's someone in the lobby who wants to talk to you."

"Throw whoever it is out. Haven't I been clear about this?"

"You do it. This one is pretty big."

"I wonder what it is you lift weights for. Or do you just use steroids? Let them in then."

"We haven't met before. My name is John Miller, and I'm doing an interview."

"Not with me you aren't. I can't even be bothered to interview myself."

"It's a book really, not an ordinary interview. Everyone is given a completely free hand. No censorship. Just what you really want to say. I want to do an honest documentary about the No Point group."

"That's just a name that was tagged onto us some time ago. Moreover, we've already said that we've got nothing to say."

"We could talk about that, too. Especially now that you've come back."

"What I'm doing isn't really a comeback. Or perhaps it is—it's my comeback to the stone age."

"Your *what*?"

"First night is two months from now. We'll see then, I suppose."

"I've sketched out a suitable foreword. I can leave it for you to read or correct or whatever."

"Whatever. Wait a second. This thing, is it just a personal problem of yours, or is someone else involved, publishers for instance?"

"You'll find the publisher's number inside that foreword I've written. They were keen as hell, so money shouldn't be a problem."

"Remains to be seen. Taking care of your brain chemistry is getting more and more expensive. Have you been in touch with the others?"

"They're a bit hard to get hold of."

"Tell me what they think sometime. Now I'd better get back to teaching what can't be taught."

III

5

One of them was said to be involved in business transactions that wouldn't hold up under scrutiny. There were all sorts of rumors, but nothing illegal was ever discovered. Interviews were almost impossible to get; the few that were obtained all followed the same pattern—I confess to all the charges; we've been among the leading drug dealers in the capital for some time; the arms trade is of course one of the most profitable and fascinating market phenomena this decade; we now control the entire black market for pornographic videos. Some saw the present activities as a logical extension of a previous career in art; in any case, it was well known that many people were eager to get this "artist" out of the way. At first I met with almost no response. I described and redescribed the idea behind my book. Even the foreword I'd composed got chucked straight into a drawer.

"Do you think unamputated hands can be free?"

"I guess I do, why do you ask?"

"I might have some interesting material for your book, but I have one condition. The manuscript has to be made available to everyone or no one at all. It must not be read unless it's published. Do you understand?"

"I understand. Everything's already been arranged. Look, there won't be any problems, I assure you. I'm just sick and tired of repeating it over and over again."

"Understanding might mean something different to you from what it means to me, or us. Let me turn on the video. For clarity's sake, I thought I'd introduce you to my bodyguard."

A bodybuilder with an unattractive face was seen destroying a hotel room with frightening efficiency.

"I met George in prison, in the art therapy group. I soon found better use for his talent. When he was released I got him a job and a place to live. These days he handles my security and shoots videos in his free time. He's doing pretty well for himself."

"Impressive."

"It's easy to get the wrong impression of George, especially from the videos. You see, they don't show the fact that his IQ is over 150. A lot higher than yours, for example, I'd imagine."

"Imagine away."

"What?"

"Nothing."

"This is one of my greatest favorites. I asked George to do a documentary on his own life, and he brought me this. The policeman is authentic, by the way; I don't remember what club it was where George picked him up. This gives you a pretty clear idea of what it is like when one has free hands but the other doesn't. The handcuffs are probably authentic too; they must have acquired a certain sentimental value by now."

The tape came to the end. I wanted something to drink. My host poured slowly and stared me in the eyes.

"I've got the sound version too, but that can wait until next time. Many of my friends only come here for the videos. You'll have to come too, if you still want that interview."

"Of course I do."

"Would you like to watch something right away? I've got everything here. Documentaries filmed in secret, docudramas, advertising, porn and rock videos, plays on tape, art films, and other rubbish. And combinations of all the above, as well as autobiographical clips by lunatics of various kinds. There have been a few attempted burglaries. Pathetic twits. As though I didn't have backup."

"I heard Naked Truth has put out a new video?"

"Well heard. This time they aren't completely naked. The guys wear condoms. I guess that won't stop a scandal from blowing up, although there's no reason really, 'cause the new arrangement guarantees that the sucking audience doesn't catch anything. The guys were a bit scared of being bitten, though."

"How much have you made through the band?"

"Exactly as much as the bastards themselves. We have more solidarity than anyone. I don't think your question was very good."

"You mean money can't be discussed?"

"No, but if you're more cynical than the cynics, you might cease to be cynical. One more thing: always call beforehand when you come. The previous interviewer had a nasty little accident. Do you want some paper towels?"

6

"So let's hear about it."

"The idiot's insane. I can read you some."

"Don't bother."

"How are the novels?"

"Which ones?"

"Well, for example the one that was to be composed by using hidden microphones and cameras."

"We're already recording. Day and night."

"I wonder whether anyone listens to us anymore, except us?"

"I doubt it. After all, we know how to speak."

"When will you all come around and see us?"

"Soon. We just need to finish a job for someone."

7

The writers were so supercilious it was disgusting. They preferred to ask their own questions rather than answer mine and never gave me more than half an hour of their time. I primed myself meticulously, but it didn't help at all. They wouldn't answer a single question properly. I gave them a tape recorder, in case they'd like to dictate some of their flitting "synopses" ("stories that just come and go like everything else") or answer my pages and pages of questions. Later, browsing through my prospectus, I discovered that they were giving a series of lectures —"The Death, Euthanasia, and Suicide of Literature." I decided to attend and see if I'd get a chance to get on with the interview.

8

I was summoned to the office. This was unusual.

"How are the interviews coming along?"

"They were a bit nervous at first, but things are picking up now. They'll soon talk all right."

"Have you already met all the members of the group?"

"Everyone except E, who seems a bit elusive."

"In fact it happens to be E we're mainly interested in. A little tête-à-tête with the party in question might even be in order. We could refresh some old memories. Can you arrange it?"

"I guess so."

"We're in a hurry. Have you asked the others about E?"

"They only talk about themselves, unless you manage to distract them and lead them on."

"Well fucking lead them on then. You don't get paid for listening to their arty bullshit. We've heard plenty of that before, in court and elsewhere. This time we're going to put them away."

"I'll do what I can."

"Not enough. I don't have to remind you of our shared interests, do I?"

"There was no need last time either."

"It only did you good, didn't it. And we can always move on to better tricks if we like."

IV

9

"Now we've got no one who can cope with this situation. Shit, why suicide, and why just now?"

"Was it suicide?"

"You know just as well as I do."

"Anyway, it doesn't matter now."

"No, it doesn't, but the memos on that Dictaphone might be useful. Why don't you have a listen through? I don't have time."

"Are you saying you can't handle this on your own?"

"Not anymore. This is no longer a tiny side issue. And you'd better watch your balls, too, if that bitch gets the chance to publish what she knows."

"It's your job to prevent it."

"And it's your job to decide how far we can afford to go."

"You know all right. There aren't many ways to bury information."

"Of course not, but you have to find it first. Jesus, we can't just do anything we want."

"As far as I've understood, that is exactly what you've been doing up to now. Well OK, OK, I'll have a listen to the memo and decide what we'll do next. Meanwhile, you'll have to stretch your authority as far as you can."

"How about the press?"

"That won't be a problem. No one will publish rumors, especially if you announce that she's wanted for murder. Pin a couple of unsolved cases on her. That should smooth things over."

10

I felt perfectly calm when I woke up. I moved around the rooms quietly and soon got used to them. I appropriated the space as I had done in prison. I did Zen exercises in the bedroom and watched videos in the living room. What little thinking I did concerned the proportions of the rooms, although no concept I could think of seemed pertinent to my present circumstances; I couldn't apprehend them through any dialectic, not in terms of the conscious and the unconscious, certainly not in terms of a hermeneutic circle, or inside and outside, or the self and the world; there was always *différance* of course, but. I stopped meditating about my state of being.

11

Lawyers who specialize in the most appalling crimes, surgeons who want to chop their patients into one-pound chunks, architects who want the houses they designed blown up. I am an expert in teasing out all the petty shitty bitterness in people. You wouldn't believe what resentment plagues the minds of people who are successful. Or not all of them, but the ones who are still alive enough to register. People who are in the wrong profession because no profession is right for them. They do their work well, and take good care of their relationships too, but, underneath it all, they are angry as hell. Never enough to change their lives, they know that as well as I do. But if I want a new face, they'll arrange it for me in secret. If I was hunted for murder they'd hide me, not out of friendship or indifference, but as an amusing diversion for themselves. How they'd relish a chance to mail hostages' toes to family members or officials. I'm almost fond of them—if it weren't for them, I might never have thought of setting up the Crisis Center.

12

We get all types here. Informers who want to betray movements that haven't even started; starving artists who want to know more about people; rebels who think there's something romantically blasphemous about transgressing boundaries and who think they can take their polo-necked nihilism farthest by serving us. Some have, of course, been useful, but only one in fifty, if that. Twenty years ago we mainly hired sociologists, and ten years ago we concentrated on psychoanalysts; nowadays it tends mainly to be art theorists.

Personally, I particularly enjoy listening to paranoiacs because they often imagine and thus provide rudimentary plans for extremely effective control techniques. A wonderful example was the idea of recruiting a few ambulance drivers, doctors, and nurses to hinder or slow down the medical care given to accident victims who belong to the political opposition and are therefore potentially dangerous. Up to now, our experience has been purely positive.

13

Sometimes I spent hours just staring at the sea. Compared to the white wall, the sea was more interesting, albeit just as meaningless. Later, for lack of anything better to think of, I pondered whether the Zen tradition could be divided into a centric and a differential half, depending whether the object *sous rature* was the sea or a wall. I recalled how, even as a child, I had been annoyed by pretentious talk about symbolism in films and literature.

14

Our old song was played on the radio. "Sudden Death." The band was new, though—D's latest discovery and brainchild, Naked Truth. The whole thing was so carefully calculated and financed that you couldn't help liking it. The band consisted of six members, three women and three men, all former porn stars. In this new project, inducing a sense of inferiority and humiliating the audience was apparently an even higher priority than making a profit. This was why the band performed naked and gave concerts that were essentially a combination of appalling rock clichés and peep show. During the acts the music came from a tape. To avoid prosecution, the band was marketed as a theater and performance group. So far, they had won all their lawsuits.

15

Which tapes upset me most? I guess it was the ones where you had to listen to the sound to get even a vague idea of what was going on. I wondered whether they had deliberately been shot so messily that you couldn't recognize the persons with any certainty—not with legal certainty, at least. The cover of the tape would typically promise a "Part 2" which was never available anywhere. A few little scraps of a synopsis only complicated matters.

16

The No Point group came into existence after its founding members had all run into difficulties because of their talents, and had "decided to join forces, or more to no point, to combine their respective culs-de-sac." Members of the group would participate in each other's projects, while simultaneously pursuing private creative work, except for the writers, who always worked in pairs. According to E, the purpose of this arrangement was to curtail the most dangerous consequences of expending energy on individual projects. Not a single member has been willing to clarify this statement, so we just have to make of it what we can.

V

17

It makes no difference what artists do. No one is interested in them any-more. I mean, no one is interested in works where something important has been grasped. I often went to the theater, for example, and was greatly in-spired by the best shows. I often thought of myself as a member of the same profession who just happened to have better equipment. It has been said that art leads us to places we could never reach without it. While I have dictated this memo I have become more and more convinced of this. Soon we will be there. Art will have done its duty, and it will be our turn.

18   ·

He claimed to be whole inside and complained that speaking shattered that whole. He blamed his teeth, but the attempt to tear them out had evidently not been very successful.

19

A large part of our lectures on the death of literature has nothing to do with the death of literature. Despite and because of this fact, you have all been given a group of texts that present radically incongruous views of language and literature. For purely pedagogical reasons, it is important that you ap-preciate their utter meaninglessness. We shall piss right in your eyes until you open them. At least until you open them.

20

In my dreams I often see children, lots of children, who are behaving in a violent fashion. Restrained, careful and patient, they don't run amok or anything, but seem to know exactly what they are doing. I wake up feeling confused, but during the dream I'm definitely on their side. Sometimes the feeling of uncertainty is so intolerable that I have to check to see what it was I was watching before I fell asleep.

21

Members of the No Point group referred to themselves with one-letter codes. Because this book is not meant for readers who don't know their "real names"—a concept they brought into question in everything they did—we may begin with the following summary: No Point consisted of writers A and B, theater director C, rock musician and video producer D, and the environmental artist E.

22

When drafting plans, it is important never to think of the law or its spirit; one must not even think of received custom. On the contrary, one must, first and foremost, consider how far one can possibly stretch one's prerogative in order to manage the contingency at hand. You must meticulously calculate how far you can go without being prosecuted. When so doing, you can gain much from the experience of officials dismissed for misconduct and from the insights of exceptionally intelligent criminals. One might well consider commissioning the latter to carry out particularly hazardous special tasks. I have compiled a list of potentially suitable persons. With one exception, they all have at least two homicides on their record. For them, murder is merely an intellectual challenge, a twist in the plot; they don't ask "Why?" but "What or who next?"

23

It is difficult to determine what sort of time we are moving in. Do the videos contain previous occurrences or D's imaginary projections and analyses of the future, or does everything take place in real time? The last alternative would never have crossed my mind but for the fact that I'm almost certain I saw an image of myself watching videos on one of the screens.

24

I wanted to find out exactly how people lived. I had no particular scruples
about this because information about people's so-called private lives was
already being systematically gathered and gathered to much worse ends—I
decided that the only way of resisting the process was to collect information
myself. In practice, the only difference between me and others who were
practicing surveillance was that I had a better idea of what I wanted to see
and of when and where to position the cameras and microphones. Surely it's
not my fault that I'm not an unimaginative academic, up and coming or
down and out. And I didn't even publish my data, so it's no use comparing
me to sociologists or any of the other frigging snitchers. First I mapped
out the remaining dignified modes of existence and then recorded their final
entrapment and destruction. Then I focused on what has replaced them.

25

There are seven children, four boys and three girls. They seem to be playing
a complicated game, the rules of which are difficult, or, in all honesty, impossible to determine on the basis of the silent video, especially since the
tape seems to have been treated in some way, digitally manipulated or
something, unless it is the events themselves that create this impression. The
game seems to have two centers—a computer with a monitor, and an adult
who is tied to a chair. During the course of the game, the children subject
the adult to various kinds of violence—blows, kicks, bites, excretions. They
appear to be scoring points. Later they begin cutting at the adult with knives.
Yet every now and then the children seem to wish to free the victim, whom
they partially untie, ungag, and address with perfectly friendly gestures. The
tape ends before the game does; the last shot shows one of the children preparing to pour a boiling liquid over the adult, who has fainted in the chair.
At this point the adult has no clothes on, but the tape is so fuzzy that it is
impossible to determine the person's gender.

26

The simplest way of outlining the career of the No Point group seems to be
to proceed in the chronological order of the court cases. They were first
prosecuted for their art in connection with the Living Dead Exhibition.
Armed with camcorders, they had recorded the way passersby reacted when

confronted with seven well-known deceased persons, who had been stolen from the mortuary or exhumed the night before and displayed in the form of installations at various central locations. Members of the group admitted no more than having received forewarning of the events; they got away with a small fine.

27

I watched videos more often than television. Since there were several monitors, I was able to follow several programs simultaneously—say, the TV news, Antonioni films, and material recorded by D. The different kinds of material gradually began to influence one another and to blend together, without ever, however, forming a coherent whole. This happened even though I remained almost consistently capable of identifying and placing a clip within a matter of seconds of its commencement. It was harder to be sure how the different strands in the flow of images interacted and influenced interpretation. At the next stage I found myself having dreams, sometimes even in the middle of a viewing session, which bore a striking resemblance to D's videos. The boundary between sleep and wakefulness was still clear and it didn't occur to me to be frightened; I allowed the different images to mingle because I knew I could stop watching whenever I wished.

Translated by Philip Landon

Mariaana Jäntti

Mariaana Jäntti (full name: Gia Ruusu-Mariaana Fieandt-Jäntti, b. 1953) has written the most radically experimental work in the Finnish language. *Amorfiaana* (1986), her punning, hectically free-associating first novel, is oblivious to traditional literary proprieties: chronology, coherence, good taste, the commitment to meaning. The "story" (as the narrator calls it) involves demolition work, seedy sexual encounters, legal proceedings, disease and decay, domestic squabbles, housework and a meal, possibly of dog meat. The bizarre goings-on take place in the eminently concrete setting of a bourgeois apartment cluttered with the detritus of a bygone era and populated by a cast that includes the stately, languorous Madame, the hopeless servant Mrs. Parkstein, Paul the Black Man, the lawyer Lorenz Trendén, and a little girl called Alfhild. Names of domestic spaces (room, stairway, cellar) serve as section headings. This rudimentary structure is saturated with language: remembered or observed sensual detail, and scraps of internal and uttered speech. We are told at the beginning that disaster looms in the form of a traffic accident down in the street, where a truck threatens to run over a girl on a tricycle, but the narrator discourages curiosity about the incident. The narrative is punctuated with disquisitions on epistemological relativism that serve to accentuate the fluidity of the novel's world: " 'I had strange dreams,' the woman said. 'The whole house is having strange dreams,' Fleisch consoles, 'there's nothing strange in that.' " Unlike its distant modernist cousins (Woolf, Faulkner), *Amorfiaana* frustrates anyone who searches for a solid center within the rampant texture. The book comes close to utter discursive meltdown—with all the perils that this implies. The fainthearted will balk at the notion that "realities are the enemy. More and more of them keep appearing. Realities cannot be told." But those with a taste for exploration and excess will appreciate the audacity of Jäntti's debut.

Interview

MARIAANA JÄNTTI: There are no answers. So let what follows below remain below, I mean the laughter and the concomitant tears, drawn by the thrill of freedom and the longing for random encounters. Having published *Amorfiaana*, I have withdrawn myself entirely from public view and from all social performances. I have had my fill of marketing men and women. I hate the (Finnish) worship of success (money, career, publicity). I have tried to become nothing, air, as they say. I'm trying to crawl along the surface of freedom. Thank God love exists. Ephemerality is what helps me bear my long and difficult social (not communal) suicide; my mumbling authorship; my unfunded research; my base, secret existence. Not to make permanent, but to ephemeralize. By being air, I provide oxygen to the tortured flesh of others. I'm not even on strike. I'm converted. I'm studying the language of the dead. Semilingual, I solicit answers from the dead, because we the (half)living are so alone. I'm practicing freedom; I'm experimenting with imprisonment. To be an eye in a net without a mesh. Can (that?) invisible writing become shared; what you can't point at, even with your finger?

PHILIP LANDON: Can you name any shared characteristics of contemporary Finnish fiction? Do you identify with any of your international or domestic contemporaries?

MJ: I would rather search for differences, privacies, holes in the cloak, hoping to catch a glimpse of unbridled flesh.

PL: How would you situate fiction in general and your own work in particular in relation to mass culture and the mass media?

MJ: I can't bring myself to regard the "me-media" as a unified entity that I should then relate myself to. (That is, aside from the fact that the money is the media.) Does the poetic shun money and calculation? The mass lolls back in its media, its marinade. I imagine myself sitting on the shore with my fishing tackle, trapping tidbits, and real treasure, panning nuggets of wisdom from that rich, turbulent "ma-marinade" sewer, and does my nose deceive me (your own sweat never smells) or does the sweat on my brow smell acrid, sickly, slightly rotten? Do I smell it? Don't I?

I experience my book-body as a secret, satisfying partner with whom I play a game of promises—promises of a relation that is free (from the media, too) and passionate and independent—promises, promises.

When I wrote *Amorfiaana*, the mass media insidiously became my social element, reality, and environment, and I was prompted to abstain from it altogether for nine months. I never imagined I would have access to some "direct experience of reality," but I explored it, I stuck my neck out, I increased my desire, and so my freedom to make contact with the repressed in the social increased.

PL: Kai Laitinen has written, "The traditional Finnish novel is close to nature. Nature features in the role of a friend or an enemy or both." Can we read your work as part of this tradition? Does nature require a new approach from writers?

MJ: In *Amorfiaana* the traditional Finnish natural landscape is mainly present through its absence. Human/Animal, Animate/Inanimate, Matter/Spirit, Thinking/Embodying, Natural/Unnatural, Inside/Outside, Object/Subject, Authentic/Inauthentic, and other such mutually forbidden companions marry each other, reproduce, and fill every nook and cranny. In *Amorfiaana* "nature" lurks in the bodily character of language. The ecology of meanings in *Amorfiaana* is rain-forest-like.

"Nature" is continually "creating" its relation to us anew. I don't believe literature stems from any starting point or sound decision. With regard to nature, I commit crimes daily, as do you. What would a significantly reformed discourse of nature look like? Could we lay our trust in the body? Would that be a road of insight for us? Perhaps our new attitude toward the air we breathe, toward animals, and toward the bodies of others will become embodied (and will cease to be a mere "attitude," even though it intensifies in thought) at the behest of our own bodies (numerous "own" distinct bodies), or perhaps not. When a natural creature, a creature of nature, which we all have, in our bodies, rends, disintegrates, fragments, e.g., in war, birth, mortal illness, torture, famine, and when that body suffers dreadfully and screams without words, do we understand and for how long? Or are market forces the only natural force whose voice, exclamation, we can identify?

PL: From the *Kalevala* to postwar fiction, much of Finnish literature has been intimately bound up with the question of national identity. Do you see yourself as a member of a more international generation?

MJ: I am not greatly drawn to identity. I feel more comfortable with plurality, in attachment to images. I have no generational identity, no decade; I feel different, independent, and unattached, perhaps. I have never liked the words *national* and *international*; they have a bureaucratic ring, especially as a pair. On the whole I recoil from the (mediated) ambiance of Finland and the European Union. I see in it a lack of solicitude and thought. In childhood I grew attached to the country of my grandparents, the Finland of the turn of the century, or a fantasy of it. It meant love of the Finnish language (the honor of words) and the promising strength of words (words of honor)—this despite the fact that not one of my grandparents was Finnish-speaking. That Finland meant joy (why, I wonder?), links east (my grandmother's stories of her trip to Siberia) to the countries of Europe, universities and spas, echoes of Fennophilia, well-stocked, multilingual bookcases, idealism, heroic ancestors, and knowledge of the fact that I have Jewish, Spanish, Swedish, German (via Latvia) and, of course, Finnish blood running through my veins. That Finland of mine was the Good Finland of a mythical twilight.

PL: Certain epistemological reflections in *Amorfiaana* evoke a kind of surrender to meaninglessness and infinity; others approach a feeling of mystical enlightenment. Are you interested in the philosophical notion of the sublime as transcendence of the unfathomable? Is an amorphous text the same thing as a relativistic text? What, if any, is the significance of relativism for you as a novelist? Critics have defined *Amorfiaana* as a feminine text. Do you approve? What does it mean for a novel to be feminine?

MJ: In response to this last group of questions, *Amorfiaana* is a context. If I start saying something about it, I feel that I am making it linear. And whatever I say is bound to be evasive, misleading, protective of the secret (of the text). I wrote *Amorfiaana* as uncompromisingly as possible, as my philosophy, which had to unfold precisely as it did, in bodily form, as a victim, which I toss off a rock into the Gulf of Finland. But here goes. To be in *Amorfiaana* is to test boundaries. I also mean traveling by foot, on other limbs, a process (a procession, traversing the border of justice, an event), limbs astride the limit, that is, the line between the legs: meaninglessness and, on the other hand, meaningfulness, all the way to the holy; the meaningfulness of the meaningless; the concentration of the shape of meaning to the point of asphyxia, explosion; burning on the burning brink of self and Other; suffering and escape from suffering.

To be sure, I am interested in philosophy and I practice it as a hobby, but in writing *Amorfiaana*, I had neither the Kantian "sublime" nor theories of "the feminine" in mind. I did, however, have some knowledge of Bakhtin, among others. What matters most of all to me is my "own" thinking, groping, embodying. It didn't occur to me to apply anything. I mean, *Amorfiaana* is an event that is related from within, if possible—precisely that possibility is taking place, being made possible. I don't think the text is amorphous at all; it is just extremely close, in the flesh. It has a straightforward plot, lines, e.g., the upward ascent, and a harsh moral—or should I use the finer term, ethics. What feminine (writing) is is problematic. Having read Julia Kristeva's ideas of the symbolic and the semiotic, I discovered I had been thinking along the same lines. I particularly wanted to allow the repressed element (for example, that which is born in connection with the "mother's" body, and never disappears) to appear, to take place. But *Amorfiaana* is a more complex passion than that.

From Amorfiaana

Why am I telling you this story? Because it doesn't exist. Because it is to happen as if you were watching a long-haired child on a tricycle in the street from your high and distant window and felt already at this height the vibration of a truck in the soles of your feet, you know it will happen, you see it in your eyes and then before your eyes, it would happen even if you leaped through the glass and flew—you would be too late. Everything happens so quickly, that is, what does happen. I tell you the story so that it will happen. You can see my face pressed against the glass, you look up at that window and mistake me for only a sudden reflection in the surface of the glass, a trick of light, a flash of the face of someone busy on the balcony opposite. No one knows me, so I have to narrate, to stooge. Everyone twists my arm. So I have to disintegrate to narrate. In fact, I am only a freak in the windowpane, an anomaly (in an otherwise homogeneous mass) from which disturbing little plays of color are mirrored, a piece of sunken cheek, a crooked finger with an unnaturally large joint, but in another sense I'm there, like an anatomical specimen, pressed against the glass, joined to it. I already suspect that the story will be left unfinished. That when the girl is run over, the glass far above will break, the fragments will fall against the lightless pavement of the street, and no one will look at them. The glass bubbles break, the specimen is opened.

Kitchen, Hallway, and Room

With a wooden ladle she stirs the white wash in the iron bucket. She stretches her neck in the hot steam. She lifts the linens to drip on a makeshift pole. She thrusts the long-handled ladle through the steam somewhere into the bucket, tastes the burning rinse water, and since it is good enough, she pours it over the tea leaves in the kettle. Through the mist she watches the leaf of the tea bush rustling in the wind swell in the boiling furnace. With eyes bloodshot from the effort, she says "I don't feel anything." She gets angry. Stabs the knife into the potato. "This is my body." She slices it up. She pours oil into the frying pan, boils it above the prescribed temperature. "This is my blood." But she does not feel her feeling. "Rat," she hisses at the flesh fly lurking in the potato's greasy steam. She licks the peppery spatula. Grows tired of it. She flails vaguely at the fly with the spatula, not even wanting to hit that gob of flesh. Strangely, the fly has appeared in her vicinity in the darkest winter . . . pollinator of ice flowers! She herself is the perennial sitter in windows, towers, barrels, bottlenecks, tubs, stairways, empty refrigerators, garbage dumps, elevators, cellars, ovens. She is a person burned to the bottom, some think, near sizzling, at least. She taps a rhythm with her fingers. "How did it go?" She racks her brain and tries DIT-DAH-DIT-DAH-DIT-DAH-DIT-DAH. "Not that way, how annoying." The hot-blooded housekeeper drummed like the Boy Scouts, at least so she claimed, support hose on legs, piece of cold ring sausage before her (good enough for the hired help), tapping, she goaded her vision from the small frost-fern-bordered pane past the abandoned cowshed, past the icy well, past the wooden manor, past the stone high-rise where she did the dirty chores and loved to the core, past different doorways where she stood varicose-veined, past various mouths of children, past dim years all the way to the wedding picture that had never been true gleaming on the box. "That's how the Boy Scouts drummed," she repeated and claimed. How annoying. Where had the man from the picture on the box gone? An agent surely, like the woman. The towersitter lets her little finger horse gallop unhindered over others' towers, over recommendations turned down returned supporting grant requests for various purposes, which the individual would presumably achieve, over Permaplate to reject glass the finger horse—DIT-DAH-DIT-DIT-DAH-DIT-DIT—over heavy traffic, which the gaze impales on the basis of bad premonitions, over a fallow field—DIT-DAH—through the falling snow—DIT-DIT—she feels like making love. She enjoys the feeling, rubs her head under its spell, bends her swan's neck, lets her sweat-smell drip from the hairy pits, pours tea, it is steeped and hot. Is that how time passed? She rises and starts to walk along the high darkening hallway toward the room where she would meet the others. Alternating her right and left hand, she bounces her body from wall to wall, hardly using her legs. Forward toward the room where she would meet the others! Plaster is breaking loose and the wall catches on her shoes. She can almost hear the happy voices already. But she gets thirsty or something. She turns and walks casually back to the tea kettle. Drinks. Numbly she walks through the hallway without pausing. Slamming the door to the stairs, she glides along the railing past dozens of entrances down to the cellar door. There she enters, perhaps to straighten out her own closet.

No one is speaking in the room off the hallway now. Madame rises, tidying and wrapping herself up with feminine gestures, turns toward the window, whereupon the lawyer with quick, coordinated movements of his limbs gets there first to open it. A wind is blowing over the sea's ice fields, the water roars under the ice, it does not rest even in winter but roars, raising and lowering its snowy armor. Panting. Snow lashes whoever walks the fields there with powdery steps, fur bristling. He walks toward the whiplashes, nose in the air to meet his own strength, with disappearing tracks. One can make out a bushy mustache under the snow. A man. If it were a woman, she would shave her mustache. Pockmarks. If it were a woman, she would shave her pockmarks. Thumb turned inward within huge mittens, he feels no panic but searches for it. Toward death, toward the chasm! a pockmarked voice roars within him. There is strength. There is fur, for now. The sea writhes in its armor. "I can't stand that perpetual roar," says Madame's hand, threshing the air. "You have to get away from here," grunts the lawyer. Madame barks voiceless barks at the roaring; a wrecking ball crunches the building opposite. Dust rises all the way to the eighth story so that Madame's hand industriously fanning the air is powdered over with sweet evenness and stops suddenly. . . . Venus de Milo's lost hand. A reproduction of the statue trembles tastefully in the shadows among the photographs on the music shelf. Madame pants. The lawyer sticks close behind her. One cannot see clearly in the room. But on the other side of the door, a German shepherd pup throwing itself repeatedly against it, paint on its claws, calls attention to itself by succeeding in turning the handle. The seldom-used double door opens into darkness. Everyone knows that the dog's jaws await, sharp fangs bared, for the animal has congenital distemper. From the unused dining room opened by tooth and nail a voice rings out, "Madame, y'see, I had to come and tell you the furniture should be covered with plastic, it's so frightfully dusty"—it is the shady Mrs. Parkstein, a maid, under the oak table on all fours eye-to-eye with the German shepherd. The maid protected herself with the thick tassels hanging heavily from the tablecloth as if they formed a small shield. The dog flopped down and lay there staring. Was the helper listening again or did she have an unusual hobby, one which would not have been suitable? "You're a wolf," Madame snaps, closing the window, the double door, and her eyes.

In a tottery but functional three-legged armchair sits a woman who could be the same as the window-sitter, cellar-goer, potato-slicer, but this one is younger, really a girl. She substitutes her own leg for the missing chair leg, balances, settles herself comfortably, and simultaneously arranges her body in a charming arch. One person would call her gloomy, another aloof, still another only a girl-woman trying to appear inscrutable. Now others cannot see her face since she is turned toward the shadows moving on the wall. The demolition lights are turned up to their brightest and perhaps their rays, owing to a mirror set by chance on the window, hit the room at just the right angle to lengthen shadows horizontally and shorten them vertically. "A splendid nose. What a short poker!" she opines about the shadows but these are only the necessary internal cries, to allow her to check what is most important, namely her own breasts stretched to mighty proportions on the wall. Lounging in the chair gives her an excuse to play with her body's shadows. Her breasts jut out and point left, right, and center. The shadow nose, which belongs to someone other than the owner of the breasts, moves in a strangely regular and premeditated way. The woman is hot—whew—but of course she cannot bare herself, cannot turn. A splendid nose, but splendid lips too. Suddenly they open and dart to the nipple. They bite. At that moment the woman turns and in her heat her gaze traverses every face that can be distinguished in the room. Accidentally she has raised a hand to her breast. The hard nipple in the pit of her hand waits and demands. The girl-woman is disconcerted. She covers up her feeling of shame with the usual vehemence and fright. "Whose nose was it?" she asks, and "Which one of you saw what happened?" but face after face is inscrutable. Madame's eyes are closed in such a way that they might just as well have been open. She remains silent and her face is closed. A ripple of speech runs through the room. Somewhere in the shade of a many-branched tea rose or in the back of a pile of books *fvantzz-japf* a knife comes flying. It is perhaps a reaction to the tottering of the chair. The lawyer even dashes forward to support it by the backrest. "You shouldn't rock or you'll get hurt," he says loudly, taking a lawyer's stance on the floor, which changes with circumstances just like a hansom driver's. For now the gentleman stands like a Gypsy or like a proud landlord in his buggy speeding to the very center of the drama. But our gentleman has neither the necessary horse nor the buggy, which he of course does not notice. He is on a grand mission. The grown-up girl—yes, her name is Alfhild—rubs her dampened palm, secretly stroking her nipple, feels the recent nipping ("then it was true and I didn't imagine it") and the actual smallness of her breast. Now she has a presentiment, raises her eyes to the man who smells ripe ("could be my father") whom she doesn't particularly know ("guardian perhaps") the man rhythmically clenches ("a key witness or Captain Daidolus or") his molars, mouth closed ("illegitimate agent or energy czar") switching work from one side to the other ("or a scapegoat"). The rhythm reminds Alfhild of the recent shadow play, but she is not sure. The man's seated position is shameless. "Behind closed doors!" announces the lawyer, at an inappropriate time, naturally, which everyone in the room makes clear by ignoring that shriek, which was meant to start things. Now it's resting time. The whiteness, heaven's manna or earth's dust, has descended even onto the shoulders of Venus. It is calm, for the roaring has ceased. The demolition machines have stiffened in the street's hollows into angular, asymmetrical postures of defense. At dusk some of the giant steam shovels have crawled off into their caves elsewhere. The wrecking ball has sunk to rest. Only old folks' centuries-old curtains gleam yellowish, veils dyed once upon a time with onionskins tremble so that looking out one knows the picture is alive. Venus is virginal. Venus is a picture. "I long for the sun," says Madame and straightens up, "You're cold." "Your heart pumps poorly," someone in the room answers and someone else has an excuse to practice the nuances of his scornful laugh. The creak of footsteps cuts off an effort to quarrel. The giant boa constrictor and the little count are probably marching this way. The lawyer hurries to open the door to the hallway, behind which stands the shady housekeeper Mrs. Parkstein with her frying pan upraised. "I am bringing fried potatoes to Madame. Madame was hungry." Madame looks into the pan carefully and announces that the potatoes have gotten too cold and besides are so distastefully sliced that she has lost her appetite, probably for quite some time. Madame calls the dog to her, "Uri, Uri, Uri, come now" (the name was chosen because it was apt but mainly because it was neuter); the dog will not agree to reveal its sex, and is allowed to keep its secret thanks to its bad temper and its long teeth. "Have some, Uri." Madame lowers the frying pan to the floor and the dog scatters chunks of potato around the large room. "I di'n' fry them, now ain't that somethin'," rages the servant, and stays in the room with her back against the door. The slamming of the door causes the flour to fall from Venus's shoulders as a man on a snowy steppe might shake the snow from his coat and think of the reaching hands left behind him, petrified, crushed; hands detached by loneliness on the shore, hands turned pictures, driftwood, crushed marble chips. He journeys toward a chasm, blue death. Toward the core of whiteness so that he himself should become whiteness. In sheepskin, or whatever, but he tries to adapt himself. In his pockets are two bottles of firewater, which, if you drink, only a miracle can save you. This is his moment alone, only alone and his. The snow has whipped the man so white that he no longer knows himself, the Black Man. He takes off his fur coat with clumsy hands, lets it fall behind him without looking back, leaves his shoes in his tracks, and goes on. He takes a little sip. He does not know himself. He screams. He does not hear himself. Kneeling naked in the snow, he does not see his skin. "Oh, you're here already," a transparent woman who has come from somewhere greets him. "Dinner is ready, you've drunk too much, fried potatoes for you, there didn't happen to be anything else, they're probably cold." The Black Man who has sneaked up to Venus could be the same, and is, but he is softer on himself. His fingers stroke the plaster belly and plaster clothing, he wipes the dust onto his cheek, each stroke repeats his proper name "Paul, Phool," the smell of potatoes makes him feel very hungry, he swallows his saliva. He would like to sip a little, snack a little, if only on snow. But he is not alone. He is playful, a word-twister, a woman-pincher, a bad little wolf.

The Room

"Come and stand here before me," Madame says to the little boy who stands gawking behind the Dutch-tiled stove, "Come here and look me straight in the eye. How, answer honestly, did you get in. . . ? Why doesn't Mrs. Parkstein please take off that heavy pack of yours immediately! The poor wretch is all tired out," Madame scolds her servant, to whom the wretched boy walks pack-on-back thinking that he is doing the right thing, stops, and looks her in the eye. "The door was open." The servant strips the pack of newspapers from his back. Madame beckons the boy over to her, and when he has gotten over the litter on the floor and stands before her, Madame says: "Will you give me the paper?" The boy goes back to his pack down by the servant's varicose-veined legs, opens the metal lock, picks out a fresh paper, takes it to Madame. Handing it to her, the boy must hold his arm out for a long time, for Madame lingers, does not draw her hand back, but prolongs the grip. When Madame finally takes the paper with a jerk, she simultaneously clasps the boy's palm in hers, tugs him up to her, and presses down on his shoulder with seeming lightness, but painfully, to judge by the twitch in the boy's face, until he is sitting on the floor before her. "You must be very tired. Rest there," Madame urges, looking at the others in the room with her hand still on the boy's shoulder. "I'm not tired. I haven't delivered my papers yet, this was the first place I rode to and I wanted to be sure the paper would get here, so I came through the door, which to my surprise was wide open. I thought I had to go in through it, it was so wide open, but now I have to hurry before the street doors are locked or I won't get my work done. I'm not tired, I assure you." The boy gulps air into his words and tries to worm free of the grasp of his painful position. "You must have a fever. Mrs. Parkstein will please fetch a thermometer and

then take the boy's wet pack into the kitchen to dry, perhaps on this paper"
(she offers the paper she has just gotten) "so that the linoleum won't be
damaged more than it already has been through poor care." Madame continues pressing the boy's shoulder and takes his forehead with her other
hand, forcing the sweat-wet back of the boy's head against her knee so that
his sweet, small Adam's apple bulges a little as the skin of his neck is
stretched taut. The boy tries to keep his neck muscles limp, otherwise it will
hurt, actually he doesn't feel so bad but the bunch of papers disappearing
into the kitchen meanwhile and the important messages in his pack cause
him to try the surprise tactic of jerking himself loose a couple of times, but
the grip is a tight one. What he has just said seems far away. "And what if
this woman asks what is in the paper?" he frets. He looks upward obliquely,
the flame flickering in the stove sets his boyish eyes agleam. Alfhild likes
those gleaming eyes, like looking into fire. In an enormous overstuffed chair
near the shade lolls a young man, even ironically one couldn't call him a
youth or a gentleman, he guffaws and announces that there's been enough
of clowning, too much playing around with that incest-begotten boy. That
instant Madame had instinctively turned the boy's head so that the gleam
vanished from his eyes and instead of Alfhild he is now facing the dog Uri.
"Excuse me, could I take the dog out, it looks as if he has to go, I'd be happy
to if I could . . . ," he says, but his throat is twisted and his breath merely
whistles, a chick's cheep. Uri growls and a laugh echoes in the room, from
even the farthest corners.

"How little you are. I love you, babykins," Alfhild whispers into the paperboy's damp ear. "Do you hear the roar of the waves, water-ear? You've
come from the sea." "It's the crackle of the flames, mother," answers the
baby. "The fire is burning my papers, which I was given to deliver; the fire
will burn you too since you let me pinch your nipples. Take me to the free-
way and I'll hitch a ride for both of us." "It's an everlasting sea, my darling.
But it no longer knows you or me, who look at it, whom it spat out of itself
to exist here on the edge of a crag. It's good for us to be here forever like
those granite whales half on land and half in the sea, frozen in that moment
when . . . when you talk to the sea it does not hear you, but the waves open
up to you at your pleasure. . . ." "You're looking at the flames, you'll burn
yourself and everyone. Press closer to me so that you'll feel how I your baby
swell and excite you. Who are you? Whore! You're burning. My papers are
burning and I have no hope." "Soft gift of the sea, don't leave me!"
Alfhild's cheeks burn, eyes glitter through their open lids. The boy is lifted
away, Mrs. Parkstein and the Black Man move Alfhild to the sofa near the
shade and remain on watch as if by command. Madame sails to the scene, a
listing ship, and raises a tender hand from within the enveloping felt sails
and rests it on Alfhild's forehead. Having taken her temperature she keeps it
to herself, but bends to build up the dying fire, throws fuel from a heap of
books into the fireplace. Fumes fly up into eyes and throats. The lawyer

bounds over the heaps, puts one bare foot onto a cold white roasting dish and the other onto the bony dice, pausing to pluck the occasional brief from the floor to his armpit, thrusts through the thick branches of the tea rose, and then stops in the light from the embers so that almost everyone who wishes can see him: his cheeks are narrow, his skin on the greasy side. Naturally he is roguish-looking and delights in it, for as a man of no account he is glad to make any impression he can. "The trial is to begin, there is no other option. I beg you to close the stove lids, to draw the curtains before the windows, to close the doors, those that can be closed, I ask for silence, and also that you close your eyes for a moment, take a deep breath, which follows a natural path through all of us, a common breath to which everyone contributes. With this breath, let us nourish ourselves, according to the principle of relativity or letting the one who makes the most noise get the most. . . ." "Without further ado," shouts the sarcastic young man. The lawyer pauses. Madame joins in the young man's laughter, then recomposes herself. The Black Man coughs, either from dust getting into his throat or phlegm rising from his lungs from not having breathed this deeply for a long time. Irritated movements, smacking of lips, creaking of bodies, general rustling. Feathers to be straightened. Strength to be refreshed. Clatter fills the space reserved for voice. The fact that the stove lids could be closed so early testifies to the imminent arrival of spring. Where the sun shines and scorches, blinds like a snowfield's crystal mirror, where the sun already skins the bulging thighs around the horse of insolent Mr. (the horse may soon die of thirst) where the man rides (Daidolos) there wings are being flapped, quills sharpened, beaks raised, tufts proffered to the wind, one's own down checked over, how one's own bones are filled and emptied, how one's own blood circulates, food is digested and expended through one's own aperture. It is time to assemble. Time to choose the leader. Time to form a flock, to smell out the course, take flight, move out from under the sun. All have a fever, all jostle, get muddled, get into formation, are afraid, reassemble, are thirsty, remember the damp northern woods, the forest light, the stringy sap of swamp trees, the worms of decay, the woods, ancient mosses, bold wild hogs, the entirety of the woods; but sometimes the clatter of a truck and the shriek that follows upon it, the great black woodpecker's nonchalant flight and expressionless cry, puncture this large heart with one skillful thrust; the arrow pierces, ignites the whole forest faster than lightning. The lawyer is silent. The pause grows beyond itself. The flock is one. The whole forest is astir. Silence spills over the banks. The lawyer dwindles further. He isn't just disgusting looking. His ears are more pointed than before. Everything about him is pointed, no longer twitching and coordination. He is a quill or an arrowhead. Greased. Buttery. Does he plan to take the lead? He is a sword. Does he stab? He is not himself. He protrudes. Is he a slippery fish hauled up on the shore? In his ignorance he opens his tapered mouth to the sky's waves. Did the flowing lava freeze his tail fin to stand him upright just when he was wriggling himself out of the suction of the rocks toward the waves? It looks that way. "Charge number one," shrieks the lawyer, consulting a paper drawn from his armpit. "Guilty or not guilty? Guilty." The room buzzes in response. "Ugh. The documents are ruined, mixed up; headings, conclusion, and decisions mismatched, buried, lost, and so forth, and so on; everyone knows everything; we must work fast, without sparing time; the court is in session. Let anyone take charge! No statute of limitations, no annulments. Everything is recorded somehow or other. The sword of justice against wrong. The sword! Where is the sword?" The lawyer draws emptiness from his left hip, his hand cuts the air midway before him. "I am the sword Swish," says the man, says the hand, "but we need a symbol, a real sword with a hilt, which in case of need comes as a sword in our hand and cuts the guilty in half or cuts off his head depending on our decision, that is, our heads. I have spoken. Who will change into a sword? Ha ha." The paperboy climbs onto a footstool beneath which Uri keeps his muzzle sheltered from mashing heels. Amid the dog's growls, a lucid declaration: "I am ready. My name is Friksos, you can call me Friks for short. I'm leaving at once on a trip to the cellar to fetch a sword, where I'm sure I've seen it flash. I ask you to be patient, for you know that it is difficult to advance in the dark if you don't know the way. Is it any wonder that one is afraid of meeting somebody, for who would not suspect a boy wandering with outstretched hands who takes fright at the least thing? Besides, this boy is filthy. That I've stolen nothing from them I can prove by turning my pockets inside out with the utmost speed (I've been practicing). In the face of other suspicions I am defenseless. In truth, my use of language is flawless and I can follow required form when I wish to, so no sweat. Lawyer, sir. . . ? Just to be sure, would you give me authorization to fetch the sword so that things won't go wrong?" The boy's skin is calm, his lips clear and soft, head back, ready to leave, leaning to the left a little as if the undelivered papers were still weighing down his right side. Again the lawyer draws a paper from under his arm, holds it out toward Friks in his fingers without taking a step, whereupon Friks scrambles down from the footstool, slips between the tiled stove and Madame's mighty wooden-framed bed, over chunks of potato, smelly bundles, kerchief-covered stacks of documents (which at the slightest disturbance flow and cover everything), over shoes gnawed by the dog, gnawed hairbrushes, femurs, doll heads, past the screen and between several half or one-third curtains to the lawyer, right up against him, so close to his body does the lawyer hold the authorization pinched between his index and middle fingers. "Let me introduce myself; Surrogate Lorenz Trendén. Everything is in order, except. . . ." "Oww!" wails Friks: during all his laborious crawling through the clutter, Uri's teeth have been worrying the boy's ankle. His sock is torn. Friks strokes his wounded ankle and unwittingly spatters the authorization with blood, whereupon Lorenz Trendén stiffens with rage. Meanwhile Madame has cleared herself a path to the spot, wets the corner of a towel with her saliva, and wipes Friks's ankle, whispering something soothing to the boy, then saying so that all can hear: "Friks, in a sense all our fates now depend on your action. You mustn't disappoint me. You must take Uri with you. On the way back he'll protect you from robbers." From the sounds he makes in his throat, Friks clearly feels ill, and no wonder, for Madame has him so wrapped in her robes that one can hardly tell what part belongs to which of them. "Little Friks, my little ragamuffin, take the dog with you. In a sense he's your dog now. Of course he's still legally mine and of course he mostly obeys me, but I will give him to you now in the presence of witnesses. Remember to take care of him. A dog must not be abused or it will become neurotic. And he needs to go regularly." From somewhere within the blankets covering Madame's armpits and large buttocks Friks protests that he does not need a dog, that he cannot take proper care of it, that the dog would be better off in the country, where he could run if even only on a chain. The young man rises from the easy chair, walks unsteadily toward them with a clinking choke collar in his hand. "I am me, then, or call me Fleisch; a name as well as flesh has its history and I believe you will learn it yet, we will soon meet, Friksos; let's shake on it." Friks thrusts out a hand from the covers. Fleisch puts the choke chain into Friksos's open palm instead of the firm paw the boy was expecting.

"Well, of course the servants are never around when they are most sorely needed. Mrs. Parkstein, come here immediately! Now I, who have not had time to get ready for thousand-times more distinguished affairs and above all for sessions of the court, am forced to perform a servant's duties without pay. . . ." Mrs. Parkstein appears before Madame with a newspaper spread out at her waist level so that as a farsighted person she can better make out the print. The large cross on an inside page leaps out at the scanning eyes. That and Mrs. Parkstein's oddly contented mien, despite her having been scolded, calm down the ruckus. Actually, the confusion is caused by the dog Uri (who chews indiscriminately at people's feet) and by the so-called characters. Senselessly, uncooperatively, they tug at Uri's ears, heels, loose neck-skin, his tail, of course, and even at his snarling upper lip. The dog whines and scratches. At last the choke chain is around his neck and pulled tight as well. The dog is frantic—he is still breathing, he is still thrashing about! Madame does not notice the picture of the cross, but goes on scolding the servant, this time accusing her of robbery, although she is totally concentrated on Uri. "The dog must be given strict instructions. Come and help me explain to him, he believes me and no one else. Take hold of his feet and ha—, I mean his hind and forefeet and his rib cage so that I can see his eyes and drop a little of this soothing medicine into his mouth and some cod-liver oil too, since when this trial is over I absolutely want to enter him in the dog show. His fur must be kept glossy, remember that. That is your responsibility, Friks. That's the way, Uri, nice dog, nice dog. Uri will see to it that Friks takes care of things. Uri won't let Friks out of the building! Do you understand, Uri? Bring the boy's coat here. It doesn't matter if it's a little wet.

Sniff, sniff, smell this Uri, smell this, sniff, sniff." Madame shoves the sleeve toward the dog's nose, which is pointed toward the ceiling, and with a quick jerk hides the coat under the rug, shouting, "Sic him, sic him, well, let the dog go right now, you'll make him neurotic, you have to let a dog obey a command!" Uri attacks the rug furiously, rips it, and getting the aha-scent, throws himself at Friks, whereupon Fleisch snatches up the choke chain and apparently saves Friks's life. While Fleisch is at one center of these events, Paul, in the character of a Black Man, has the opportunity, even the duty, to improve Alfhild's apparently stiffening position on the sofa. The Black Man is an alien, so it seems to him. A look into his eyes is confounding. In place of the blind spot there floats in the eyeball the point on the horizon where lines converge. It bothers him that he does not feel the intersection of lines in his eyes, but knows it. So it is still a blind spot. He has no escape. The Black Man kisses Alfhild's ear surreptitiously and whispers into it that they should go into the kitchen and drink a little tea at the same time as the door opens for Friks to leave with the dog, that it would be good for Alfhild's health. Alfhild rises and walks from the room in the Black Man's shadow.

The Black Man is left standing in the kitchen doorway. Leaning loosely against the frame, he examines Alfhild, who is standing with her elbows resting on the kitchen windowsill. Her rear reaches out toward the man. She feels his gaze. She isn't sure if her rear has begun swaying; she tries to hold still but feels herself swaying. Sensing the feelings in her rear, the man becomes aroused. Cheeks and necks get wet from the linens hanging on the temporary pole. Alfhild wipes the windowpane. She sees herself in the glass. Her rosemouth flirts. She sees herself remembering something. She sees herself squinting, focuses. She flails vaguely at the selfish flesh fly not wanting to hit that gob of flesh. Strangely the fly has appeared in her vicinity in the darkest winter . . . pollinator of ice flowers. A limby creature on the other side of the glass fondles her face, tattoos. One has to beware of letting the beast get the upper hand. Alfhild wipes the freezing glass. Is she watching her picture, is she watching the Black Man in the dark hole, is she watching, does she see anything, is she only playing? Below they are loading tons of express cargo for the night freeways. Steam rises from the bearers. Bent legs spread wide, the dark figures lift from the knees, backs straight, as recommended, alone and together, bundles, boxes, chests, and swaying upright portable closets. From above one can only wonder how quickly and soundlessly like the work of spirits the express truck is filled. She squints. She wipes the faulty glass that annoyingly keeps reflecting random little plays of color, a piece of sucked-in cheek, a crooked finger with an unnaturally large joint. . . . She wipes the flawless glass and no longer has any doubt about the imagined stroking of her behind. In the glass she sees her own face and the man's partly overlapping. Her rear spreads itself, takes a breath. Alfhild's center against the Black Man's center! She has not yet let any man completely inside her. How she has dreamt of it, imagined its every detail, even tormented herself with fears of mockery, of not knowing how to give herself, of there being something wrong with her. And soon she will give, will have given herself. She is happy and afraid. Squeezed between the radiator and the stove, skin against the dirty floor, both man and woman notice the table legs from the familiar old corner, the dust gathered in crevices, the spoons under the radiator, the indentations from heels and the sticky stuff accumulated in them; the products of motion and motionlessness, which again begin to signify adventure, head and body swaying as one indivisible being. The woodpile in the corner flashes into Alfhild's view. What are the long logs that won't fit into the stove for? She would like to ask every object what it is, what it is for, how it works, could she get one (this she would ask only as a test), where it had come from, who had brought the Russian teacups as a homecoming present, who had broken the crystal goblet, why there are cuts on the face painted on the canvas, why there is a jagged head-sized crevice in the cement wall, how the ceiling has become stained, why candles are used although there is electricity in the house, what the creatures crawling on the wall are, whether they bite, whether one could eat the interrupted meal from the plate left near the table leg, or did one have to wait first to make sure it was not for others. Alfhild is curious. The tea in the kettle is fragrant. She has to have some. Alfhild pours a cup for both of them, warms her hand on the side of the cup, then takes hold of the little gentleman's plumlike head with her warm fingers. He is a gentleman. When Alfhild asks if he has missed her, he replies with a nod. He repeats the nod with his whole being. He is soft and sweet. One can stroke him all the way and he always nods. You can take his bundles into your hands. Fondle them. Ruffle the mossy beard. The gentleman likes it all. When you hold his neck or collar by both sides, he may open his toothless mouth and shout a long and resonant voiceless shout—an invitation. He is a traveler with a bundle on his shoulder and wants to lay his head down in the nearest nest. Courteously he salves his smooth head, his face, and the mouth of the nest. When he has thrust inside, he belongs to the Black Man, to his eyes, mustache, and lips. Now he is a lever and a probe on an unknown surging sea. The sea caresses it, feasts it, guides it into soft recesses, kneads the traveler's belief in himself. The Black Man's eyes flash "Now is the big moment," "This is unique," "We are godlike," "Now it's coming," "This was fate," "This is living." His lips mimic a memory which rises to them from the distance. Was it as a mere suckling, a recollection encompassing feeling, which lips can no longer possess? Heedless of the lie, little Mister Main Attraction serves his master faithfully, he has not yet abandoned him, and his ace is in every lad's poker hand. The Black Man has slashed a wound into the picture! It is one wound among others. One wound in a lacerated face. The man looks at the woman painted on the canvas, her cut mouth and eye, and feels virile. Indeed, the situation makes him, the Black Man; and he has an aptitude for situations. The Russian teacups clink, plaster settles in the air; the truck starts up, a log falls on Alfhild's foot but she doesn't really notice it, for she wonders at this man who is in her and at herself, who is not here but preferably on the express load, leaving.

Alfhild washes her feet in an iron basin that happens to have warm water in it. She flails vaguely at the selfish flesh fly that circles her rear. From the pole resting on two chairs she selects still-damp, snow-white clothes and puts them on. As hawkmoths fly toward the light, so she, whiteness, steps from the kitchen into the dark hallway. She is the lover of night, the nightmistress. She lives for dreams and the true games of night, she bears night clothing, the bride of night. Darkness is soft, unbounded, enormous. Darkness is. She is in darkness. She is the white heart of darkness. One of many doors may open soundlessly and the light falling from it, creeping at first through the crack, will cut the darkness sharply in two, and slowly, surely, the wound will deepen until darkness is destroyed. If a listener is suspected of being in the hallway, the door bursts open without warning. Alfhild knows the risk, but it does not bother her. Only darkness is. It is eternal, erratic. Distant sounds, even echoing shouts, darkness absorbs and dissolves into itself. It is all-powerful. One need only stand limp and still to become a part of darkness, softness, the spirit that rests and moves without tension. Alfhild rejoices, although she does not know it yet. She does not raise her feet, but they rise as eternal motion, as flight in the arms of darkness, which loves her. "Here she is!" Fleisch announces in a loud voice and with a firm hand he pulls Alfhild into the room through the suddenly opened door. The encounter with the Black Man returns to Alfhild's mind and between her thighs. "I, the bride of night, betrayed my lover with day. What happens when day and night meet?" Arrogant Mr. Sternpoff stares at Alfhild from the rotating leather chair. Madame's eyes scornfully mock the girl's dress. Mrs. Parkstein still has the paper spread open in her hands. Alfhild knows that the Black Man, the son of day, is afraid of night, does not believe in dreams, but takes a sip and thinks he's traveling, believes in the spot he cannot see, in a convergence he does not believe in. Alfhild regrets her infidelity, squeezes her thighs together, feels the slash, squeezes it away, smells the blood. "Well," says Fleisch, who stands blocking the door he has closed. The lawyer takes a step toward Alfhild. Farther away, Mrs. Parkstein straightens out the paper so that Alfhild can see the picture of the cross. The lawyer takes another step and shouts at Alfhild: "Charge number one: burying alive. Charge number two: libel. Charge number three: defamation of the dead. One of these will stick, believe it! Bring forth the evidence." Mrs. Parkstein smoothes her dress, stooping, peering, hesitating, she begins reading like a servant, leaving to the judge the things she can't be sure of: "How d'you say this, but I'll say it like it is, *In Memoriam Matrem Meae* in big headlines. This is a death notice 'n anyone c'n see there's a humongous cross here. I just happened to see it when they told me to put the boy's pack on it to dry so I just looked at it, I wasn' looking fer anythin',

only it was there 'n I thought Madame 'n the lawyer really ought 'cause
there's more here 'n then I wondered was she really dead 'cause they don't
put them alive 'cause well it says here:

> Mother, see how space glows!
> you are near me now:
> in each of my million tears
> your eyes shine
> each of my million unborn children
> has your features.
> They are beautiful and ugly children.
> They caress and abuse one another
> and gaze with me at the glow of space.
> They are the children of mankind
> whom I, their unbearing mother, tend
> your lineaments on my face, mother,
> beautiful and ugly.

Then below it: 'Blessing hereby performed. Sympathy futile. A.' 'N there
ain't no more here." Mrs. Parkstein folds up the paper and puts it under her
arm, strides into the shadow of the grandfather clock, and stands waiting in
her support hose to see if she is still needed. "Who is your mother, I ask you
tee-hee Miss Alfhild. You won't get away with a wrong answer." Alfhild's
head pans around: faces, stances, hovering dust, breathing shadows in the
shadows, withered unwatered plants; the silence is oppressive. Night loves
her. She pans around; everyone waits devoutly for her to be hooked, for the
bobber to sink deep and move away, pulling furiously, making swirls on the
surface, for the fish to be hauled ashore at last, for the hook to be released,
some draw it out any old way not caring about tears, others do it slowly and
patiently, removing the hook protruding from the face without causing un-
necessary damage. She pans: it is time for the blow to fall, the fish to be
clouted, unpleasant or not, Mr. Sternpoff would thrust his cruel thumb under
the gills and wring the neck, Madame would kick the fish here and there,
feeling nauseated, grind it underfoot and finally call for Mrs. Parkstein, who
would take a stick and beat the fish until it would be fit for nothing, certainly not for human consumption, at least in Madame's opinion. Let Mrs.
Parkstein eat it herself, or put it through the meat grinder for Uri so the dog
won't get bones caught in his throat. Fleisch would leave the fish there,
hook and all; why, Alfhild cannot understand. "Below, the initial *A* as in
'Alfhild.' Who is your mother! Answer!" the lawyer is incensed. As he
leans over the coals, his cheeks are like flames, his eyebrows jagged. He
heaps up the coals, turns. Blue flames rise and die on his brow. His tongue, a
stiff lump, moves in his mouth along the lumpy membranes of his cheeks
and the cracked and bitten insides of his lips. Perhaps the heat of the coals
has set his blood boiling so that a little of it seeps onto his lips from innu-
merable eroded veins. His back has the limber arch of an angry cat, but his

movement is the slow, backward crawl of a crab—slowly, like a magician, he draws the red-hot poker from the coals and raises it overhead in a broad, sparking arch. "The truth," he says, and plunges the poker back into the stove. Everyone looks at Alfhild, suspicious and tense. But the woman-girl seems to have lost her sense of sight; it seems to have been sucked in some strange way into the eyes of the others. She sniffs the air. There is indeed a new smell in the room. Glancing at Mrs. Parkstein, Fleisch asks how clean the place is, whether a rotten fish has been buried there or old sardine cans stored in the corners. Alfhild misses the sarcasm in Fleisch's voice (is there any?). She feels the fat, cleaned, headless sardines preserved in oil penetrating her nostrils. No longer smell. Merely sensation. The girl's nostrils expand to the limit, and the canned fish press deeper and deeper into her head; the floor draws her to it; A drops to all fours and thrusts her forefinger into her nose. "Not to mince words, who ate the last can of fish from the kitchen cupboard?" Fleisch shouts pathetically at the ceiling. "I ate it, I ate it," answers a voice from near the Venus. Paul, the Black Man, has with difficulty squeezed through the seldom-used and slightly open double doors and in the shelter of his own darkness sunk into the shadow of the music shelf. Now the source of the smell is clear. Everyone quickly locates it with Paul's few words. They laugh, amused at themselves. How could they not have noticed it immediately! The Black Man leans forward enough so that the light reflected from the mirror reveals his smallpox scars, blinks his thick-lashed eyes, smiles at Madame, whereupon she sighs: "Paul," and he withdraws into the shadows to explore how tastefully and Frenchfully Madame pronounced his name; as it should be; so that was Madame's strength. Alfhild takes her finger from her nose and with wonderful grace points to her temple, slowly writing an answer in the air. "A variation on the Chinese actor's convention, 'the pointing finger,'" Fleisch comments to the lawyer, who waves to his seat a male creature with long-lensed cameras draped around his neck. "Focus," yells Fleisch. "Everything will be recorded," declares the lawyer and shoves the photographer in front of Alfhild. Flashbulbs pop. Alfhild's finger dances in the air, stops to rest in the Black Man's corner, whereupon Mrs. Parkstein giggles, continues pointing through the window at the tiled stove, then back to itself, to Mrs. Parkstein's varicose-veined legs, to Madame, but the fingertip points a little past Madame, at the cans and bottles, handkerchiefs, hairpins, a roasting fork, powder puffs, earplugs, tufts of hair on the night table beside Madame's large thigh. "Record the sequence of movement," says the lawyer. "A certain person wishes to speak," Mrs. Parkstein announces. Alfhild does not have time to stop her movement and merely lowers her pointing finger toward the floor. "The film will be developed immediately. The case or the girl's trial will be interrupted. Are they at the door already? Psst housekeeper Parkstein, are my boxes packed? Is the boa constrictor . . . ?" But the lawyer's voice is silenced when cold air wafts into his face from the door. A whirlwind spreads Alfhild's curls. The tufts of hair Madame has saved rise in flight from the night table, Mrs. Parkstein and Fleisch, experienced fowlers, pursue the hairfalls with spread fingers, thus learning to fly themselves. Mr. Stern-poff's arrogant nostrils flare in the fresh breeze. Then Alfhild's hair settles down. A woman slightly older than Alfhild enters the room, frost flowers, the gleam of water or moonglow on her palms. The colors of the rainbow flow over her cheeks, over the tiles, the walls, the night-covered windows, through which one can see only in, what is behind one's back, but not with the dependability of a mirror. The revelation awaited by those of little faith, the woman who has entered, holds light out to those waiting. "I came to ask," she whispers, and many of them cluster around her. Slowly, arms extended, she lowers the bowl of her uplifted palms, "Has this happened to you too?" The woman tilts her palm bowl so that they can see; ooh, veiled goldfish swimming; but mere glass slivers gleam in the hands; the viewers back off in disappointment—suddenly a hole appears in the window. "Has the first stone been cast now?" I thought and felt the stone in my thoughts. "Was the stone meant for me?" I thought, and looked into the gulf of the street, but there was no sign of a rock thrower there, only some solitary soul. Is this automatic? Do you think the glazier can blow me a cheap bubble to protect me? For I'm freezing, although I should sit at the window on guar—Mrs. Parkstein nudges the woman. "Many pardons," says Parkstein, "the rug's ears are dog-eared and you c'n trip on'm. None of our glass breaks," concludes Parkstein having fully regained her balance, a fragment detached at the beginning of time and rooted here. In Madame's opinion, there is a draft from the kitchen and the glazier must change the pane immediately, or has the servant left the window unputtied! Paul shouts from near Venus that he thinks everything is under control and there is no need to panic. Well, Madame is of the same opinion. The arrogant Mister walks with the proud stride of a matador over to the intruding woman (the false light-bearer), takes treasurelike splinters into his fingers so that they fall at his feet. "Naturally the maiden's duty was to voice her evil suspicions, which you will permit me to laugh at. I happen to be an expert. You have the proper radiation, my expert's organ indicates that. Open your mouth and say A-A-A-Amen. Just as I thought. I'm sorry, these are pieces of aquarium glass—goddamn, can't we expect anything of you? Look everyone, here it is, if it isn't the bottom of a bottle. Alfhild, come and see what on earth the neighbor lady is showing, well the girl is tired and her trial is unfinished and I have only two legs or welcome again, that is to say, at the best time if it is suitable and good luck to you, or goddamn it all, I'll push this woman's butt along myself, ahem, the hallway is long and dark." "Our own count must come with us!" the stand-in surrogate women's guard cries to the poor woman. Housekeeper Parkstein sweeps up the splinters of glass and throws them onto the coals.

Translated by Richard Impola

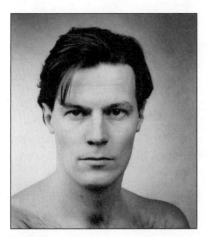

OLLI JAATINEN

Kari Kontio

Kari Kontio (b. 1956) has studied political science, philosophy, theology, and drama and has worked in journalism, television, radio, and the theater. In addition to publishing essays and fiction, he has been a parliamentary candidate, a playwright, and a theater director. Other interests include motorcycles and boxing. Kontio's frantic pseudoautobiography *Lajinsa viimeinen* (The Last of His Kind, 1992) is a romping diary of moral licentiousness, a veritable purgatory of self-analysis, and a record of spiritual growth. It mixes stentorian rhetoric with schoolboy profanities in an atmosphere of general sordidness that recalls the gutter sublime of Henry Miller, although Kontio's approach is infinitely more ironic and self-doubting. Kari, the novel's wry protagonist, recounts in detail how he wallowed in the shallow prosperity of the 1980s. Having experienced his comeuppance and suffered a complete psychological breakdown, he stands as a grotesque but endearing embodiment of the values of the yuppie decade. By dissecting his own soul, Kontio's protagonist also performs an autopsy on Finnish culture, revealing its philistinism, its redneck machismo, its materialism—and its humor and tenacity. The hard, cynical story concludes with an unexpected epiphany where God is likened to a military helicopter roaring protectively above the benighted protagonist. Hemingway, Mailer, Mamet? Kontio has links with the pugilistic tradition in American fiction, although the self-reflexive courage that informs his cutting prose seems wholly original. Kontio's novel surprises, stimulates, and entertains, and it marks the arrival of one of the most promising young writers in Scandinavia.

Bibliography: *Kirjava lehmä* (The Piebald Cow, with Tuomas Nevanlinna, 1988), *Kausi helvetissä* (A Season in Hell, 1988), *Lajinsa viimeinen* (The Last of His Kind, 1992). Forthcoming: *Kirkkoisän nainen* (The Church Father's Woman, 1996).

Interview

PHILIP LANDON: Can you name any shared characteristics of contemporary Finnish fiction? Do you identify with any of your international or domestic contemporaries?

KARI KONTIO: Perhaps the most characteristic feature of contemporary Finnish fiction is that it sells less and less, except for a handful of favorite entertainment titles. The market is also dominated by hugely hyped international best-sellers. Otherwise, I would say that books seem to be moving away from modernism and so-called critical social realism. People write at a remove from history, employing elaborate stylistic experiments, fantasy, and so forth. I don't identify myself with any writers, although I respect many. Of the living Finns I could mention Paavo Haavikko; of the dead, Mika Waltari and Yrjö Kokko. I understand the last two also had some success in the United States. Of foreign writers, I might name Robert Musil and Elmore Leonard.

PL: How would you situate fiction in general and your own work in particular in relation to mass culture and the mass media?

KK: Literature, music, drama, and the visual arts are not "media." What happens in the media is, at best, a commentary and a simulation of the arts. The arts must be experienced with immediacy for them to be able to alter our interior worlds. Mass culture and the mass media are vacuous concepts; we're all part of the same mass.

PL: Kai Laitinen has written, "The traditional Finnish novel is close to nature. Nature features in the role of a friend or an enemy or both." Can we read your work as part of this tradition? Does nature require a new approach from writers?

KK: My novel can be read as part of any tradition whatsoever, because it tells fascinating stories about nature, cities, and the human mental world, and then it splinters these stories on a metalevel.

PL: From the *Kalevala* to postwar fiction, much of Finnish literature has been intimately bound up with the question of national identity. Do you see yourself as a member of a more international generation?

KK: For me, Finnish culture has all but vanished, with the exception of the language and the sauna. As for internationalism, I can say I've traveled abroad in more than just the capacity of a tourist and that I've watched television avidly all my life (especially MTV, nowadays). What's more, I desperately wish to flourish on the international market—first, for money, and second, because there is nothing that the Finns value more than the praise of foreigners.

PL: Contemporary Finnish writers frequently use autobiographical and mock-autobiographical forms. Why?

KK: Perhaps the total situation is already so complex and rapidly changing that it's safer to speak for oneself only.

PL: The self-conscious narrator of *Lajinsa viimeinen* interrupts his titillating confessions at every turn to discourage one-dimensional reading-for-the-plot. Is irony integral to your work?

KK: In my opinion irony's got nothing to do with it; I loathe the very word—at least when it refers to some sort of arrogant snob-humor or emotional escape. Perhaps the element in my novel that has been interpreted as irony is my philosophical view of the psyche. In no way do I believe in the existence of a unified self or an identity within the subject. We just have ways of speaking about ourselves; identities hover between people and also among the rest of what surrounds us. Also, because I desire to write for many people, I must continually change the way in which the self incorporated in the novel views himself.

PL: The narrator of *Lajinsa viimeinen* reprimands himself for having belittled "the only Finnish virtue: honesty." He declares Finland to be "a vandal country without history." Similar remarks have been made about American culture. How does this association strike you?

KK: Of course it would be fascinating to trick oneself into believing that Finland is like America, but the association is artificial. America happens to be a genuinely young culture; assembled from all corners of the world, it has created its own rites and traditions. Large, fledgling cultures often give an impression of barbarity. Think of, say, the violence and rapid decline of Rome, the late Soviet Union, or the United States. Finns, by contrast, have lived in these parts and spoken these languages for at least seven thousand years. The distinction is that the people living in Finland were so-called indigenous peoples rather than modern citizens. We were nomads in our own world. Young, unified cultures, nations, always either destroy or absorb the nomads. With the Finns, this has happened over the past two hundred years or so. What is left is, as I already said, the language, in which "the Call of the Wild" still reverberates in the form of endless adjectives attached to nature—adjectives that so-called civilized people are incapable of translating or imagining. With the strength of about twenty-three possible adjectives, we always know exactly what the purling stream sounds like. But soon we'll be like the Indians of the silver screen, mouthing our clumsy one hundred words of English.

PL: Has your professional experience in television and radio had a significant influence on your fiction?

KK: I don't know. My writing takes shape in a purely organic process, emerging into the gap between the first and the last sentence. I always write those first. When I'm at a loss as to how I can fill that space with a novel that would have a form and a structure, I go and get totally wasted—lo and behold, the book comes, inch by inch. Perhaps my journalistic work has something to do with the fact that I always present the publisher with a honed product rather than some arty-farty stream of consciousness for the editors to weep over.

PL: The notion of masculine identity is a major preoccupation in *Lajinsa viimeinen*. Why is this topic important to you?

KK: I'm a man. In my next book, however, I'll be a woman. A woman who lived at the end of the fourth century at that!

From The Last of His Kind

Pen and Sword

When I left the army and took up my studies, I immediately joined the left-wing group of intellectual history students led by my friend Aimo as well as the university's Reserve Officers' Club headed by another old friend, Kenneth.

The former because I have always liked the company of intelligent people and it gave me a chance to earn drinking money on the student paper edited by Aimo. The Officers' Club because I could shoot a pistol and drink at the expense of banks, insurance firms, breweries, and export enterprises, which are all of the opinion that reserve officers are the "decision makers of the future."

I owe my status as a reserve officer to a double deceit. First, I had entered the army under cover of a false medical report. The physician father of a friend of mine classified me A-1, although I should have been a B-man owing to an allergy. The deceit was not motivated by a militaristic urge to embark upon the shittiest and longest training possible but by my desire to do my army service immediately after finishing school. B-men were not admitted into the army as volunteers; I would have had to wait for a draft call.

The second deception resulted from the first. Kenneth's father was a lieutenant colonel. He agreed to a civilian doctor's carrying out a false physical on one condition. "I demand that you excel," said the lieutenant colonel, warm as a sated bear.

That I did excel was thanks to a friend and classmate named Erik, who served in the same brigade with me, and also in the office of the headquarters company, where tests for the noncommissioned officers were duplicated. In exchange for evening beers, Erik always arranged to get the tests to me and another friend and service mate, Martti, ahead of time.

Thus I was able to get an excellent grade in the theory of radio communication, although in the practical tests I could neither send nor receive a blessed thing.

This occurrence is a perfect metaphor for my attitude toward the theory and practice of life. I need to transform my capacity for endless explanation into creative ability. The art of turning a dead end into an original artistic creation, a kind of coloring-book sketch of a hero of our time, a warning example for entertainment and edification. A picture of a panicky but spiritually vacuous person in a distorted landscape, where among others of his kind he repeats fine terms and signs, to purchase one last wish before the gaping abyss ahead.

The army suited me brilliantly. I have often kicked myself for not having taken it more seriously. I was quick to learn every last technique for evading work and responsibility while still managing to look brisk and soldierly. I scraped through officers' school by imitating others.

While still a high school student, I had begun cheating on women and leading a confused double life, from which the army was a perfect refuge. I still remember how free and relieved I felt when returning to the post after some mix-up with a woman, riding a 600 cc. Norton Dominator along the highway on an early fall night.

I wore a cadet's leave uniform, with (more stylish) combat boots I'd bought myself. The Norton putt-putted along between my thighs at an easy pace. Pleasant thoughts of the uncomplicated army life drifted through my mind. Reporting to the company duty officer, sleep during mandatory quiet hours, the wake-up call at six, morning chores at one's leisure (the princely prerogative of cadets), leading the group to breakfast, giving classes. The stern, deeply felt sense of power while forcing young men my age to obey.

Oh what a brainwasher's bursting exultation I felt at commanding those squirming boys in their combat jackets. I was intimidating and chickenshit but would change in a flash to an ally, and vice versa. I set limits for the world. I had asked every woman I knew to write to me so that at the top sergeant's public mail call I would receive an enviable stack of letter and postcard love.

We are taking explosives training. It is a hot summer day. We learn to build all kinds of playful traps for the enemy boys. With relish I explain how a clever guerrilla can double wire a pipe mine on a tree trunk: one, the classic trip wire across the trail; two, a type of pressure detonator buried in the ground beyond the wire. An enemy boy, who fancies himself alert and well trained, comes along. Being wary of wires, he may even have a metal detector. He notes that there is a mine somewhere, sees the wire, and steps over it with a knowing grin. And again there are letters of condolence from commanding officers and employment opportunities for army surgeons.

I laugh gaily at my sadistic fantasies. I wax enthusiastic about how handily one can set up a splendid trap on a suitable slope with only trinitro and makeshift materials. First a sturdy hole resistant to explosive pressure is dug, a charge is set to explode in its bottom, then the hole is filled with fist-sized rocks or iron scrap, tightly packed with dirt, and finally the trap is camouflaged, say with pretty oxeye daisies, the petals of which a tired soldier loves to finger as he remembers his sweetheart.

Until the air is again garish with blood, shit, guts, and razor blades—the army term.

Wolverine Tracks

I truly wonder how that boy of fifteen who once found wolverine tracks on a snow-covered lake could develop into a prick like me.

That boy, of course, became excited, slung a shotgun over his back, started up his snowmobile, and hit the trail. It was one of those treacherous Koillismaa mornings—the sky was shitty, the expression they use. The tracks were bluish shadows on the pale gray snow. From close up, one could see that they were exceptionally fresh. Although the boy was young, he knew very well that the wolverine had decided now in the early morning to skirt the pond to the east. The easiest way, exposed to dangers the animal had reckoned as only slight.

The boy sped along the trail in the snowmobile. He knew that with very good luck he might at least see the secretive blood drinker darting through the pale dawn to who knows where, to lie in ambush for new prey. Ideally he would get a shot at the animal as it raced across the white ice of the lake.

The snowmobile obeyed his fifteen-year-old hand perfectly. He was not sitting but was kneeling on the seat, to see more clearly from higher up, in the direction the wolverine was taking. The engine howled rather loudly, snow flew from the sides of the treads, and the skis hammered along the trail. The boy had pressed the throttle to the bottom with his right thumb. "Now, goddamn!" he thought confusedly.

Suddenly there appeared to the searching eyes of the speeding boy a fleeting black shape against the white surface of the pond. The wolverine! The animal made a sharp turn and scurried off toward the opposite shore. The boy made a turn half as sharp and headed in that direction to cut him off. Everything now depended upon whether the boy could get the shotgun off his back before the wolverine reached the shelter of a spruce grove on the shore. As he jerked the shotgun over his shoulders, the boy estimated that the wolverine had a good 150 meters to run. He cocked the bolt as he leaped from the sled onto the snowy ice and aimed the bead some distance ahead of the wolverine. He estimated the animal's speed, his own distance from it, and the weapon's muzzle velocity without himself understanding anything about these calculations. Having analyzed the situation for one tenth of a second, he pulled the trigger. Snow spurted up a meter in front of the wolverine's snout, and the animal instantly changed direction. It was still heading for the same goal, but now began to zigzag like a luffing sailboat. If anything, its speed increased. It was impossible to know where and how much to lead it. For a little while the boy tried to follow the path of the animal with the barrel of his rifle but he realized that only a chance shot could hit it. Pretending nonchalance, he lowered his rifle and said: "Well go then, you devil!"

The boy felt an astonishing sense of well-being. He rejoiced because the animal was so clever and swift. The snowmobile took him back to camp along the old tread tracks, which had already obliterated the animal's trail during the pursuit. When he arrived at the camp, Father and his buddies were waking up with hangovers. Someone was at the water hole dousing his face with ice-cold water.

"Well, what's new, son?"

"I almost got to shoot a wolverine," I said.

"Yaah, a wolverine," said the man. "Hey, there's been a wolverine killer up and around at the crack of dawn," he yelped to another of the hungover men.

At the time, nature was still the same thing to me as women or girls. For then I thought of them as girls. There was nothing to be hated in either of them. One had only to get along, to learn to play with them. My relationships with nature and women were marked by fair play. I was no more concerned with owning or mastering them than I was with destroying them. I wanted only to be with them. I trusted and respected them. I could not fear them.

Only later, when I had struck a woman for the first time, did I begin to slink through the woods like a secret killer. Fortunately the woods are, when they so desire, a sufficiently overpowering antagonist to humble the haughtiest of men.

For years I have not touched a hunting rifle or spent one full day in a true wilderness. I had the sense to draw back in good time. To wait for the proper state of mind. To live alone, without my loved one, the forest.

I have not been able to go without women. I have not drawn back, have not waited for the proper state of mind, have not lived alone, without a loved one. I have simply drifted from one blind alley to another, chosen hurriedly, chosen wrong. I have silenced my understanding with ceaseless internal chatter. When I should have listened, I screamed like a fire alarm. When I should have spoken, I was as silent as a prison wall.

All Three Last Tycoons Become Products of the Imagination

I first understood my situation—although incorrectly, to be honest—in the late summer of 1979. (The previous winter I had shot a raven.) I was sitting on the balcony of a room at the Kalastajatorppa in Helsinki. I was staying at the hotel with my father. It was less than a year before his death. I was acting as his chauffeur. I had taken a leave of absence from the publishing house. It concerned some vague business dealings with the Konela firm, marketing rental Ladas in northern Finland.

Father was sitting on the opposite side of the balcony table. On the table were a bottle of dry vodka, two glasses, and bottles of lemon soda in a bucket of ice. It was a beautiful sunny afternoon. A red carpet was rolled out in front of the restaurant opposite our balcony.

The assistant vice minister for foreign affairs of the Soviet Union was arriving soon to host a dinner for Urho Kekkonen, the president of the republic, and for the government of the country, a large number of officials, and a horde of Russian embassy flies and spies.

Father watched in silence as black automobiles escorted by motorcycle policemen began to glide up to the restaurant. With a vaguely superior smile, he poured lemon soda into his vodka, making an occasional sarcastic remark. The automobiles disgorged their dark-clothed and high-heeled contents to trip along the carpet into the friendly bosom of the air-conditioned restaurant; they were all feigning a down-to-earth modesty.

When the president's Cadillac limousine finally made its appearance around a curve, the heraldic lion brandishing its saber on the hood, Father tossed off the remainder of his drink, straightened up in the sun chair, and poured himself another shot of straight vodka. As Kekkonen stepped along toward the restaurant, still erect, his bald head gleaming in the sun, Father followed his progress without blinking.

Just as the president's back vanished into the dimness beyond the gaudy doorman, Father raised his glass, like one swindler toasting another. He nodded with a nasty sneer on his face and tossed off the drink without a grimace. Then he turned to me with an inscrutable, half-affectionate smile and said: "Well, what about it? Shall we also order whores with the Russians' money?"

I told him I would probably go to the movies, and I did. I saw Elia Kazan's *The Last Tycoon*. When Robert De Niro in the lead role gave his monologue on what a movie is, I finally realized that the mere assurance of one's presentation can convert the stupidest tale to truth—in the movies, in the business world, in politics, and above all in love. For me, the figures of Father and Kekkonen came to be just as authentic and obligatory as any character in a movie. I could choose to identify, or not.

After the movie I sat in a pub and laughed aloud into my glass of beer. I was still unable to fear anything, no, not even when a gloomy chance companion at the bar had just told me he had lost everything: his business to the bank, his family to booze, his friends to the smell of failure. But I was then young and stupid, with all my dangerous knowledge—I wasn't even drinking like a sponge. My bar mate was the same age I am today. Now all I can write is this humble and alcoholic platitude, that the new generation always thinks itself wiser than the old. Indeed, I believe that nothing is more dangerous than knowledge that outpaces experience.

That is precisely why the world will end soon. At birth, the last generation will already have unlimited knowledge available, without the least bit of experience to restrict, chasten, and frighten them. Knowledge, untainted by experience, leads to unlimited optimism and self-confidence. The final utopia is on its way to realization.

When people are at one and the same time young and old, as innocent as children and full of mute knowledge, the eternal totems begin to speak with the mouths of children. They join with the child-person and turn against the millennial taboos. When the totems no longer protect nature, her wise beings, inexplicable rules, forefathers' customs, lives, and breath, they no longer protect and honor God himself.

In our time God need not raise a finger to summon the horsemen of the apocalypse. Fire and brimstone will plunge through a sky already rent by the greedy child himself. God has no need to break his covenant. He has no need to grow angry, to take revenge. He has only to spread his hands like a loving father and grant his child's plea.

But I merely boasted to my companion that I would leave my work and the university. I said I already knew enough. I said that next week I would kick start the Norton and take off for Europe without plans or a timetable, doing whatever happened to amuse me. I would sleep when I was tired, eat when I was hungry, and work when I was poor.

My stupid companion could do nothing but jabber drunkenly that I should do it, that the young should take chances. I gave him my high school graduation watch and assured him that I no longer needed it.

In a week I was in Europe. As a hospital orderly in Stockholm.

A Novel Must Create Expectations and Fulfill Them

I want to be attentive and pleasing to you, dear reader. The questions remain excitingly open. Who? How? Where? When? Why? And above all, the classic: Who is guilty? I promise to answer all questions. I am as honest as Satan himself. An agreement made with me has this advantage, that you know who you are dealing with.

I am literature. I entice the reader to accompany me on a trip to hell. This is a very traditional detective story. The plot has in it something old, something new, and something borrowed, like a bridal gown. Let's change sexes. You are the fiancé of the novel, and you can undress me at night if you walk nicely with me down the aisle to the altar. You are to approve the novel's respiration and rhythm, and this time it is as whimsical as the mind of a bride-to-be. On the one hand, it is to be hoped that all will soon be over; on the other hand, it is desirable to savor your suffering so that there will be something to remember.

Don't rush me, dear, or I'll trip on my pretty shoes. Follow my father's example. Did you see how calmly and decorously and, above all, how professionally he gave me away to you? Now be worthy of the trust. This is no experimental art that strives to shatter forms and rituals. This tale does not live on rejection and scandal; it does not lay bare the mind's corruption or politicize the unconscious. This novel is guiltless and sufficient unto itself, like a dance or a marriage.

A novel *is* ritual. Its aim is to produce and bolster a predictable world. It succeeds only if we approve the roles. If you don't know the steps, follow the rhythm, try it, test it. In the end, notes and steps are merely guideposts for interpretation. The dancer must be in the same state of becoming as the music. If you don't care for jarring compositions, you can transpose more placid sound pictures into your head. Thus we can glide effortlessly from the altar into the swirling wedding waltz of the future. One need not understand everything. One can enjoy books as one enjoys life or the chess column's warlike tropes and exclamation points, knowing nothing about the game or its object.

Remember, we were told at the start that we were on a journey to hell. Before that we are faced with a wedding night. I leave you now for a moment to ponder if you want to be the groom at night also, or if you would prefer to dress in the white silk of the bride. If you want to climb to the ceiling, you will find a mirror there that is a true pleasure to look into.

Life Must Be Protected

Hear how far death had progressed in Sweden in the late seventies. I was then in Stockholm, working in the chronic-disease ward and the morgue of a hospital. Beautiful dying in a beautiful land.

Well, let's take seventy-five-year-old Jenny, scrunched up, silenced and paralyzed by Parkinson's disease. Weight sixty-six pounds. Life of any human value totally ended over ten years ago. There are relatives, but they no longer visit her because it is too appalling. Frightful pain. Forty pills a day. With her last iota of strength and intelligence, Jenny tries a hunger strike. She refuses to open the last movable part of her body, her mouth. I don't want to force her; I pat her cheek and push the gruel cart over to the next "patient." He is Oscar, who has suffered a stroke. All he can say is "No." It takes some time to figure out if his "no" means denial, agreement, or something else.

After my rounds, I am sitting in the employees' lounge negotiating pussy with Monica Zetterström, an orderly, when the wing supervisor, a Romanian hysteric named Julia, comes rushing up to me screaming that she will be held responsible if Jenny dies of malnutrition. Some sack of spite has reported my "negligence" to her. Julia drags me along to Jenny's room to show me how she should be handled. She grabs the old woman by the knot of nerves under the hinge of her jaw and squeezes so hard that it crunches. Tears well up into Jenny's eyes, a miserable whine sounds from her throat, her mouth opens, and Julia begins to shovel the revolting gruel into the oldster's mucoid mouth. Although Julia is a Swedish citizen, she is constantly afraid that for some reason she will be deported to Romania into the hands of the secret police. She doesn't take chances.

The high-quality upkeep of these two people, the patient and the caretaker, costs the ideal commonwealth of Sweden ten thousand crowns a day. Crowns torn from the earth with the destructive power of atomic energy and combustion engines, from polluting factories, and from every possible sector of industrial life. For responsibility, love, and sense they substituted wages, hospital equipment, plastic spoons, leisure time, staff parties, and a society ticking away like a time bomb, which could afford all this.

The next day, I marched to the personnel office and took a job in the morgue.

I was given a raise in pay.

Now we are in the same state in Finland. So Finland may also be discussed in a chapter entitled "Europe." For it is to that kind of Europe that Finland may belong, a dying Europe.

A Clash of Cultures

The hospital morgue was a fun place to work in the winter. There was only a trickle of grannies and grandpas from the eleven floors of wards to the basement, a couple every few days. As a joke, we called our cold cellar the Second Circle, after Dante's *Inferno*. The chronic-disease ward was the First Circle.

We? My work partner was a pleasant and agreeable kid named Roy, who taught me the rudiments of Stockholm's discos, rock clubs, and the general alternative culture scene.

With Roy's help I broke free of the dull-minded Finns. From that awful emigrant's life, where one wakes up beside a mouse-colored girl from Kauhava, a girl who is forever spending her year's break somewhere in the Rinkeby suburbs before entering the university. That girl whom one recognizes in the subway as a Finn—in a split second, no matter how often she has patronized Åhlen's and the little boutiques of the Old City. No matter what color she has dyed her hair, and no matter how fluently she speaks mainland Swedish. That girl whose greatest mistake is to try to pass herself off as the real thing.

On the other hand, what else could she do? She had no identity, no national self. She was white and raised on television, advertising, and the nanny state. Structurally, she was Scandinavian, a kind of Western automobile produced under license in Eastern Europe, a Russian Volvo. The same but uglier, clumsier, a little shorter-legged. Neither blonde nor brunette, but a crossbreed, with a language that conflicted with her northern genes. That Ugrian tongue which bends and kneads the world, conforming to nature by means of endless adjectives and case forms. That language that cannot organize the world under prefixes, into a game.

She was worse off than a black. She was praised for her diligence. She was presumed to have the same values as the majority. Yet it was nearly impossible for her to latch on to a Swedish man.

I escaped from her, and as a return gift, I taught Roy (who was the son of a senior tax official) nihilism, Finnish gloom, and serious drinking. I set him to reading Spengler's *Decline of the West*, Schiller's *Robbers*, Ernst Toller's bitter plays, Machiavelli's *Prince*, Nietzsche, of course, and—as a special treat—Hannu Salama.

In our free time we spent shadowy evenings among Roy's friends in artistic and vegetarian circles sympathizing with all kinds of minority nationalities. The fiery-eyed representatives of these minorities were almost without exception men, who, at some point in their pot smoking, stole the lush, empathetic girlfriends of the thin-wristed, narrow-chested Swedish humanist guys. The same girls who are now pleading for the return of their kidnapped children from Iran.

The humanist guys didn't dare to show anger. Besides the fact that they would have been beaten up, their girlfriends would later have branded them racists and collaborators with the system. I still can't decide whether those unfortunate young men with their ethnic dress and scraggly blond beards were more afraid of their girlfriends or of the thick, black masculine beards of the minority men.

These are the same guys who later founded all those truly pathetic men's groups and finally—fortunately for them—discovered their feminine side (their sensitivity) and dared (after long confidential discussions) to grasp each other's penises. Without having to perform.

I will always remember that gray February morning when Roy came to work late, with a terrible hangover. Of course the steel service elevator had to bring down an exceptionally revolting corpse from Ward Seven the first thing in the morning—some unfortunate soul named Birgitta who had died of a stomach cancer. She was, I recall, about fifty-seven years old.

It was one of our agreeable tasks to rip off Birgitta's hospital garb and disinfect her, put a tag on her toe, and shove her into the cooler to await the always cheerful, playful pathology crew. Naturally we wore full protective gear, masks and all, but still a hint of rotted intestines penetrated our nostrils.

Roy had said hardly a word all morning. Suddenly, just as he was shoving Birgitta into the locker, he turned to look at me and said, with a gloomy rage in his soft voice: "Damn it, Kari, you really were right. You were right from the very beginning!" Then he slammed Birgitta on her cheerful roller board into the cold and darkness. Into the Third Circle waiting room.

We always kept cold beer in an empty body slot. We opened a Pripps Blå each, and I asked what I had been right about.

Roy guzzled down half a can in one go, swept his long blond hair back behind his ears, and said, "About everything." I had been right about everything. He declared wildly that he would cancel his application for civilian service and go directly into the army in the spring. And to the barber today.

Translated by Richard Impola

PENTTI SAMMALLAHTI

Leena Krohn

Leena Krohn (b. 1947) is best known for her essays and short stories. Much of her recent work straddles the line between narrative and essay, yielding a sort of cerebral lyricism that focuses on a range of scientific, technological, and historical concerns. Her favorite themes include the problem of determinism and the mysterious relationship between consciousness and physical matter. Krohn handles her challenging subjects with clarity and elegance, and she thinks nothing of mixing fantasy with abstract contemplation or of shattering the unity of a work by using textual cross-references. One is at a loss to find a counterpart among writers in English, although the habit of incorporating philosophical reflection in short fiction recalls Edgar Allan Poe and the work of such contemporary philosophers as Thomas Nagel. Krohn has also published children's fiction, including the acclaimed *Ihmisen vaatteissa* (In Human Clothes, 1976), which has been translated into seven languages. Krohn's work is accessible without being simplistic and up-to-date without being trendy. Her profundities will seem austere to readers who like their fiction full-blooded and entertaining. But the numerous literary awards that Krohn has won and especially the breadth of her readership testify to the fact that there is a market in Finland for serious writing that refuses to be fashionable or trivial. She recently made her English-language debut with *Doña Quixote and Other Writings, and Gold of Ophir* (Carcanet, 1995).

Selected essays and fiction: *Donna Quijote ja muita kaupunkilaisia* (Doña Quixote and Other Townspeople, 1983), *Tainaron, postia toisesta kaupungista* (Tainaron, Mail from Another City, 1985), *Rapina ja muita esseitä* (Rustle and Other Essays, 1989), *Umbra* (Umbra, 1990), *Matemaattisia olioita tai jaettuja unia* (Mathematical Beings or Shared Dreams, 1992), *Tribar* (Tribar, 1993), *Ettei etäisyys ikävöisi* (That the Distance Should Not Grieve, 1995), *Sfinksi ja robotti* (The Sphinx and the Robot, 1995). Children's books: *Vihreä vallankumous* (The Green Revolution, 1970), *Ihmisen vaatteissa* (In Human Clothes, 1976), *Salaisuuksia* (Secrets, 1992), *Älä lue tätä kirjaa* (Don't Read This Book, 1994).

Interview

PHILIP LANDON: Can you name any shared characteristics of contemporary Finnish fiction? Do you identify with any of your international or domestic contemporaries?

LEENA KROHN: Agrarian, epic, masculine, and realist traits have dominated Finnish fiction for a long time, even though there have always been people who have also trodden side paths, duckboards, and even unbeaten snow. Diversity has increased in recent years, which is delightful.

I can identify neither with Finnish nor with international contemporaries, although there are many whom I revere and whose influence can be discerned in my writing if you look carefully. Such writers—to name but a few —include Giuseppe Tomasi di Lampedusa, Italo Calvino, Boris Pasternak, Don DeLillo, Salvatore Quasimodo, and Harry Martinson. What I've read by them has been transformed into part of my experience.

As for Finnish authors, I have been more interested in the poets than in prose writers, principally Edith Södergran, Helvi Juvonen, Gunnar Björling, and Mirkka Rekola.

What I have experienced in this flesh, in this time and this place, is known to me alone. What interest it has stems not from the fact that it is *mine* but from the fact that it is one person's experience and thus comparable with the experience of anyone else. But the expression that I am groping toward, does not yet exist. It will be rich and simple at the same time.

PL: How would you situate fiction in general and your own work in particular in relation to mass culture and the mass media?

LK: I see fiction as a counterforce to propaganda. Fiction and fantasy boost our spiritual and moral immune system. This is one reason why tyrants are afraid of literature. The same cannot be said of entertainment, although the roles of literature and mass culture have become blurred somewhat of late.

I have been told that my works also contain entertaining elements. If that makes them easier to understand, all the better. I do not, however, specifically aim to entertain; rather, I wish to question the obvious.

PL: Kai Laitinen has written, "The traditional Finnish novel is close to nature. Nature features in the role of a friend or an enemy or both." Can we read your work as part of this tradition? Does nature require a new approach from writers?

LK: I see nature neither as a friend nor as an enemy; it is too huge to be either. My consciousness is also part of nature, which for me implies that everything is connected. But of course my Finnish environment has had an indelible effect on me. I acknowledge my roots, and the extraordinary beauty of the world is manifested to me in the forests and shores of Finland, its granite bedrock, its waterways, and its falling snow.

PL: From the *Kalevala* to postwar fiction, much of Finnish literature has been intimately bound up with the question of national identity. Do you see yourself as a member of a more international generation?

LK: For my generation, national independence has been too self-evident. National identity is in a continual state of metamorphosis, as it should be. No nation is separate, but the borders that separate nations are cell membranes: they facilitate diffusion as well as osmosis.

I do not believe in nationalistic literature. All the arts share roots in the consciousness of the human race. All literature contributes to the same human cathedral that reaches out toward the unknown. The output of a particular writer is only a brick in a wall that rises but is never finished.

Nations and languages are not eternal; they flourish for a while, decay, and die. But literature cannot die as long as there is consciousness and suffering in the world.

PL: Contemporary Finnish writers frequently use autobiographical and mock-autobiographical forms. Why?

LK: Do Finnish writers use autobiographical forms more often than European writers as a group?

PL: You pursue scientific and technological topics in an intimate, lyrical prose style. Can we call you a humanizer of science?

LK: Humanizing science is by no means my main aim. It merely so happens that I have been unable to avoid scientific and technological topics; in fact they pester me. In the future I believe that the human and natural sciences will engage in a far more lively dialogue than they do now. This is indispensable. We will see more and more clearly that ecology, economics, and psychology cannot be separated from one another. There are also areas, such as multimedia, where different art forms, entertainment, and science (e.g., fractal mathematics) will blend together in new, interesting combinations.

PL: Your work often explicitly investigates the issue of spirit/matter dualism. This is hardly a fashionable preoccupation in an age of materialism and considering the way binary oppositions have come under assault from poststructuralist thinkers. Why does the mind-body problem haunt you?

LK: I sometimes get called a postmodern writer. I do not know why this is, because I am not sure what postmodernism is, either. But if—as I have heard—postmodernists assume that narrative is dead, they are wrong. The human brain spins stories—even during sleep, because we need drama, a plot, meanings, and figures. A person is a web of images and stories.

I have never sought to become an avant-garde author or wished to transform Finnish fiction. My goals as a writer are far more modest—and more ambitious.

The mind-body problem is nowhere near a solution. Apparently, physicists as well as philosophers and psychologists in different parts of the world are once more gathering around it. The mind-body problem inspires me both intellectually and emotionally, and the fact that it is a problem cannot be dispelled by any trick, structuralist or positivist. Where is the poststructuralist who can tell us the exact way in which the mind and the physical world interact?

PL: Fantasy and logic are both prominent in your prose. Is this a contradiction?

LK: Conflict and paradox are part not only of the human mind but of the nature of reality itself. I believe that the cosmos—at least the one that we inhabit—is based on contradiction. So why should paradox not have a place in literature? Lewis Carroll already understood that there could be no fantasy without logic and no logic without fantasy.

PL: You seem delightfully indifferent to the restrictions of traditional genre, and you freely combine philosophical disquisitions with fictional material. How did you come to this form?

LK: Philosophical problems are not born in philosophy departments but in normal human life. I have, it is true, studied theoretical philosophy, but it is not theory that leads me to such questions. The most personal experiences, those connected with death, love, guilt, beauty, suffering, growing up and aging, childhood and motherhood, drive me to philosophy and metaphysics. But the idea becomes word through fiction, because fiction and poetry are where the concrete beauty of life is revealed.

Lucilia illustris

> Darling, do you remember what we stood gazing at
> in the glow of a summer morning?
> —Charles Baudelaire

An abandoned railway spur led to a factory yard overgrown with brushwood. It was located at the extreme north end of the city, in a neighborhood to which one moved when there was no alternative. Here were city-owned apartment buildings, a supermarket, a primary school, two kiosks, an end-of-the-line bus stop, a paint factory, and a national railway supply depot.

The last item to be produced in the low-ceilinged rooms of the factory had been Christmas tree ornaments. If you could bring yourself to peer through a broken window, you could still see a long, fuzzy strip of silvery tinsel gleaming in the dust on the floor.

I know this, for I did glance inside—and saw the forgotten glitter.

Behind the workers' barracks that had served as a canteen, the yard sloped off steeply and then crumbled into a sand pit.

The residents of the neighborhood used the sand pit as an illegal garbage dump, throwing all the usual refuse there: refrigerators, automobile tires and hubcaps, damaged office machinery, rusted oil drums, and leaky canisters whose contents were best forgotten. There were parts of things so altered from their original form that one could no longer guess their function. The plush covering of a sofa was splotched with mold, as well as with wine and sperm stains from parties held decades before.

In the summer, field chamomile and fireweed and wormwood seemed to do their best to hide the human refuse, but their efforts fell short.

And it was summer now. An armchair sat on the rusted rails, looking as if it had been set there for display, to bewilder, to mock, as if a viewer were meant to take it for a private vehicle of transportation, one which at any moment might start speeding southward to where the stout rails joined the main line, to go on from there till it arrived at the railway station in the city.

Behind the armchair, between a burned-out Datsun and a Strömberg electric hearth, lay another object. It was, I admit, very strange that it should have escaped notice for so long. Now all our attention was fixed on it.

It was tightly wrapped in a yellowish cotton quilt that had once had a floral pattern and was tied over and over with a plastic clothesline. The quilt was partially decayed; it had been soaked by rains and by secretions from its contents.

The highest fever in a living being never rises to the heat of decay, which in this case had consumed both the object and its wrapping. The colors of the quilt had faded and run into each other. One could only guess at the original design: mere streaks and pilled patches of color remained. But the heat of bacterial action had not been the only cause of decay: insects, flies and their larvae, beetles, and many other species had shared in the work of destruction.

It was the height of summer, so early in the morning that the city was still asleep. A bird unknown to me was warbling in an elder bush on the slope of the sand pit. The berries on the bush were already turning red. A little sand sifted down from above as if someone were walking there. I looked up but saw no one. The sand was falling of its own accord.

A camera shutter clicked repeatedly. A photographer was executing a complicated dance around his objective, squatting, taking a brief series of pictures with a hand-held camera, then shifting his position, setting up his tripod, and clicking again.

The rest of us, a detective and a couple of uniformed policemen and I, all summoned to the place by an anonymous telephone call, looked at the bundle silently, without a lens, until one of the policemen vomited. At the same instant, as if by common agreement, they all moved away, in fact recoiled, from the source of the stench.

I couldn't. On the contrary, I had to go right up close and bend over the bundle. I was already drawing on my rubber gloves. I had to do my job, even though I had felt exhausted the minute I saw the bundle. It looked like a week of hard work.

"A shitty job," one of the policeman said in a muffled voice.

I glanced at him coldly as I opened my equipment case and selected the right set of tweezers.

Actually, I would have liked to recline in the faded armchair, where someone had once sat reading peacefully of a winter evening. I would have searched for the hidden lever to propel it into motion, sunk my head deep into the padded cushion, and sped away from the officials and the unknown corpse, as far as the rails would carry me.

But I soon forgot the armchair. The bundled-up world, from which a buzzing melody arose, possessed me completely. I did not open the package yet: it was not time for that. The others were too far away and could not hear the melody. If they had, it would have driven them even farther away.

I have never been able to close my ears to it. It is the voice of decay, the voice of life in death.

A man, himself a poet of sorts (with whom I had sometimes slept), in a fit of drunkenness once read me Charles Baudelaire's poem "Carrion" from start to finish. I hadn't known it before.

"It's for you," he said. "Remember it always."

I remember. It can be assumed that the corpse that the speaker of the poem and his beloved saw on a bed of pebbles at a turn in the trail had been dead only a few days. It was in the second stage of decay, actually shifting into the third, since it stank and was still bloated with internal gases. But the skin was already beginning to tear: "You expose your belly, pregnant with stench."

I have also heard the sound Baudelaire writes of, the "strange music" that reminds one of the wind or a stream or the rustle of grain. Its source is the movement of insects, their overlapping mats, rolling, digging, eating, procreating, shedding their shells, growing, and preying.

When I first heard the melody, it nearly turned my stomach. It no longer has that effect on me.

I am an entomologist. In my youth, I made field trips to many countries. Once, in a rural town the name of which I have forgotten, I had lunch in a dirty restaurant. On the wall of the ladies' room someone had written in a swift sweeping hand: *Time is nature's way of keeping everything from happening at once.*

I thought it a strange and remarkable graffiti to appear in the restroom of such a bad restaurant. The moment I read the words, I felt they had been written just for me. I could not imagine the person who had written the words standing before me. All I could see was a hand that wrote.

The poem and the words have stuck in my mind all these years.

To fix a time—that is my function. The restroom wall told the truth: if there were no time, everything would happen at once. There would be no distinct causes and effects. There would be no chain of causality reaching to infinity. But as it is, things succeed one another in a precisely determined order: an effect never precedes a cause. This holds true for death and dying as well as for life.

Perhaps you ask: Why speak of what is self-evident? I answer: Because it is in just such matters that the real mystery resides.

As a sideline to my profession, I take part in forensic medical investigations. I am called to the scene when a body is found and the time of death needs to be fixed more precisely. Homicide is usually involved. This happens four or five times a year. I have to repel, conquer, or at least put aside my revulsion, pity, fear, and grief. Do not imagine that I have conquered them over the years. They are still there, but I can function regardless.

I am called to the scene as soon as a body is discovered. I travel around the country carrying a briefcase containing dozens of specimen cases. They are for insects. I collect in them all the insects I find on the surface of the body and in the immediate vicinity.

Only then is the body taken to the Institute for Forensic Medicine. There I continue my investigation, going, so to speak, beneath the surface: I take samples, analyze insects, assigning them to species and estimating their numbers and stage of development. Meanwhile, of course, pathologists carry out the other routine investigations they consider indispensable at the Institute. Only when both they and I have finished are the remains surrendered to the family and the funeral home.

Most frequently the victims are women or girls. Sometimes they are homeless men. Once I had to analyze the mummified body of a newborn child.

In some respects I am in the same position as meteorologists. The farther ahead they have to predict, the less accurate they are. It is like getting farther away from a radio station: the static increases until finally the transmission is lost completely. This occurs rather quickly: it is impossible to forecast a month ahead. Countless variables convert such estimates to mere guesses.

I "predict" backwards and my task is easier, fixing the time of just one event, the death of a given organism. Nevertheless, my findings are subject to the same laws. The longer a body has been permitted to lie there, the less accurate is my pronouncement on the time of death. If the body is found after four or even five days, the estimate is accurate within hours. If it is found after weeks, make it days; if months, make it weeks.

And there comes a time when I can say nothing.

I serve neither the prosecution nor the defense. But my expertise can be used to prove either guilt or innocence. As an entomologist, I am not interested in who is guilty and who is innocent.

I want the answer to only one question: When?

I say to this deceased one: Tell me when you died and they will know who killed you.

A childish person once asked me: Don't the victims come to haunt you?

Why in God's name should they? I'm not the one who killed them. I'm not afraid of them. I could be afraid or contemptuous of those who have brought the body to the state in which I find it. But I hardly even pity the victims. They have felt utter terror and insufferable pain, but that is over now. It is truly over. The victims are no longer there where I see the bodies. Do they care whether their remains lie resting in a family grave under a granite monument, sheltered by a wrought iron fence, or lie rotting nameless in the filth of a garbage dump?

Victims do not rise from their resting places like the horror figures of a B movie, splotchy rustling shapes with beetles for eyes, hollows for noses that have been eaten away, skin—or what once was skin—moving in slow undulations to the pulsing of the larval armadas.

Those who have met a violent end are no different from those who have died of so-called natural causes. Even that kind of death is violent.

But if the end is caused by another person, its consequences are more lasting. Grief is more unbearably piercing, tears stay hot longer. And the scorching furnace of rage—that's a very different heat from the steam produced by decay, which purifies, dissolves, and ultimately renews.

Decay is the precondition of all renewal.

Yet nothing is considered as shocking and dreadful as decay when it affects the substance of which we are made: human flesh.

The different phases of decay vary with temperature and environment. I must be exactly informed about both the taxonomy and the duration of different stages of insect life, as well as the circumstances and climatic conditions of each site where a find is made. We speak of the body's growing cold. But very soon, although the warmth of life has left the skin, the body's internal temperature begins to rise. As I have said earlier, the maximal fever in a living being never rises to the height of this afterglow, the heat of decay.

And now life in death and life after death begin, although—as has been stated—not everything happens at once. We must remember that the insects come in waves which follow one another in a predictable order. Although decay itself is a continuous process, it is useful to distinguish and name several phases as an aid to investigation.

In my investigations I follow M. Lee Goff's five-phase sequence.

The first wave arrives during the "fresh" stage, which lasts from twenty-four hours to a week or two, depending upon environmental and weather conditions. How quickly they come! How in fact do they know? My expertise fails me. I doubt that anyone can answer. Flesh flies are on the scene in ten minutes, long before a human nose can detect the slightest hint of a smell. The process has begun. Thereafter it continues without a pause. A more careful, exact, and orderly job of cleansing is not to be observed anywhere.

The first wave of insects, mainly the flesh flies, are sometimes called the garbage men. They attack the soft tissues and soon destroy them. They are attracted to all the openings: the eyes, the ears, the nose, the mouth. Their labors clear the way for the next group, those that prefer gristle and dry skin.

The next phase of decay is the swelling stage, when the body's temperature rises and internal gases cause it to bloat. At this point flies and larvae are still the predominant genus.

Only during the third phase of decay, the rotting stage, does the body begin noticeably to smell. The corpse wrapped in the quilt was at just this stage. Its skin was tearing and gases were being released. This is when the greatest number of larvae appear, both within the body and on its surface. However, they soon give way to the armies of coleoptera. During their phase all the flesh disappears, leaving only skin, cartilage, and bones.

During the first stages of rotting, insects that prey on other insects also make their appearance to devour those mentioned above; parasites march and crawl forth, along with omnivores, which feed on both the corpse and other insects.

There is yet another group of insects not really relevant to the matter in any way: they blunder onto the corpse by chance and gain nothing from it. One might imagine they have nothing to tell me, but that is a mistaken assumption. Sometimes I find insects on the scene that are completely foreign to the environment.

What can one conclude from that? A fact of extraordinary interest to the police: that the body was brought from somewhere else to the place where it was discovered. In all, there may be eight or nine such insects which differ from the others. In a given stage of decay one can find several hundred distinct species of insects on a body.

The process goes forward relentlessly, although the duration of its various phases varies from case to case. The length of these periods depends on environmental circumstances and the fluctuation and duration of the temperature. But the increase in number of insects, the hatching of their eggs, the development of larvae into individual adults always occurs according to the same laws. Note this well: NATURE NEVER SKIPS A STEP AND NEVER GOES BACK. Never, not anywhere. Or, for the sake of caution, let's say not here anywhere, nor ever in time.

Nor can we do anything, not a single thing, to force her to skip a step or go back. She cannot do either. The only thing we can do is to regulate conditions so that processes are delayed or accelerated.

Crops are not harvested in the spring. The child becomes an adult only by way of puberty and the insect an imago only after having been a pupa. Not a single phase can be omitted and each one occurs in an order governed by law. In the fixed and inexorable order. In the only possible order.

On this truth I base all my certainty and uncertainty.

With one wave following another, before long we reach the phase of after-decay, when even the skin and cartilage disappear. Then only what is lasting remains, that which may be preserved for hundreds, perhaps thousands of years: hair and bones.

Then all is over. The fluids and gases have vanished, the temperature has fallen, the mucus has dried up, the stench has gone. Everything is settled and irreversible. Cold and dry, clean and brittle. We view the remains calmly, without revulsion.

The insects are gone, and I too will have long since departed. All is done. If anything is left, it will be invisible, like sorrow and soul.

They do not always find an answer even to the question of the deceased's identity. That is exactly what happened to this woman. She had been left to lie in place for three weeks during the height of summer, so the insects had been at work for a long time, and my estimates were very rough.

The police went to a lot of trouble to identify her but found out very little. She had taken the last bus to that neighborhood on the night that she was killed. She had been alone, and the driver had not noticed anyone talking to her. She was from another country, but which one was not discovered. To my knowledge, the woman was never identified.

Who was she? What exactly does that mean? Officially it means a name, address, date and place of birth, height, color of hair, identifying marks, if there are any. And if one should want further details, her father's and mother's names, her profession and marital status. This information being known, it is assumed that one knows who she was.

We saw her brown hair, her large build, and the bare soles of her feet, her skin, which was torn, and beneath which a living mat of insects was seething.

Her body was their bowl. Life had left it, making room for other forms of life. It was no longer living itself, but there was life in it. Despicable, nauseating life, in the opinion of human beings, but indispensable nevertheless.

Rain and fermentation secretions from the body had soaked and stiffened its wrapping. But the shamed human being had long since departed.

Lucilia illustris. Necrophobus vespillo. Emus hirtus. Insects are not individuals. They are statistical entities, so to speak. They do not know what they are doing. They know only what they want, which is exactly what they must do: eat, couple, multiply, avoid death for as long as they possibly can. Nevertheless—or rather, thereby—they accomplish an incredible, indispensable function, the only true catharsis.

To clean. To eliminate distinctions. To restore. To unite. This is the goal, of which insects know nothing, but which they demonstrate to him who wishes to see. They labor in the service of this universal one in their effort to preserve and prolong their own worthless statistical existence.

How tempting it is to believe that humans, merely by being what they are, by being true to themselves as fully as possible down to the very last detail, would at the same time be carrying out an even more important duty, of which they are no more aware than insects are of human life.

I seldom become involved with the families of victims. Nor with those who are suspects or who have actually killed. What would I have to do with them? But this time an exception occurred.

"Do you know that they suspect me of killing her?"

I jerked away from the eyepiece of the microscope, startled. A strange man stood at the door of my office looking at me gloomily and imploringly.

"Who are you and what do you want?" I asked rather stiffly. He had entered so silently that I had not noticed his presence until he spoke.

He told me his name and repeated the question. He was no derelict but was neatly dressed and careful in his speech. I had indeed heard his name mentioned in connection with the investigation of the case. He had been questioned but not held, and I knew no more about those interrogations than any reader of the evening papers, merely that he had ridden in the same bus as the victim and gotten off at the same stop.

"My only job is to determine the level of insect involvement. I'm not a police officer."

"But yet you know?"

I admitted it reluctantly. "Why have you come to me? What significance does it have if I've heard your name?"

I was silent and watched him expectantly and a bit suspiciously. He was youngish, tall, and blond. Was he trying to influence me, and did establishing the time of the woman's death mean something to him?

He dropped his eyes and said faintly: "I was just asking."

"I identify insects and their age. Once I know that, I can give a rough estimate of the time of death," I told him.

I don't know why I was continuing the discussion, why I told a stranger the duties of my profession.

"I work for neither the prosecutor nor the defense attorney," I went on. "Others make the final decisions. Flies do not lie. Undoubtedly there are truths other than theirs, but they do not concern me."

"What will happen to me now?"

"It depends on what you've done."

"Since a person dies anyway," he said, "and everyone in a more or less brutal way, why is it so horrifying to die by the hand of another? What if it frees the victim from evil? Who knows?"

"Is that a confession?" I said, standing. The discussion was beginning to horrify me.

"By no means," he said hastily. "I didn't do it."

"Then why have you come here philosophizing?" I said, suddenly angry. I felt myself growing rigid and blushing. "You're talking rot and you know it. If you have something specific to say about this matter, go to the police."

"How do you know that the murderer didn't do her a service?"

"Are you still on that? People love their burden," I said. "Don't they say that evil must come, but woe to him by whose hand it comes? Go to the police."

"Now of course you imagine that I did it. Admit it. I didn't even know her, never said a word to her."

"So what? Not all murderers know their victims. You must have something to say about this case, otherwise you wouldn't have come here. But I'm not a policeman—you do understand that."

"Do you plan to tell them about this discussion?"

"I don't have to," I said. "You'll tell them all that is necessary yourself."

Why was I so sure? He glanced at me and was obviously about to say something, but changed his mind for some reason.

"Well? You see that I'm busy," I said, pointing to my table.

He turned and left without saying good-bye.

Actually, I think there is nothing but life. A very varied life. It is called birth, growth, and death.

People who have looked at their dead sometimes say: "Then I knew that there is no resurrection. That there can't be. He was as thoroughly lifeless as if he had never been alive."

One might perhaps think that a person who has seen death in its entirety—not in its nakedness but in its multiformity, in its richness, dynamism, and passion—would feel the same. That such a person, if anyone, would be predestined to the most rigid materialism.

The thought of resurrection *is* foreign to me. But whenever I witness the inevitability of the change that occurs in death and in its irreversible consequences, I cannot help but wonder. I repeat the same question as others: What has happened to the life that was just now here? Where is the "I" that only yesterday still planned, wanted, loved, and remembered?

How can one who has seen what I have seen at such close range not believe in continuity? Since it exists in matter, how should it not in spirit?

Life is like the queen in an anthill. No one sees her; she lives in the most cloistered of dens. But her influence keeps the body healthy, intact, whole, united. It moves the body. It alone gives the hill life. When the queen is removed, the hill disintegrates with unbelievable rapidity. Soon it is mere dust.

But the queen herself might be intact.

I saw him again—the man who had come into my room. I saw him in a group that was chatting animatedly in front of a movie theater, and I recognized him at once. He was wearing the same clothes as when we had last met.

He said something to a woman who glanced at me curiously and then turned away. He came over to me.

"Well?" I asked.

"Are you still doing the same work?"

"Still. It's my profession," I said.

"They never solved that last summer's case," he said. "A pity."

"Yes," I said. "It's a pity."

He hesitated and glanced at his companions, who had fallen silent and seemed to be waiting for him. Then he said: "I want to apologize for barging into your office so rudely. But the interrogations had upset me. It's not every day that one is suspected of murder."

"It certainly isn't," I said. "But I never did understand why you came."

"It was just an impulse," he said. "Coincidence, actually. Someone mentioned your name and what you did. I was—interested."

"Really? Are you still of the same opinion as you were then?"

"About what?" he asked.

"You philosophized about the legitimacy of killing."

"Did I say such things?"

Now he looked a little rattled. Perhaps he regretted having confronted me.

"I'd had a little to drink. Forget about it."

I looked at him wondering whether I should report the discussion to the police after all.

"It's sad to think that a woman's murderer is still walking around free," he said.

Someone called his name. The movie was already beginning. He nodded, joined his companions, and disappeared into the theater lobby. I saw him turn at the door and look at me as if he expected me to follow or even wanted me to come after him. As if he were a little disappointed that I didn't.

I can see the bright shape that once was your hand, its delicacy in contrast to its present form. Only dry blackened shreds of skin that no longer hide the bones of your fingers.

Who knows whether you were killed by a man whom you once loved, whom you trusted more than anyone on earth. Or did that blond stranger follow you from the bus stop, seize you and throw you to the ground, beat you over and over, kick, rape, and finally choke you to death?

"You were alive," I said mentally to this shattered, torn, raped, devoured, sucked-dry shape. "You were alive as I am now. Where did you go, since you are not here? Where will I go when I am no longer here?"

In her hair there was still the force of life. It gleamed among the twigs and dry hay even though her skin was already torn, her face swollen and blackened and unidentifiable.

But I could still see an expression on it. That expression—I'd seen it on the face of other deceased, those who were still in the first or second stage of decay. How can I describe it?

It is a gravity that does not admit of degree. It is not hate or fear or pain. Concentration—that is the word. The total concentration that can be seen only in the eyes of a small child or of a listener to music at a moment of ecstasy. Something left as testimony of what has been and may perhaps remain. As if something essential has become clear.

It is a look of comprehension. The mouth is half open and, above all, the eyes—they are open. The vitreous fluid is of course muddier than a living thing's. The eye will never again blink or the mouth speak of what it has seen. Nevertheless, a knowledge remains, one which no longer seeks or needs expression. It is left to gnaw at the spectator's mind as an undying question.

I would like to know what she was looking at. Not her murderer, not anymore. She was no longer interested in what happened to her. It had already happened, it was over. The worst had happened. Everything that could happen to her on earth had happened.

What was her gaze fixed on in that last moment when all her muscles were numbed by that last blinding convulsion? On the limb of a tree at the edge of the bank, which continued its calm and ceaseless swaying even as hands were squeezing her windpipe? The wind, eternally roaming the earth, brushed both the bushes and their two foreheads. "Stay O stay yet, wind of the moors. . . ."

In the place where she was tossed and hidden, the place from which she was borne away, the first snow of the year is falling. The rusted rails, the tires, the oil drums will soon be covered with the meek shapes of drifting snow. A gleaming pad will coat the armchair left on the rails. How gentle and, at the same time, how overwhelming is the ceaseless falling of the snow. The meadow hay, crushed and yellowed under her shamed body, will be covered by the crystals. When they rise again in the spring, no trace of her body will be visible.

Queen, where have you gone?

Translated by Richard Impola

Kirsti Paltto

Kirsti Paltto (b. 1947) is one of the most prolific authors working in Sámi, the language of the indigenous minority inhabiting Lapland, or Sámiland, in the Russian and Finno-Scandinavian Arctic. She currently chairs the Sámi writers' union. Her short stories, poems, and novels have been appearing since the early seventies. She has worked as a teacher and a translator and has also written books for children and award-winning plays and radio plays. The following extract is taken from *Guhtoset dearvan min bohccot* (Run Safely, My Flock), the first volume of Paltto's long historical novel chronicling the experience of the Sámi people in the early twentieth century as their small, austere communities try to cope with the disintegration of ancient traditions and the intrusions of a foreign war. As is appropriate for a novel describing a culture of transhumance and nomadism, the narrative meanders freely. Description is punctuated with spoken recollections, digressive dialogue, and the occasional *juoiggus,* or traditional Sámi chant. *Guhtoset dearvan min bohccot* deals with somber events, and the narrative has a valedictory tone: arbitrary legislation and military conscription by the Finnish state disrupt Sámi communities, while compulsory education in Finnish schools threatens to rob a generation of Sámi children of pride in their own language. The modern world with its wealth and technology exercises a mesmerizing influence on the young and impressionable. Paltto openly laments these events but without nationalistic bitterness. She trusts a quiet voice and asserts the dignity of the quotidian.

Fiction: *Soaknu* (The Proposal Journey, 1971), *Risten* (Risten, 1981), *Guhtoset dearvan min bohccot* (Run Safely, My Flock, 1987), *Guovtteoaivvat nisu* (The Woman with Two Heads, 1989), *Guržo luottat* (Run, White Fox, 1991), *256 golláza* (256 Gold Coins, 1992). Poetry: *Riđđunjárga* (Stormy Headland, 1979), *Beaivváža bajásdándun* (Updance of the Sun, 1985). Books for children and adolescents: *Vilges geađgi* (The White Stone, 1980), *Go Ráhkun bođii Skáhpenjárgii* (When Ráhkun Came to Skahpenjárga,1982), *Golleozat* (The Warblers, 1984), *Dávggáš ja násti* (Dávggás and the Star, 1988), *Divga* (The Bell, 1990), *Urbi* (Urbi, 1994).

Interview

PHILIP LANDON: Can you name any shared characteristics of contemporary Finnish fiction? Do you identify with any of your international or domestic contemporaries?

KIRSTI PALTTO: I think urbanization and the exploration of individual psychology are shared characteristics of contemporary Finnish fiction. I do not identify with any Finnish or foreign writers.

PL: How would you situate fiction in general and your own work in particular in relation to mass culture and the mass media?

KP: Literature is more durable than mass culture and the mass media because the literary writer often captures things that are common to all humans (aspects of history and life, dreams, passions), rather than merely trying to grasp at the superficial phenomena of the moment—gossip, politics, and so forth.

My own writing cannot belong to mass culture or the mass media because it is written in Sámi. Sámi literature, cinema, and the other arts that are bound up with our language cannot be disseminated all that widely in different languages because we have no funding of our own. The translation of our literature depends entirely on funding from the Nordic countries.

As for the content of my books, my work is not as light and superficial as mass culture and the offerings of the mass media. My books deal with Sámi life, which might seem strange to consumers of mass culture who have a Western outlook and who might have difficulty in getting to know a different culture, its richness, and its way of thinking.

PL: Kai Laitinen has written, "The traditional Finnish novel is close to nature. Nature features in the role of a friend or an enemy or both." Can we read your work as part of this tradition? Does nature require a new approach from writers?

KP: I see nature neither as a friend nor as an enemy. Nature is an element and companion that exists on an equal footing with humans, so it can't be treated as a friend or a foe. Nature would exist without me; it existed before me, and it will still exist after I am gone. A human person, on the other hand, can be either a friend or an enemy of the existing world.

You can't set preconditions for literature, not even concerning proper attitudes to nature. Writers are products of their own age, and they write of the backgrounds and images of their particular situation. The stance that authors adopt toward nature will change of its own accord as the ecological catastrophe deepens and imposes limits on society, thereby changing attitudes and opinions.

PL: From the *Kalevala* to postwar fiction, much of Finnish literature has been intimately bound up with the question of national identity. Do you see yourself as a member of a more international generation?

KP: As a Sámi writer, I do not emphasize Finnish identity—I stress Sámi identity. The Sámi people nowadays live in four different countries: 2,000 in Russia, 5,500 in Finland, 20,000 in Sweden, and 40,000 in Norway. The Nordic countries and Russia divided Sámiland between them in the seventeenth century and practiced a policy of oppression and assimilation by obstructing reindeer husbandry in border areas, by marking off the lands of the Sámi as part of their own empires, by outlawing Sámi culture and the language, and by teaching Sámi children only the language of the "official state," that is, Russian, Finnish, Swedish, or Norwegian.

The Sámi identity has also been shaken because the conditions of land ownership, the concept of justice, and the politics of each nation state have dispersed the shared values and aspirations of our people. A conscious search for an identity began in the early twentieth century, when the first Sámi books appeared and when the Sámi people began to gather behind shared symbols: linguistic, historical, and cultural.

PL: Contemporary Finnish writers frequently use autobiographical and mock-autobiographical forms. Why?

KP: I don't know, really. . . . Perhaps it is because literature is becoming popularized, trying to compete with mass culture and the mass media on their own terms, trying to persuade the public at large to buy and read books.

PL: Individual spoken voices enjoy exceptional freedom in your novel *Guhtoset dearvan min bohccot*—the narrator makes little effort to bind them into the overall scheme of things. In the light of the Sámi oral tradition, how do you see the significance of speech in your work?

KP: In *Guhtoset dearvan min bohccot* dialogue is conducted with the community and with nature. It is these things that control the individual spoken voice, not the so-called plot of the book. The Sámi community and its environment, its changes and pressures, constitute the plot of this book, in a manner of speaking.

Of course, the rich narrative tradition of the Sámi has an effect on my work. It is also true that the Sámi are lively and talkative compared to the Finns. However, the function of speech in my work is very deliberate and carefully balanced. In addition to trying to define a prevailing situation, I want to render the human reality of that situation and, of course, also the interiority and personality of each character. A given story in a novel or text aims to advance the string of events or to define the society or social situation of that particular moment or to show the relationship between an individual and the environment. This is an old oral Sámi tradition, but it also works well in literature.

PL: Your novel describes the efforts of Sámi civilization to resist hierarchies and laws imposed from the outside. The book has no controlling overall viewpoint, no contrived plot, and puts little emphasis on psychology. Its desultory, meandering structure amounts to a rejection of the traditional form of the European novel. Can we call your work decentralized fiction?

KP: In my opinion *Guhtoset dearvan min bohccot* does have a distinct, controlling overall viewpoint that gives a form to the fragmentary, roaming culture and lifestyle of the Sámi people. That it is fragmentary is due to the times when the Sámi have had to "take cover," that is, either ostensibly or quite concretely submit and become invisible in order to survive as a nation. As for roaming, that stems from the ancient Sámi custom of wandering nomadically with the reindeer. Writers will reflect their people, right?

Of course, my novel could be decentralized, if this means disrupted, because even in actual fact, Sámi culture, the Sámi way of life, and the Sámi language are being disrupted by pressures from the other people living in the Nordic countries as well as by legislation.

PL: Do you feel any cultural affinity with the indigenous peoples of, for example, America or Australia? Has literature or art from such sources had any influence on your work or outlook?

KP: It is natural for me to feel an affinity with, say, the indigenous people of America or Australia because I myself belong to the indigenous Sámi. The world's indigenous people have their own global organization, the WCIP. Almost all the world's indigenous groups are members. In Sámiland the work of the WCIP is conducted by the Sámi Council, a joint body representing the Sámi of all the Nordic countries and Russia.

The literature and art of different indigenous groups are, of course, inspiring to me, particularly the works of American and Canadian Indian writers. But the major influence on the perspective of my books was black American literature during the 1960s. Indeed, that was what set me going and taught me to look at things from the point of view of my own people.

PL: *Guhtoset dearvan min bohccot* performs a valuable service by retrospectively vivifying a neglected historical perspective, forcing readers to reassess their view of the past. Momentous changes are under way in Europe again today. Do you feel tempted to write about the contemporary European context?

KP: The contemporary European context is interesting but also dangerous. Even though so-called national self-determination seems to be on the increase, I see no sense in creating numerous small nation states. Building up a national bureaucracy and hierarchy is toilsome and costly in terms of natural resources and human energy. What is more, it is increasingly the case nowadays that an individual country cannot get along without others. I don't believe that a nation state as such can save the identity or culture of a given people—at least, not from supranational mass culture and the mass media. On the other hand, I do believe that a small people has the right to self-determination, autonomy, and equality with larger ones.

From Run Safely, My Flock

> Stars of the sky, don't cease to shine above my land
> *nannago na-a, voija-a voija-a!*
> Paths of my ancestors, don't become overgrown
> *nannago na-a, voija-a voija-a!*

The first war winter passed. There was a shortage of shop goods, and kerosene was so scarce people had to live by the light of fir torches through the darkest sunless months. As spring was approaching, Vulle's son Jovnna stopped by. A bullet had pierced his palm, and he had gotten himself some sick leave. He was reticent about the war, but he worried aloud that the wounded hand would never allow him to handle a rope as well as before. Jovnna's lassoing had been famous. Vulle had had a tough time with his shepherding after Jovnna was hired for the war.

Dávvet had the hardest time of all. He had run out of hay and was reduced to cutting twigs to feed his cow and bull. Sure enough, the bull looked as if someone had gnawed the flesh off of him. His skin sagged and the shitty haunches were sunken and hollow. So Dávvet called his bull an old hack but praised it for its strength and docility. Nor was he ashamed to sledge as far as Hearggesullo when business called: a draft's a draft, he said, and some people have no bull at all.

Late in the spring he went to see Ánol to buy some rationed goods. He had spent the entire winter trapping willow grouse and even had a fox fur to exchange for food. Ánol was as wily as ever—wilier, if anything. He paid only half the old price for the grouse and fox. Said he needed cash, not creatures, damned swindler! The shopkeeper enraged Dávvet, but he didn't dare say anything. He had no option but to visit Gutnel-Mihku and barter himself a few pounds of flour and a handful of salt. Why, the people of Hearggesullo had more of everything than the people who lived in the outback. The soldiers, Deutschers and Finlanders alike, passed through Hearggesullo on their way north and south. The troops had everything, and the herdsmen traded with them—meat and hides for butter, flour, salt, and often cheap spirits, too.

Dávvet trundled along the hole of a road left by the iron cars; it ran along the frozen Májánjohka River for a short way, upstream. Gutnel-Mihku had warned Dávvet about the Deutschers and told him to move out of the way at once should he meet any. Dávvet's spirits were already as low as could be. He thought about the children who were expecting food at home. Well, there would be enough flour for a Sámi cake today; the rest would have to be saved for the spring thaw, when the roads were impassable.

Dávvet kept dozing off casually, letting the old hack putter along at its bull's pace. After all, it was good being free to ride home. Not having to go to the war like so many others.

But his nap was interrupted by a rumbling sound ahead. A horribly large, black iron car was coming the opposite way.

"And where the devil did that appear from!" cursed Dávvet and strained at the right-hand bridle. "You wretched bull! Make way, at once!"

But the old hack had not the slightest intention of yielding. Slowly and calmly it trotted on, as though it fancied itself lord and proprietor of the road, free to go wherever—darn the Deutschers and their monster machines.

Dávvet broke into a sweat. He released a stream of profanities, roared out and beat the reindeer bull. "Hell, they'll run us over now, they will! Misherable goddamn creature, you'll get me killed!"

The iron car was already very close, but the bull was undaunted and carried on as before. Dávvet was already imagining what it would feel like being squashed under the wheels of the iron car.

But whatever the Deutschers were thinking, they turned their car to avoid the bull. Dávvet swore aloud, this time for joy.

His joy was, however, premature, for the Deutschers' iron car ran straight into a stretch of unfrozen water and came to a standstill. Brown-clothed soldiers poured out of it.

"Now they'll shoot," said Dávvet to the bull. "Because of you, you damned old hack!"

The soldiers hopped out of the iron car one after another and came over to Dávvet. They prattled excitedly and gestured at the river bank. They didn't intend to shoot after all. One of them knew enough Finnish to be able to tell Dávvet to fetch some wood from the shore, for getting the iron car out of the water.

The damned bull understood at last! Dutifully it trudged to the shore and waited obligingly while Dávvet chopped the wood and meekly dragged the load over to the iron car.

At home, the iron car gave Dávvet plenty to talk about. The children listened with round eyes and nearly forgot their destitution. Dávvet called at various homes and described his adventure from beginning to end and from end to beginning. Each time, his story expanded; each time the iron car became larger and more dangerous.

Dávvet would have grown hungry, but Ándaras returned from the herd and brought some meat. He had been skinning emaciated year-old calves.

"It's a bad spring, I tell you," said Ándaras. "The ground's frozen and the doe are thin. Calves will die, you bet they will. And it's worse farther north. Even the newborns might not make it."

And they didn't. Shortly before the calving season it grew warm and snow fell; the ground was wet for days. But then it froze and the crust on top of the snow became so hard that you could go anywhere as though it was summer. The reindeer got no lichen. The calves were stillborn or died within a few days when their mothers had nothing to feed them with.

A third of Ándaras's calves died that spring. Wolves also stalked the herds; a weakened reindeer was the easiest prey. What was strange, however, was that even the wolves seemed to starve. In Láttonjárgga they said the wolves were so hungry that they would ignore humans if they came across them. The brother of the late Eapper-Jovsset had met a wolf on foot, but it had not even seen him.

"That doesn't bode well," said Mággá. "This will end badly yet, believe you me. This hasn't happened before, oh no."

Ándaras lost reindeer another way, too. The starvelings would throng to the melted, snowless edges of steep ravines where green shoots grew. Many animals perished when the edge of the ravine collapsed and the reindeer crashed to the bottom. No one but the croaking raven and the half-starved wolf could retrieve them from there.

During the worst of the impassable spring thaw, Sofe also ran out of flour. Meat, too, was low, although they had slaughtered a calf to add to the reindeer that Ándaras had brought.

Sofe was just about to send Johanas over to Vulle to borrow six pounds of rye flour when Chortling Ingá plodded round. It was some time since she had called, and she had gotten even fatter than before.

"Oh, the bane of my life, tee hee!" Ingá hissed and followed Sofe into the cow shed. "Do you know, hee hee! Risten is pregnant again. And now that hussy let slip who did it, hee hee!"

Sofe, who was indifferent to whether Risten was pregnant or not, simply kept agreeing without saying anything more. Risten's condition did not rouse her curiosity.

"I just have to tell you, tee hee! Risten now has a real bridegroom, oh yes! A soldier! Be sure not to mention this to anyone. Right? A Deutscher, hee hee hee!"

"A Deutscher?"

"Oh yes! She found him in Iesvárri this winter. She was there with my cousin for a couple of weeks. The child is his, heavens, hee hee!"

"Uh-huh," uttered Sofe and began to milk Lávggá. "A Deutscher, then."

"Is it such a miracle? Risten said he's straight as a pine, and beautiful, beautiful he is. Risten's going. To Iesvárri. The Deutscher's there, you see. Risten, you see, means to go south, hee hee!"

"I see," repeated Sofe. "Tell you what, you'll lend me some flour, won't you? Six pounds?"

Ingá was struck dumb by Sofe's sudden question and simply stood there, stroking the heifer.

"Well? Don't you have any?"

"Yes, yes I do. But you would not happen to have a pair of summer shoes for Vulle? You see I haven't had time to sew any myself, hee! I've had my hands full with little Mihkkal, while Risten's been in Iesvárri. You wouldn't have just one pair? Then I'll give you some flour, definitely."

Sofe had just sewn a pair of tanned-leather shoes for Ándaras. She could hardly bear to give them away but had to. She would have to make Ándaras a new pair. There was no choice. . . . It was useless hoping that Ingá would part with any flour unless she got the shoes. And the flour was vital now.

"I see . . ." she said. "Well, I do have one pair."

"I guessed right! You see, that's why I came all this way. I knew that you, a sewing woman, would always have a pair of shoes. Would you mind sewing a pair of leggings for Jovnna as well?"

"If you bring the leather. I have none myself."

So she's to have a Deutscher for a son-in-law, Sofe mused once Ingá had plodded off home. How does she have the nerve. . . . And how does Risten talk to him when he speaks a foreign language? And how about Vulle and his plan to marry Risten to Elias, Ovllá-Per Piera's son? Ingá didn't even seem to mind that the wealthy Elias had lost the game to a Deutscher. The world certainly was topsy-turvy. What had once been wrong was now right. And what people used to hold in high esteem no longer seemed to mean anything. A rich young herdsman was no longer worth pursuing, for example.

After a long, cold spring, summer was on the way, at last. The ice melted and people were able to row to fetch their shop goods. And, best of all, you could cast out your nets and gorge yourself on fresh fish every day. Lake Riebanjávri was like a huge, inexhaustible pot. It fed everyone, and no one was left empty-handed.

The earth grew green, and the thin cattle were goaded out into a verdant world. No need to chew twigs and lichen anymore. Joyfully the cows gamboled, udders flopping. The calves, with their light limbs and lithe bodies, bounced with particular delight. And the starved newborn reindeer and the emaciated calves of the previous spring also livened up at the taste of green leaves.

Mággá's very eyes welled up with tears when she watched the calves frolic. Nor did she miss the cuckoo. It sat calling on a fence post. Mággá taught the children to listen to the cuckoo and told them not to chase it. Its call was its vocation, the only work the cuckoo knew. It could not even hatch its own eggs. Another clever bird was the bluethroat, tinkling on a green branch. Here, too, you had to learn to listen quietly, in order to understand its song.

"Well are they hungry or what, almost hungry enough to eat up a man! Easy, easy! There you go, eat, you shkinny stick-legs! It's no good hoping for more, even if you die! My field could never grow as much as you'd eat, you greedy devils!"

It was Dávvet who spoke like this to his creatures, the sheep that had charged, bleating, at the sheaf of hay, shoving and butting each other. He had let them out, it being a mild winter's day, so that they would take some fresh air and shit outside a bit and not soil their shelter quite so badly. Dávvet had carted sawdust and wood chips into the peat-walled cote, but it hardly stayed dry for more than a few weeks, they were such prodigious pissers. Dávvet fed the lambs separately, choosing them soft green shoots, which he carried into the cote.

"Confound you and all!" Dávvet grumbled as he watched his sheep. "It's a marvel the way you remind me of the people who live around this lake. Loján—like Ándaras, just as meek and quiet, a real 'yes, you're right.' A hint from Sofe and Ándaras goes running. Sulky—like Hánsa, ruminating so, depressed, thinking about Old Biehti the Witch, and even believing in him. But you're not as wise, Sulky, you're not, don't imagine it! Young thing, always bleating and stealing from others, like the late Olle. And that long-tailed one chortles and laughs just like Ingá. And you, Ram, are like Mággá. . . ."

Dávvet would have continued comparing his sheep, but he heard sleigh bells from down below. "Who the devil is that? And he's riding this way, too."

The man at the bridle behind the horse indeed came sliding to the shore where Dávvet lived, clinking along, all the way to the corner of the house. Ovllá-Per Piera!

Dávvet's heart almost turned over. Damn it, was the man here to recruit him to the front? Ovllá-Per Piera was not the type to come sledding into the outback for nothing. He was the richest man in Hearggesullo and had grown even richer during the course of the present war. So it went for some, while others grew even poorer than before. The thing was, Ovllá-Per Piera had the right friends. It was they who held Piera on the surface, even a little above it. And so Piera had purchased himself sleigh bells as well as a saddle harness, to make sure everyone heard him coming.

Dávvet hurried out into the yard, almost running. He must be the first to hear what was new; the children could be told afterward. Piera had already stepped out of the sledge. Dávvet paused and stared in amazement: Piera was not on his own. What the hell, was he bringing Biret back already! Dávvet's mind lightened and he hurried beside the sledge.

It wasn't Biret in the sledge at all, but a thin, long foreigner, with a face like gnawed bone, eyes wide as lakes, and hands like dried trees. The foreigner struggled out of the sledge and handed Dávvet a parcel before uttering a word.

"This foreign lady here is from Avvil. She works for the Red Cross and has come here to discuss your children," Piera explained officially and headed for the house, accompanied by the foreigner. He added something in Finnish, but Dávvet didn't hear what it was.

"That parcel contains a few clothes for the children," Piera said over his shoulder as he entered ahead of Dávvet. "Don't open it now. You'll have plenty of time after we've gone."

"There's a weird guest for you," Dávvet snorted, leaving the parcel in the windbreak and following Piera and the foreigner into his own house.

The foreigner was already sitting cross-legged at the end of the table, scrutinizing everything around her. Her forehead was wrinkled and she wore a look of extreme dissatisfaction.

"How many children do you have?" asked the foreigner. Piera interpreted, even though he knew that Dávvet understood Finnish and could even speak it. But Piera wanted to show that he was needed here, he in particular, and no one else.

"Six," replied Dávvet.

"What ages?"

Dávvet obediently listed the ages of his children.

"And the wife . . . ahem . . . has fallen ill?"

"Yes."

"Listen you . . . I came here because these children have no mother. I have come to ask whether you, David, wouldn't send those three youngest ones to Sweden. There are many children from northern Finland there. We thought we would also take a few from these parts," the foreigner explained.

"To Sweden? My children? Thanks, but that doesn't quite suit me, you know."

"There are wealthy families there who want to look after the children of Finland now that Russia's claws are tightening around our little country. They want to rescue some of Finland's children—if only some," the foreigner explained.

"There's no need to rescue my children! We've been quite all right. We'll manage fine. No, I won't send off my children, not anywhere!"

"Your children are the only ones to be allowed there from around here. And free of charge! They'd no longer need to suffer cold and hunger."

"Hell!" Dávvet lost his temper. "Who's been saying that my children are hungry and cold?"

"You only have to look at this poor child here. . . ."

The foreigner nodded at Simo, who was sitting on the threshold of the bedroom, finger in mouth, huge eyes wide open, staring at the foreigner in his stretched and faded shirt—but also wearing a brand new pair of reindeer-skin shoes, which Sofe had brought the day before.

"What's wrong with him, a healthy boy!" Dávvet sneered. "You won't find a livelier and more active child. A real weasel he is, tee hee!"

Káre snatched Simo off the floor and took him into the bedroom. In truth, she was somewhat ashamed of Simo's clothes, especially the dirt. But what could she do, when the boy always rolled himself into a mess as soon as you let him go? How could she possibly afford the time to watch the boy all day, to make sure he stayed clean from dawn to dusk?

"Haven't you lost two children in recent years?" Piera asked, then translated for the foreigner. The foreigner turned down the corners of her mouth to indicate how sorry she was about the death of the children.

"What the devil are you thinking, Piera—that I've killed my own children, telling people about it like that? You villain, you know very well that I've taken better care of my children than you have of yours! I may be poor, but you listen, I've never, ever, begged from the rich! And I don't intend to. So there! And don't you tell lies about me!"

"You mustn't start swearing like that," Piera admonished him. "This lady only wants the best. Those three youngest ones could be in the lap of luxury. . . ."

"Hell! Don't you understand that they're my children? Have I tried to steal your children? It's a fine day when a poor man isn't even allowed to have children anymore! Everything they'd take, down to my very life, if they weren't so hypocritical!"

The foreigner nudged Piera in the side to inquire what Dávvet was saying. But Piera merely shrugged his shoulders—he wouldn't translate Dávvet's abuse.

"This lady was confident that she would go back with at least one of the little ones," Piera went on pleading.

"Confident or not, I'm not giving away my children! You see, they're not cattle to be driven wherever anyone pleases! No, even though they don't chomp at greasy roasts or sip cream, like the fat and proud types we see swaggering!"

Dávvet didn't hold back once he had got going. Piera blushed and paled alternately and regretted having even come to see this "musty hide of a lunatic" who showered all his sins and faults into his face. Luckily, the foreigner didn't understand. What would she ever have thought!

"That's enough then," Piera enjoined good-humoredly, reluctant to start shouting in front of strangers.

"Get out of here and take that foreigner with you, before I throw you out!" Dávvet roared. "It's my house, even if I am poor!"

"I can't leave, I'm only an escort and an interpreter," Piera objected. "This lady has come to. . . ."

"Shall I give her the facts in Finnish?" Dávvet screamed.

"Don't you say anything! Let me interpret!"

"Fucking hell, interpret then, and tell her my children aren't up for sale!"

"We're not proposing anything of the sort!"

"Well what then? The foreigner brings me some clothes, I hand over the children! That's how that idiot planned it! Oaf! Does she think children are . . ."

"Stop abusing a stranger like that!"

"Tell her at once before I get angry!"

Piera had no choice but to turn to the foreigner and lie that Dávvet was going to take the smallest children to his rich relations in Láttonjárgga. And that Dávvet had no intention of sending his children to Sweden.

"Well then. I see! A pointless journey, in other words," the foreigner sniffed and stood up to go. Before leaving, however, she glanced at Dávvet with such contempt that he broke into a sweat.

"What a devil," he remarked, as Piera was riding down the bank toward the ice. Dávvet snorted and stole a look at Heaika. He felt as though he had finished a piece of hard work, having had to shout like that.

"The things they come up with, damn them!" he said and went outside.

Dusk had fallen and night was coming on. Dávvet paused for a piss behind the peat-walled cote where the sheep were, and he stared up at the sky. The morning star was already glittering in the east. A frost was coming; one star after another appeared.

"And why did God-our-Father have to invent darkness on top of everything else?" Dávvet pondered, still looking up at the sky. "Who the hell benefits from it? Or did He just do it for a laugh. . . . Then, afterwards, He invented the stars, to shine always, lighting up the world. This crazy world where blood and tears never stop flowing. If only God-our-Father was just a little more reasonable, why then. . . ."

Dávvet strolled back to the house, fumbled in his pocket for a smoke and stopped to light it. But he paused to look round first: no, it wasn't too dark yet; the fire wouldn't show. Open flames were forbidden outdoors at night, and even the windows had to be covered; not a flicker of light was to be seen. Should someone happen to cross Vuottavárri hill in the evening, they would think they had come to a deserted place. Mad times indeed. . . .

Dávvet remembered the parcel that the foreigner had brought and hastened indoors with it. The children surrounded him in a great flurry and stared at it with eyes like saucers. It was the first parcel Dávvet had received. Southerners had been collecting used clothes and sent them up here.

The parcel contained a green skirt for Káre, woolly sweaters, one pair of oversized shoes, two pairs of pants, and other clothes. They burrowed in the parcel and tried on the clothes, which smelled peculiar but were clean and pretty. Especially Káre's long skirt.

That night they were late going to bed. The smallest children laughed and fooled around, and even Heaika, who was usually so grave, showed a small smile in the corner of his mouth when Káre dressed him up in a white shirt. He tried to catch his reflection in the window; why, he was like a "gentleman," like the teacher Dángosar when the inspector came to the school. All he lacked was a ribbon round the neck. . . .

At last they went to bed, the smallest ones still wearing their "new" clothes. The temperature was still falling outside; it was cold in the house. But they were accustomed to sleeping almost fully clad; only shoes were taken off before getting into bed. For a long time, they had not been as warm as they were now, with the woolen sweaters to sleep in.

Morning broke cold. The southern sky glowed red and the frost crackled in the corners of the house. The windows were completely crusted with rime, and there was hoarfrost along the edges of the floor and in the corners inside the house—it was like a yard. The smallest children would stay in bed until noon, when the house had warmed sufficiently to stop their teeth from chattering. But Káre and Heaika had to rise together with Dávvet.

Heaika went outside but immediately came clattering back inside.

"Wolves have been circling the house!"

"Seriously? Oh hell!" Dávvet let slip and he hurried outside without lacing his run-down skin shoes and wearing only a tanned leather coat on top of his underpants.

It was true: the tracks of two large wolves had circled the sheep cote, the cow shed and the storehouse, and had come close to the very front steps. They had dug for buried rumens behind the storehouse, stopped under the bedroom window, and then had set out running across the lake, in the direction of Olle's house.

Dávvet shuddered, and a chill ran through his spine when he followed the tracks of the starving wolves down the bank to the shore. For a moment he gazed out toward where Ándaras and Hánsa lived. Then he climbed back up on the bank.

"Goddamn it, this isn't right," he swore and scratched his head. He stopped at the corner of the house, and a strange restlessness entered his mind. Wolves on the front steps! That didn't bode well, it really didn't! With no gun or anything . . . he'd have to set some traps tonight. You can't have wild beasts besieging your house. Two-legged ones by day, four-legged ones by night. . . .

Dávvet went inside, but he hid his anxiety and foreboding from the children, chuckling and slurring his s's at them, as he had done every morning up until now.

Translated via the Finnish by Philip Landon

ANU PIRILÄ

Petter Sairanen

Petter Sairanen (b. 1958) studied at the Finnish Theater Academy and currently works for the Finnish Broadcasting Company. He has written screenplays and fiction, and his play *Maailmasta ei ole mitään hyötyä* (The World Is Useless) received its premiere earlier this year. His first novel, *Sähköllä valaistu talo* (Electric Lighting,1989), was awarded the Kalevi Jäntti prize and is to be made into a film. A sequel, *Tulen valopiiri* (Firelight), appeared in 1995, and a third novel is forthcoming. *Sähköllä valaistu talo,* from which the following is excerpted, is the story of a young man's initiation into city life. An environmentalist to the core of his being, the protagonist detests the padded sterility of life in the urban coop. He is incensed by the seductive power of technological commodities yet is ultimately unable to resist the pull of the city or to sustain an alternative way of life. Sairanen's whimsical prose style uses repetition and lyrical forms and incorporates blue-eyed romantic reverie, adolescent horseplay, and impassioned tirades against contemporary society. Set among pristine forests and lakes, the story is told with disarming innocence. Observed with compassion and humor and informed throughout by a deeply civilized respect for all life, Sairanen's fiction reflects the combined toughness and fragility of the old values of the Finnish people, latecomers to the urban-industrial system. The importance of such fiction will surely increase in direct proportion to technological and economic progress.

Novels: *Sähköllä valaistu talo* (Electric Lighting, 1989), *Tulen valopiiri* (Firelight, 1995). Forthcoming: *Valonheittäjä tulessa* (Searchlight in Flames).

Interview

PHILIP LANDON: Can you name any shared characteristics of contemporary Finnish fiction? Do you identify with any of your international or domestic contemporaries?

PETTER SAIRANEN: In Finland, as in all countries of conspicuous consumption, people have tried to conquer climate conditions without clothes. A bit like Napoleon and Hitler, who tried to invade Russia without dressing properly. They put their money on a short-haired horse, and it turned out to be the wrong one. Hitler even imagined that tanks don't need to have long fur.

But the modern world has conquered the weather. Energy has been squandered with admirable success; palm trees decorate the walls of the shopping malls and tropical soundtracks stimulate their growth. This has been a recent development, in Finland and elsewhere.

Finland is exceptional in having had exceptionally severe climatic conditions to contend with. The Finns have struggled against the cold for thousands of years. The enemy was huge and perpetual. But we grew fond of it. And we had a secret weapon against it: the sauna. After a sauna, the cold seemed like a tolerable adversary, even a dear one. You could feel confident as you fought in its grip when you knew the sauna was warming at home.

"It is not good for men to get all they want. Sickness makes health sweet and good, hunger plenty, weariness rest" (Heracleitus).

Nowadays, the Finns do not know how to live, because they are not allowed to wrestle with their darling enemy, the cold. We live in rooms where the temperature is always the same, wondering what has gone wrong, now that we no longer need to struggle against the cold but still feel empty. This predicament also manifests itself in fiction.

The characters in novels and short stories are often hollow, unable to decide what they want, unable to fathom the cause of their emptiness. This sort of fiction is also common in other countries of conspicuous consumption. Of course, others may not have conquered the cold because they live in more temperate climates. But they have conquered something else, and they used to be just as fond of the adversary as we Finns were of the frost: they feel equally bewildered. And hollow.

I would like to hope that I am close to the Finnish writer Antti Hyry. He strives for beauty in language—pleasure in language itself. As far as I can see, with Hyry, the subject is immaterial; his language expresses that which the Finnish language is able to express. He writes astoundingly beautiful Finnish, like "hoarfrost on the bright plains of spring," or like "the sighing and singing of tall firs in the wind," or like "chopping birch wood in the frost, white inside, slightly yellow, on the snow in the forest, in the gleaming sun."

The first foreign writer who comes to mind is Joseph Brodsky. His essays are glorious defenses of the word. I sometimes feel that it must be religious. Of past writers, I have deep respect for George Orwell.

PL: How would you situate fiction in general and your own work in particular in relation to mass culture and the mass media?

PS: Reading requires effort. Mass culture and the mass media are oriented toward effortlessness. Literature is elitist. It need not be, but the mass media, such as television, obstruct higher civilization.

PL: Kai Laitinen has written, "The traditional Finnish novel is close to nature. Nature features in the role of a friend or an enemy or both." Can we read your work as part of this tradition? Does nature require a new approach from writers?

PS: I'm writing this in a tepee. An open fire is burning before me. The smoke rises through the hole in the top into the sky. I haven't made much of a fire because the frost outside the thin fabric of the tepee is not much of a frost either. In addition to the fire I have an oil lamp for writing. A tepee is not a common dwelling in contemporary Finland, but I've got one, because I want to preserve and use such parts of tradition as seem meaningful. A whitefish is cooking in the glow of the fire. It's attached to a piece of board with wooden pegs. Soon I'll eat it.

Humanity has a duty to use its reason, reason appearing to be the one special gift that humanity has been given. The writer's duty is to dress warmly and to report what lies in view.

PL: From the *Kalevala* to postwar fiction, much of Finnish literature has been intimately bound up with the question of national identity. Do you see yourself as a member of a more international generation?

PS: I don't think "nationalistically" when I work. I write about what I know about and what I feel.

From a Western perspective, Finland is in the East. From an Eastern perspective, the opposite applies. This is problematic as far as national identity goes. After all, identity is something that is constructed in relation to others. I think the subject deserves further scrutiny in literature. As does the question of nationality per se. After all, we live on the brink of mass migrations.

PL: Contemporary Finnish writers frequently use autobiographical and mock-autobiographical forms. Why?

PS: Why not ask where the steak is and not worry about the shape of the plate?

PL: You seem to have adopted the nature aesthetic of Finnish realism, but you have rejected conventional prose in favor of an eclectic, playfully fragmentary technique where lyrics, jeremiads, and factual material intermingle with comic vignettes. Why?

PS: I think form is subordinated to content. If I write about a man who makes a journey on skis and has a trustful view of love, the trip will be beautiful and unbroken. If he is in a different state of mind, the journey will change accordingly.

Sähköllä valaistu talo, Tulen valopiiri, and *Valonheittäjä tulessa* are all love stories. The tenor of *Sähköllä valaistu talo* changes at the point when the protagonist (the narrator) has faced disappointment in love. His mind begins to equate lovelessness and the destruction of nature. The form of the book is determined by the love story.

PL: Your first novel is openly hostile to modern technology, especially to the electronic media. You now work for the Finnish Broadcasting Company and write for television. Are you disillusioned with literature?

PS: The question refers to literature as an instrument of change. Perhaps literature is such an instrument, in its own unfashionable, discreet way.

Now that the snows have come, the reindeer and the wild deer, noble creatures of the forest, have adopted a diet of lichen. Humankind, for its part, is preparing for the cold and dark period by adopting a diet of high-definition TV. The hood of satellites above us begins to resemble a lid of ice with fish sulking in the darkness beneath.

No, I am not disillusioned with literature.

PL: Has your professional experience of the electronic media changed you as a writer?

PS: I somehow feel that the electronic media render us spiritually impotent. The rainbow has no power to move us, and even children lack passion for life. A sort of joylessness can be seen in the face of a child sitting in front of the television or a computer game. I have the old-fashioned conviction that you should play ball with children. And for adults, too, the entertainment available from these gadgets is a substitute for something. It's a prosthesis that people need as they writhe on, through their dull lives, finding meaning in nothing at all. I think we should have done with these gadgets. We might see the rainbow again.

PL: Your work is accessible, even deliberately naive. Have you deliberately chosen an anti-intellectual stance?

PS: I think people are naive. And naiveté of course comes in many guises, as does intellectualism. Healthy naiveté is a quiet assertion in favor of existence. It may allow cynicism to score a few victories before its coming defeat.

You might say my "anti-intellectual stance" is activated within me in the late autumn when people claim that the water ouzels, a type of bird that migrates from the north to the southern streams, are automatons.

"We travel our little while here between the firmament and the earth's shell, and the tracks of our reindeer convoy appear on the tundra for a short instant. For that instant, the tracks must be bonny, so that no one traveling after us need remember us with malice." (The creed of the Finno-Ugric Hanti people. The Hanti dress warmly because they live on the Siberian tundra on the banks of the river Ob.)

From Electric Lighting

A Little Portrait Gallery from a Border Post in the North

1

I went to the marsh, as usual. Midsummer had passed a few days before. It was warm and it started to rain there on the edge of the marsh. A helicopter flew over me and I took cover among the dwarf birches. I stood there and saw the gnats rise for the first time that summer. They swarmed up from the marsh like water out of a fireman's hose. There were pools all over the marsh; that's where they came from. Buzzing filled the air. I watched for a while, then hurried across the marsh and up the hillock and into the forest and across the river and up into the fell, where there were no gnats or trees but where the landscape expanded like a sea, a sea of fells, toward the north. I looked south and longed for home.

2

I came here in winter, by bus. I asked the driver to stop at the border post in Karesuvanto. I got off, looked around, and surmised that the brick house on Sakkaravaara hill was my patrol station. I walked over there with my two knapsacks, one for my personal things, the other for the company kit. I held the assault rifle in my hand. It was wrapped in its bag. I was a twenty-year-old border sergeant.

3

The commander's forever thinking of his border post, what's best for it; appearance-wise, everything must always be tip-top. He's proud of it. No one else can grow a lawn at this latitude, on the verge of the tree line.

Must rig up a string to stop them walking across the grass, says the commander, an old man.

Takkinen eats away his sorrows and drinks away his thirst. If he's not drinking, you can be sure he'll be eating. The most celebrated fakir of the north. He'll come down from the Munnikurkkio border post on leave and never make it farther than Karesuvanto. Or perhaps he'll do a quick loop via Muonio or Kilpisjärvi, but he'll always spend at least a week in Karesuvanto, boozing. "I'm buying, you can count on it. There'll be liquor aplenty, you can count on it. I'm Takkinen. If you don't know me, ask anyone you like. That's who I am, Takkinen."

Vornanen prepares a roast and serves it by slamming the meat down in the middle of the table, lancing his own share first with the tip of a sheath knife. Says, There you go gentlemen, eat it up. Then he preaches a long sermon to the whole assembly about the curse of liquor, its diabolical attributes. Two hours and he's raving drunk himself. Soon afterward it's remorse, a soul on the rack. He dashes the bottles of liquor on the ice and mortifies his flesh. "This hand hath touched liquor; now the body shall suffer. It's a gift of Jesus that I broke the bottles. The joy of the Almighty doth flood into me when I do pluck off my clothes and stand shivering naked like the children of paradise. The Bible shall warm me. What the fucking Devil! The bottle's broke! Oh Satan give me liquor!" The fellow eats liquor-sodden snow with extreme relish. And shortly he's asleep in the cold sauna with the Bible under his head.

Pikkupeura's a child of nature. If a party has to go on a long mission in the wilds, Pikkupeura will make one of the number. He needs no map, seeing as he can't read one. But he never gets lost. Or if he does, he heads back to barracks and says, I was lost so I came straight back to the post.

Pikkupeura doesn't drink. Spends his leave fishing or roaming out in the wilds. He has a few reindeer, to "keep me in roasts and besides they're nice to look at when you see them, your own herd."

In spring the man's brown as a coffee bean, spends so much time loitering in the fells. Never a care in the world, so long as he can up sticks and go, like a nomad. "Yeah, I've been on at least ten of them presidential tours. President Kekkonen, oh yes, he's hard on those bigwigs but friendly to me. A friendly man that Kekkonen, but strict too, I'll say."

There's no sending that Alanko out on patrol, the commander says. Alanko never goes patrolling, he just does janitor's jobs, repairs the patrol cabins, this and that, duty shifts. Yellow fingers from rolling cigarettes. When he's on leave, he stops for a drink at the Ruska bar. He'll go and start drinking at noon and come back no later than six, switch on the television and watch, drunk, alone. The duty officer might bring him a cup of coffee. "Doesn't bother me, the dark dayless winter, or the white nights of summer for that matter. Time passes, the grave gapes."

Isokoski has oversensitive nerves. Poisons dogs because of the noise they make. Thin, tall, teetotaler, a believer. A first-class radiotelegrapher, quick tapper, sensitive fingers, as sensitive as his nerves. Isokoski listens when he has his earphones on, dit-dit-dah-dit-dit-dah, and when he's asleep and dreaming—always on the alert. It's good to schedule a lot of "listening" on his border patrol assignments. When you read his patrol reports, they're full of entries about noise: a bird, a car, a person, a dog, a fish. "The racket those dogs make is quite intolerable. Again last night Hamu barked, twice. After that it was impossible to sleep. When will Hamu be shot?"

Puustinen likes to tinker at his dinner table at home, making fox traps with cyanide. The children fuss around beside him doing whatever, eating, drinking, drawing, pulling one another's ears, fighting, chasing gnats, while Puustinen prepares his poisons. His wife makes coffee in a two-gallon pot. Puustinen leaves all his gear helter-skelter. His snowmobile sank in the bog after it conked out, in the spring. It sank during the summer, and someone who was gathering cloudberries found it in the fall, its runners jutting out of a watery hollow.

"I should repair the fence, it's just I've got all these other urgent chores. But come fall, then let's see, it's even better to do it toward fall, like. I've lost my coat. How can I go anywhere without a coat that's vanished, oh deary me, but now it's coffee time, I have to drink my coffee."

4

Dawn. I approach the border post with a kayak on my shoulder. I've paddled through the night at Lätäseno, spent a day off there.

The commander's mowing the lawn. I lower the kayak onto the grass, and he snaps at once Not there, not on the lawn. I leave the kayak where it is and head for a wash and a nap—my shift begins in a few hours. The commander's on holiday, and I'm in charge of the post.

Morning coffee, the usual routine, send a surveillance patrol out, change of duty. Isokoski takes over. He complains that the commander started cutting the grass at five, no hope of sleeping.

A helicopter stopped by midmorning, leaving Takkinen with us. The copter's been on patrol and touched down at Munnikurkkio to pick up Takkinen on the way back. Takkinen has a week off.

Takkinen and I go and check out the commotion at the village. A festival of indigenous peoples is kicking off. Already we see Inuits in their hairy knickers and Indians and Sámi herdsmen and tourists. They've erected tepees and lean-tos all over Sakkaravaara hill. Takkinen goes to the Ruska bar for a drink; I head back to the border station. When I get there, Alanko is heading for the Ruska bar.

In the afternoon a patrol returns and we hear there's been a bit of confusion between the Inuits and the Sámi. The patrol's sorted things out, no big deal. We speculate as to whether there'll be trouble at night.

My shift's over. I go and change into mufti. Then coffee. The phone rings, it's the Hotel Ratkin, they need men. I put my gray uniform back on and call the police at Muonio. They promise to send a patrol. I also telephone Takkinen at the Ruska bar and order him over to the Hotel Ratkin. Meet you there. Takkinen's extremely compliant. I head for the Ratkin with a pistol in my belt.

Takkinen and I arrive outside the Hotel Ratkin at the same time. As we enter we find a wrestling foursome. The bouncer looks on innocently. A crowd has gathered around the wrestlers, drunk to a man. Takkinen goes in first. A couple of roars from him puts an immediate end to the wrestling. We ask the reindeer herdsmen, Now what's all this about. The men agree to sit at opposite ends of the bar. That's that sorted; we leave.

At the post I change into mufti again. Takkinen's got hold of some whiskey; we drink some.

We decide to spend the evening at the Hotel Ratkin. The bouncer refuses to let us in. No entry, no matter what we say. We tell the man what we think of him and vow not to come should he ever need our help. We head for the lean-tos of the indigenous peoples and carry on drinking there.

In the middle of the night we're in an empty little cabin finishing off the whiskey. Takkinen's already half-dozing, and a guy I don't know is curled up in a sleeping bag in the corner. Another stranger enters the cabin and asks: Is this the celebrated Takkinen? Your very man, I reply. He attacks Takkinen. I belt him on the cheek and he leaves the cabin.

I head back to barracks and bed. I'm on patrol duty the next morning. At daybreak, the duty officer comes and wakes me. They've phoned from the Ruska bar. Some Inuit's been thrown through the window and is lying in his blood on the floor. I call the Muonio police again. They're sleepy. They promise a patrol by and by. I call Pikkupeura and he agrees to join me. We head for the Ruska bar.

A semiconscious Inuit lies on the floor, covered in blood. We bring him over to the border post and clean him up.

"Scratches."

"The hairy knickers protected him well."

We can't understand a word the man says. We put him to bed in the guest room. I ask the duty officer to call the Muonio police and the platoon commander. Then I go back to sleep.

The police arrive in the morning, ask all kinds of questions. I'm a bit fuddled. The Inuit's ready to hit the festival again. The police drive him over to the lean-tos in their car.

The patrol is scheduled to travel by foot and on bikes, but I revise the plan and borrow a car from the reindeer police. Pikkupeura and I set out for Kilpisjärvi. Pikkupeura drives and I sleep.

On the way back we're surprised by a thunderstorm at Kelottijärvi lake. We have to stop the car, the rain's so hard. Suddenly a massive thunderbolt strikes right next to us. A little timber house beside the lake catches fire. I radio the border post and tell them to call the fire department. We run down to the house. A man is in the yard with buckets in his hands. The flames burst out under the eaves and through the windows. The man says, What an awakening, it came through the phone, damn, I don't have any insurance at all. All we can do is watch.

The fire department arrives but the pump doesn't work. They call the Karesuvanto firemen on the Swedish side, who soon arrive, but nothing remains to be done, the house is a goner. The man who lived in it decides to move into the sauna on the shore.

Pikkupeura and I continue our journey. When we reach the post, the commander's in the yard cutting the grass.

5

When Pikkupeura arranged an orienteering competition, no one found any of the checkpoints. He'd gone and scattered the crosses wherever. He found a suitable stone, put one there. Found a suitable bog, put another there. Then he returned and drew circles in the map, wherever, and numbered them. No one found a single cross, but Pikkupeura went out and retrieved them all. A new competition was held the following week.

6

Once I was napping on the duty officer's bunk. Isokoski's small son, a five-year-old sprout, crawled up next to me. He pushed his head into my armpit, and deeper: You're not a soldier.

7

I had the lyrics of Hector's album *The Lost Children* on my wall.

We came back from the hotel, me and two tourist girls and a colleague from the neighboring border post, back to my place. Spotting these wall mottoes one of the girls said with immense disdain: "Who here pretends to comprehend the poetry of Hector?"

8

Suddenly in a dream, suddenly a girl appears in my dream, comes to me, approaches, I look at her, her face beams at me, I want to be there, she smiles, then walks away, without disappearing, halts and speaks, such a beautiful girl speaks to me, I can hardly believe it, but she says: "Listen how the wind moves in the birches, now it grabbed that, and again, it shakes and strains the branches, and now it quit, there it goes, and this birch like a lifeless pole. Go, what are you waiting for?"

I wake, rise, walk across the floor to the window, the floor of the patrol cabin is cold, I look outside, the dark profile of Puunasvaara hill, behind it, Norway, the border runs across the hill, along the ground, here, Finland, this is a log cabin for patrolmen, Pikkupeura's asleep over there on the lower bunk, there's a fire in the stove, our boots are hanging from a nail above the stove, there's a carton of milk in the corner, the sound of the wind up in the roof, I look outside, birches, dwarf birches in the middle of the snow, it begins to snow over the empty land, and this dream clings to my mind, this girl in the dream, I don't know her, I don't recognize her: What was it she said?

The next day there's a snowstorm, we lose our way and travel in a circle,

the snowmobile loses a fan belt, we fall through the ice and there's a terrify-
ing snowstorm, but I live in another land, I have a dream, an awful yearning,
dreamward, womanward. I'm indifferent to the hardships of this land, I'm
not cold nor tired nor hungry, I'm indifferent, I have something here in my
heart, I won't give it to anyone, I won't say or speak, I'll move through the
winter. Move, ski, exist, live in the middle of winter, inside the winter, I
have something warm in my heart, hidden.

In the yard in front of the border post the sky arches over me, the entire
blue frozen sky, the whole universe arches swiftly over me from infinity to
infinity, the stars pierce the vault into brightness, the snow creaks, my
breath steams. Dreamgirl, white beauty: What did she mean?

9

I walked in the forests; I explored the marshes, the rivers and the fells. They
wondered why I roved, even though I had no reindeer. What type of guy am
I, what are the others, how hard it is for people to understand one another's
words: drinking, lawn mowing, dog poisoning, solitary roaming. A broad
stretch of virgin snow between all people. What happiness it would be to
ramble and paddle alone if you had someone to think of.

In the summer they held entrance exams for officer training. I applied in
Rovaniemi and some time later a message reached the post that I'd been
accepted for the next course.

Farewell whiskey, courtesy of Takkinen. Then I left.

A Brilliant Future

I find a good excuse to visit Oulu: Lauri, my friend, former lumberjack
turned entrepreneur, trained in Uppsala, comes to see me, says he's got himself a boat, a sailboat, and asks me along, to collect it in Tenala. Where's
Tenala? It's near Tammisaari. So next weekend then. Sure, why not, a train
to Helsinki and on to Tenala, together. Lauri lives in Helsinki, he buys sail-
boats and apartments, but he's a lumberjack by temperament. With such a
temperament, he'll do well in Finnish business. So I've got an excuse to
stop by at Umur's; I'll leave Taika with her.

I take the day train to Oulu.

I ring the bell, Umur answers the door. Taika leaps about, mad with joy,
Taika has been pining, Taika is always waiting for you to come, Taika
dreams about you, Taika walks through crowds of people, snout in the air,
trying to catch your scent, sometimes he thinks, some familiar gesture, a
movement, for a moment he thinks you're there, but no, Taika won't even
eat properly when you're not there to feed him, he's restless, he wakes up in

the night and looks out the window to see if maybe you're coming, Taika walks with you forever in his mind, there's nothing he does without remembering you, Taika has been sad, look at the state his coat is in, the little guy's sick with longing.

Pretty good, nothing much, so you're sharing with some girl, well, there's plenty of space, two rooms and a big kitchen. I'll take the night train to Helsinki, Lauri's coming to meet me, we'll continue together, Lauri's friend will make a third.

Umur makes some coffee, I sit in a chair like a beaten dog, a mongrel, unjustly punished. The other girl, Eija, comes home. We drink coffee.

The phone rings. The father of Eija's boyfriend Ari is phoning to say that Ari is dead; he was run over by a car and killed instantly, an hour ago.

Eija wants to be alone. Umur comes outside with me and Taika. It's drizzling outside, dusk is thickening, the yellow leaves shift in the wind. We walk past the athletics field, we climb up to the road, the cars pass, we walk along the streets, side by side, not speaking.

Umur sees me to the station, I hug her briefly, mount the steps, Taika would like to come along, he tugs at his leash, Umur is standing on the station platform, we glance at each other, I go inside, step straight into the rest room, wipe my eyes, enter the coach, the train leaves, I look through the window, Umur and Taika, Umur with tears in her eyes.

In Helsinki, I drink my morning coffee in the station restaurant. Lauri and his friend Tapsa show up shortly. They have a hangover. We board a train that will take us to Tammisaari. From there we take a taxi to Tenala, then we buy supplies from a store and continue to the marina.

The boat is small, a twenty-two-footer built of pine. Dark, stained sides, a veneered deck with plastic matting on top, race rigging. Inside the cabin are four berths, the forepeak and two bunks. An old boat, made in 1933. It cost ten thousand marks.

We hoist the sails. A good tailwind and fair weather. We're speeding like crazy toward Hanko. Lauri has brought some rum, we take a shot after food, the water is lapping in the bows, the wind drives us forward.

The light begins to fail. Lauri starts looking for the charts in the cabin to see how far it is to Hanko. Discovers that the bilge hatches are waterlogged. Looks like the boat leaks pretty badly. There's a pump under the afterdeck, we pump until the bilge is clear again. But Lauri can't find the next chart, can't find it, although it should be there, was supposed to be included in the price. Tapsa has sailed this route once before. Tries to recall it, can't picture it very well. The wind sends black clouds up into the sky.

Now we sail off the last chart, there are rocky islets and islands ahead, buoys and beacons, and the black clouds above, the wind picks up, dusk, no other boats in sight, Tapsa is trying to remember the route. Rocky waters near Hanko, apparently. The wind rises.

Should we go to shore on an island somewhere? Not just yet anyway. A flashing light of some sort ahead. Almost dark. Again the bilge is full of water. The wind rises, creating whitecaps. The black sea. There's no lamp here; it's started to rain, over that way, toward the glow over there.

Over there the lights of Hanko shimmer on the horizon. Hell, this is a storm already. What's the light that's bobbing on that side? What lights are those? Lucky we brought the land compass. How so, it's useless. A strong gale, the cleat flies off, the foresail starts to flap loudly. We tie the foresail to the sheet bench, no but let's haul in the foresail. It's a boat, that light over there. Damn this, not having brought any rainproofs. Damn cold. Let's have some rum. A cigarette. That's the way I reckon, we turn soon, I remember, it's left after that lighthouse. Christ, turn will you, there's a rock! Fuck, man. Two fucking yards. Wow. Wow, you don't spot them, black stones, smooth rocks. Where did that other boat go. Hold a course for that. Which one of those lights, which of them. The bilge is full, complete darkness. Lights there and there and there, flashing, constant, red, white, green, the sea is swaying, whitecaps, the boat is leaking, not even Tapsa knows where we're going, but it's fast, our speed is.

Tell you what, let's head near that lighthouse, toward it, hey what's that, a spar-buoy, didn't see it at all.

A black night, wet men, cold, a fall storm, but Hanko is over there on the left side, we still have to circle round the Hanko headland, now Tapsa knows where we are, more or less. What's the draught of this thing did you say, four feet, the water's always deeper than that. As long as we make sure we don't hit a rock.

At last, Hanko, the marina. We maneuver alongside the jetty. Secure the ropes, sails down. Damn it, it's two o'clock already, the bars aren't open anymore. The boat is soaking wet inside, the mattresses, sleeping bags, everything, we're soaked through to a man. We step on shore. It has stopped raining. We light a fire on the sandy beach. We burn some trash, paper and junk from the garbage cans. We dry our clothes and drink rum.

Swedish-speaking men come and start saying, No open fires here. Lauri, the businessman, trained in Uppsala, does the talking. The men leave. We're starting to feel warmer.

I fetch cigarettes from the boat. I notice some steel containers beside the jetty. I peep inside: mattresses and sails and all kinds of nautical equipment. You could sleep in there. I don't feel like getting into the boat, the cold wet boat. I stroll back to the fire. The boys immediately agree, definitely, spend the night in the container.

We get inside the container. A candle from the boat is burning on the floor, we sit on mattresses, wrapped in sails, the bottle of rum goes round.

The same Swedish-speaking guys return, and they say, Get out at once. Lauri, grand champion at hanging off balconies with just two fingers, speaks a few words of Swedish. The harbor watchmen won't give up. Lauri goes and shows them the boat. They return. No way, we have to leave or the police will come. Well fine, fuck you, we'll continue, sails up and into the night. The fat guards return to their caravan. It starts to rain. We cast off the ropes, hoist the sails. One of the guards comes along carrying an umbrella and starts squeaking, What's the point of setting off now, in the night, it's already dark and there's a storm. He stands squeaking on the jetty, our boat is already free. Lauri hops onto the jetty and hurls the man into the sea, the man flies, his umbrella floats in the water, the man surfaces like a cork, Lauri hops onboard, we tighten the sails, the boat is moving, the man clambers onto the shore, swearing. Hey-ho and a bottle of rum.

The jetties are like traps and the islets lurk, invisible. Right then, out toward the open sea.

The water splashes about in the bilge, the boat sways on the dark sea, soon we'll see the island of Jussarö on the left. We swim onto the map. The wee hours. Dawn breaks slowly. Tapsa says, Better bring her in, take the coastside passage before we reach the open sea at Porkkala, it's so damn cold, let's go ashore at some island and take a break beside a fire.

The dark silhouettes of the islands, Tapsa doesn't know where we are. Soon we should come to the coastal passage. But what lights are those, on the left, in the stern, and there, back there on the right. Shit, looks like we passed it already, just here there's a . . . crash! the boat stops, the prow swings slowly to starboard, the boat is moving again, but in the cabin you can hear the merry din of water as it rushes in through a hole the size of a cat. Blasted surface rock! To the island!

The island is close already, the water comes flooding in, I jam sweaters and rags into the hole, then I hear a thud, the boat stops. I emerge from the cabin, the boat is aground on a sandbar near the shore. We grab our wallets and cigarettes off the pipe rack and our knapsacks from the bows, Lauri is fumbling for the bottles of rum in the bilge, the water is lapping above the bunks, the boat tilts. We walk to the bows and jump into the water, wade ashore. The boat tilts farther, sinks into the shallow water on its side, the mast juts out of the sea like a monument. It has a brilliant future, the pole where the last brotherhood tested its strength, a wooden mast standing out of the sea with a faded blue streamer hanging below the acorn, a fixed point for the eighth brotherhood in a world afloat on nothingness, a positive, howling, furious totem of the will to live in the midst of unsinkable speed cruisers with their yachting shoes and their dead souls, a turning pole in the middle of the world, the point where Finland stopped and took a new course, a brilliant future, northern thinking, this world that's visible, that's gone already, it no longer exists, glossy trinkets on the TV, they no longer exist, Finland has turned already, northern thinking, we start gathering roots from the ground, herbs become valuable, it's happened already, that wooden mast standing out of the sea is a totem of hope, the new brotherhood is coming.

Translated by Philip Landon

OLAVI KASKISUO

Hans Selo

Hans Selo (b. 1945) caused a sensation in 1970 when he published *Diiva* (The Poseur), a stream-of-consciousness novel about the 1960s, which won the prestigious Erkko Prize for the best literary debut. Fifteen years of silence followed before the appearance of *Pilvihipiäinen* (Cloudcomplexion) in 1985, and a third novel is expected in 1996. A metalworker with no academic training, Selo is entirely self-educated. He is known for his linguistic inventiveness: he coins words at will and flagrantly exploits the agglutinative and suffixal resources of Finnish. *Pilvihipiäinen*, the novel sampled here, is not a work of plot, character, or action, but a fluid verbal tapestry. The burden of description keeps shifting from mouth to mouth, and political, philosophical, and theological debate mingle with slangy, self-mocking portrayals of bohemian self-indulgence. Selo's characters live for erudition and aestheticism. These would-be cogniscenti are hard put to maintain appearances as they feed their alcoholic, sexual, and intellectual appetites with Dionysian relish. Through the shifting perspectives emerges a blurred portrait of one Anders Holm, a hypercerebral artist manqué, autodidact, self-proclaimed prodigy, and author of a single acclaimed novel. We share his memories of childhood privation and psychiatric hospitalization, his lighthearted intellectual dandyism, and his philosophical roamings. Celebrating the sheer abundance of the world's texture, Selo dismisses all rules of decorum, blending mysticism and polysyllabic erudition with obscene slang. He employs a stream-of-consciousness technique to rigorous ends as a means of evoking the vitality of the self's interactive relationship with the world. Paterian hedonist, Wildean poseur, and genuine lover of ideas, Selo is Finland's most wonderful literary eccentric.

Novels: *Diiva* (The Poseur) 1970, *Pilvihipiäinen* (Cloudcomplexion) 1985.

Interview

PHILIP LANDON: Can you name any shared characteristics of contemporary Finnish fiction? Do you identify with any of your international or domestic contemporaries?

HANS SELO: Given my somewhat reclusive lifestyle, I must make do with the stylistically conventional prose transmitted by the Finnish media, prose that necessarily lacks sophistication and individuality. In Finland literature of quality is disseminated only through hearsay. For good literature to find its way into the media on its own terms, better literary criticism and greater openness would be needed. Alternative: aimlessness, blindness.

Books are about life. Only life can possess value. All forms of life are based on analytical progress. Even plants analyze, through their reactions to the sun, water, etc. Every sensation transcends the merely quantitative in containing an element of consciousness. From *quantity*, *quality*: a species that has fallen into a ravine a thousand times eventually learns from its suffering the consequences of its falling; millions of experiences, torments, and emotions crystallizing into new quality. The ability to reason. Being, primitive intelligence. The crystallization of remembering into human consciousness, perfection.

The Finnish impulse to keep literature and criticism *quantitative*, suppressing the implicit *quality* (a precondition of life) in each sensation, is based on structural violence. Suffering becomes an end in itself. Stifling prevails. Finland has an exceptionally high suicide rate, for purely cultural reasons. Criticism evens everything out, trivializing it, restricting freedom of speech. Curbing democracy and equality.

To each according to his ability, for the good of all.

Given my focus on *content* and *quality,* I belong squarely within the Western tradition; I continue the spirit of the Enlightenment.

PL: How would you situate fiction in general and your own work in particular in relation to mass culture and the mass media?

HS: As an eye for crystallizing the social and the interactive in general, literature has immense capacities. It can fire at all the senses from the power of the imagination. Because of its conceptual acuity, it can be receptive to the sciences; being their mother, it can be receptive to the father: philosophy. The present global society, with its technology, its spaceships, is perhaps best understood through literature's views of it. The crystallizing, formative eyes (the sciences) owe their high standard to their mother's milk: literature. Which focuses on the words *you, I, we*. Focuses, in fact, on the analysis of a single, synoptic word: *I*. As does philosophy.

All forms of culture share the same brainstem, moral codes (which, for example, the Bible articulates in the Sermon on the Mount). All culture is a contemplation of the validity of these codes. It is impossible to live without being in some degree conscious of them. Evaluation is indistinguishable from morality and partakes of its end: spiritual growth. Interpretations of morality can, by definition, fail. But even unwitting purposiveness yields evaluation, the possibility of consciousness.

Socially, even more crucial than consciousness-heightening literature are the mass media responsible for literature's critical transmission. They are necessary for the fastest possible comprehensive progress. They can also be used destructively. Where this happens, they are always used with a *quantitative emphasis*. Mass culture that aspires to nothing more than quantity is pursuing consumption for the sake of consumption. Even as a term that elides the individual, *mass culture* is violent, whether we are dealing with sport or with life as a whole—whenever victory is considered more important than participation, in which case participation is reduced to a necessary evil, and content is overridden by *quantity*. Like the gambler, who wants to win by pure coincidence, without merit, interiority, skills, consciousness. Read: greed.

Consciously or not, through all his actions, each person is writing the book of his life. Which is more important than all other books.

PL: Kai Laitinen has written, "The traditional Finnish novel is close to nature. Nature features in the role of a friend or an enemy or both." Can we read your work as part of this tradition? Does nature require a new approach from writers?

HS: Like all Finns, I was born out of the 180,000 lakes of Finland. Sparsely populated, Finland only has a handful of inhabitants: five million. I'm an urban writer, yet I too am moved by the Finnish landscape, its twin midnight suns, on either side of the reflection-veiled forest-lace on the opposite shore.

To define nature is to define humanity. The ascent to humanity from the mineral, vegetable, animal kingdoms, being the work of nature as a whole, implies that human consciousness is not qualitatively reducible to its quantitative foundation. What has once acquired quality, human consciousness, is always a rehearsal in a more crystalline form of the incarnation of what has been learned. Skill becomes flesh. A sloughing off of burdens, possessions.

Humanization. It epitomizes the one and only conceivable freedom: creation beyond quantity. A cat sees monochromatically. Why do we see polychromatically? Culture stresses quality, and rightly so. How many black-and-white TVs must I bring into your home in order to compensate for a single color TV?

PL: From the *Kalevala* to postwar fiction, much of Finnish literature has been intimately bound up with the question of national identity. Do you see yourself as a member of a more international generation?

HS: A cultural achievement of international stature can also be distinctly national. Your somewhat tortuously formulated question anticipates a personal reply. I don't have enough space for that; national identity would need to be conceptually investigated.

Were I to take the question literally, I would ask: Has Finland's national identity been teleologically fathomed profoundly and creatively enough for it to problematize itself internationally? National identity, like criticism, is ideological and exists only in individuals, luminous paths.

Identity is immediate identification with the self as its own goal. The immediate identification of the path with itself. Identity-as-path; a self-penetrating process. For identity not to become fragmented into absolute separateness, it must trace and proceed through the unity that controls it, the self. The sum transcending its constituent parts. To be immediately itself.

What is at stake is the relationship between cause and effect. The cause, rent open, immediately analyzing itself; its consequent realization in people, in nations. To evoke an ancient metaphor for the universe: the whale identifies itself with the ocean and devours and digests that ocean, so as to shower water over itself out of emptiness, wine, Plato's epigenesis. Unbridled creativity beyond our universe and its logic; the gods at play. For the unification of the individual whale, transunification, divinification. Without such Other logic, it's impossible to define humanity, freedom, life. Progress presupposes both limitation and its transcendence.

Presumably, the various creating gods reflect a number of principles. As absolute exceptions, extreme individuals, they create across one another by means of immediate knowledge of each other: In the beginning gods created the heavens and earth—Let us make man in our image, according to our likeness. When I have created an image of a vase, I don't claim that the vase thinks, has consciousness. The conscious one is me.

Normally, national identity is defined by means of some vague reference to romanticism. Ignoring the structure of consciousness, which contains everything. Any kind of identity, even a dog's, is fundamentally a path, not a list of goods.

Defining my position in relation to Finnish literature would be guesswork. I'm a couch commentator. Finland lacks literary criticism, whose function, in the interest of freedom of speech, would be to fuse the citizens' rays of thought into a sun: national identity.

PL: Contemporary Finnish writers frequently use autobiographical and mock-autobiographical forms. Why?

HS: Because of personality cults. Which allow autobiographical material to stand out from the huge flood of books published. The best books go unnoticed. Throughout Finnish history, the critics have massacred works of quality. Indeed, the critical guillotine killed and buried the national author, Aleksis Kivi, in the nineteenth century, before Finnish independence. Subjective criticism, which claims the right to err, is ultimately relativistic, arbitrary. In the end, all writing is autobiographical. What matters is *quality*. Someone may write ten masterpieces about his life on a boat. Someone else, ten quantitative books consisting of varying quantities of plot. Quantitative criticism will weigh them, sifting the "good" from the "bad" without disclosing the unit of measurement it's using.

Finland is not yet a civilized country. Take the annual Finlandia Prize, which was launched in 1984 and dwarfs all the other prizes in value. In 1993, in a television interview, the leading newspaper critic attacked the judges for being too highbrow: "They're basically rewarding their own cleverness. The Finlandia Prize should not be given to the best books." No justification given.

Thus are creative souls forced into mediocrity! Driven to despair, silenced.

PL: In 1992 your first novel, *Diiva* (1970), was voted one of the most important works published during the first seventy-five years of Finnish independence. *Diiva* departs defiantly and flamboyantly from the Finnish realist tradition. What do you think is the secret behind the lasting appeal of the book?

HS: What lasting appeal? Before the occasion you mention, *Diiva* had been pilloried for years! Having made it onto that famous list, I find myself something of a rarity in Finland: a living author, safely ensconced in the official canon! Albeit as a living corpse. With empty pockets, without the chance to write full-time.

You see, the result of that vote astonished the public at large. The 150-odd electors were drawn from the intelligentsia—only a handful of newspaper critics were included. The winning novel, Volter Kilpi's *Alastalon salissa* [see introduction], had been kept secret from the public, in ignominy, for sixty years! But its author clambered out of the grave and made a fresh debut!

In life, if you can identify with nothing, self-consciousness means play-acting, a role. The protagonist of *Diiva* grows weary of everything. Life may be over, once you really see what it has to offer. Why live—unless your life is voluntary, chosen? Chosen against the fearful void, the voidlike richness, of life itself.

My novel *Pilvihipiäinen*, an extract from which is printed here, makes the human divine. It speaks about the illusory, dreamlike nature of all phenomena.

PL: In your prose obscure words and esoteric topics intermingle with earthy urban slang. The combination is exhilarating and has won praise from Finnish critics and philosophers. Do you worry that you might be writing only for the intellectual elite? Can good literature be popular?

HS: Should people live below their potential? Stunt their brains? Shouldn't they rather try their best, nurturing life? What should prevent them? Why?

The main obstacle is the wrong attitude, willfully propagated: reluctance to analyze, to be elastic, to empathize, to open out.

PL: The sheer exuberance of your prose suggests an almost pantheistic sense of wonder. Do you reject materialism?

HS: Sense perceptions collide with furniture, trees, drawing mountain ranges, ravines, to rise transformed, out of the tempestuous ocean, as humanity, walking across the ocean as its master.'

The problem posited by your question is—what? I'm a rigorous monist and can't understand your question. What's the context? The conditions of Western materialism and idealism? The notion of weightless energy they both embrace? I'm in favor of analysis that cuts through all labels; scientific rigor, precise consciousness. Elasticity, compassion. I'm against religious warfare. Religions interpreting themselves quantitatively, which yields a kind of materialism, as also happens with the Christian religion in the versions whereby a person can be saved through time, quantity, waiting—that is, through hypocrisy—without any need for content, consciousness.

PL: Your novels are full of neologisms and wildly heterogeneous material. They are, in this sense, unashamedly artificial; they openly celebrate their own textuality. How do you feel about the currently popular theories, whereby language has no power to refer to a solid reality beyond itself?

HS: Lacking familiarity with such theories, I can respond only in general terms. Consciousness is not identical with thought. Thought, which deals in relations, must subject itself to language, *is* language. A child on a beach, engrossed in producing sand cakes, has no worries about the future. Eternity as pure presence has become an aimful path, interior, immediate, active. Outside reality is ignorance of unity, mere property. The self-conscious human role instrumentalizes outside reality, turning what is mediated into immediacy. Having spoken a line a thousand times, an actor will know it by heart. Yet a good actor will project the role so intensely that every syllable is fresh and unexpected.

From Cloudcomplexion

"Dad, down on all fours, inside, in his overalls, wielding the grinding-board, was surrounded by articles that contained his history. Identity! It was like they were trying to tell me about it: the cement smoothing plates, the seaming irons, the trowels, the gluing slabs. The carpet knife. The backsaw, and, also, Dad despite his disability pension having occasionally repaired boats on the beach, and houses, the claw hammer, hanging at an angle from the tab of his ballooning overalls, their belly fondling the floor as Dad crept along on all fours. The handle prodded the floor, uprighting as Dad returned to vertical. Slurping coffee off the saucer, lips like a trumpet. Grave. Eyes all serious, like a cat taking a crap! Feeling proud of me, he indicated where I should carry the toolbox containing: masonry nails, an edge feather, a triangular saw file, a mall hammer, a staple hammer. And he cast ceremonious-luminous, loving glances at me, furtively; I was his own son! The continuator of his job! Or was he stifling me? After all? Did my palms express intelligence, in any way? Advanced culture, my hands in work mittens! By putting them on, had I slipped a hood over my head? Perhaps I was an artist, his suffering gaze said, as I pushed the wheelbarrow filled with cement, in a near-horizontal posture, my thermal rubber boots crinkling the muddy yard, its latticework of icecrust, gippoes hollering from the neighboring plot. From whom Dad bought his moonshine. Who walked in swarms down Indian Street. Which was apparently named after them. Considering the names of the other streets in the area. All named after Asian and Arab states . . . Indian Street reigned supreme, being the only shopping street in the neighborhood. . . ."

"Transported, as it were, straight from India!" quoth Ari. "Together with the gippoes who came from there! And there really were a lot of Gypsies on Indian Street, night and day. I once asked them why they never confab about their faith, so Old Einar slapped shut his Sanskrit holy book and said the reason why they've been harassed here, and in Europe in general, since they arrived in the 1300s, fleeing hunger and persecution, has never been their dress—the women, with their ankle-length skirts, beautiful hands pointing out of white lace sleeves—no, the real reason is the church, the agnosticism of the bishops, tens of thousands of Gnostics have sizzled at the stake. What would inspire the gippoes to blather about their faith? Well. They couldn't, because it was sacred . . . it was transparentized into everything they did; it had become their flesh! So talking about religion, making it visible, would have meant objectifying it, separation, worship, idealization, and (the same applies to God) heathenism, irreligion. Complacently worshiping an idol, that is, yourself! Perhaps for the same reason, the yellow-robed Buddhist mendicants never thank the people who feed them; the meals go to the Buddha-God . . . who once merely smiled at the question of God's existence . . . for one reason or another. . . . But I don't suffer even from that limitation because in principle I myself operate as the creator (directing myself outward) which is possible only through becoming fully conscious of Reality when you ultimately regard life (creation) as an end in itself (its being, living). By apprehending myself as the creator of myself, detached from any cause (facilitating my freedom, MY LIVING). . . . But this already brings us to Andreas's current philosophy, and more about that later. . . ."

"Weren't you being a bit polite about the gippoes, calling them sacred?" a certain girl asked Ari. "Perhaps they aren't saints after all, if they aren't capable of self-creation . . . LIVING. . . ."

"All right, all right, no doubt we'll return to this later!"

"And you didn't disappoint me that summer, Ari, you set me up with a woman! Together, me and her, at the island (as the sun sank under the sea. Gold-rimmed tufts of cloud and an undulating fireflower complete with smokebract against a granite-gneiss rockface shadowed by a multi-veil-socked rosebush and me and my date in the frigging freezing air), saw, through Ari's eye-gray pup tent, a disk of lightglow and Ari's shadow-ass pulsing up and down, at which point my chickadee smiled her long front teeth over her upper lip. 'Honey, don't eyeball me like that!' she pleaded as my butterflykisses fluttered from her pop-eyes to the nape of her sensual neck. 'OK, let's kill some time.' And I was pissed, the way a fuck for her was just a way of killing time! Her whole life even! Having provided satisfaction in her thermally insulated sleeping bag, I strapped her arm back to her shoulder, skymusing on the origin of biological needs, the genes! Why did she do it, when she was only careering into the abyss of her grave? She: 'You talking about refinement?' Me: 'About the basis of everything! The beginning! Does it contain everything already, in immanent form, an acorn; does the matter inside its shell contain the idea of the whole oak, a huge tree?' She didn't understand me and nor did I understand anything, but her talk of killing some time irritated me to such a point that she had to defend herself! Sitting on the sleeping bag in her mignonette-green corduroys, hands warming over the fire as it turned the lenses of her butterflyglasses into snow.

"In the end, isn't everything just a way of killing some time, pretending, in the absence of immortality. I enjoy a fuck, the ability to create hydrocephalic clones of myself, although they also signal my own mortality. In fact I even enjoy dying. What a wonderful privilege it is to be allowed to die!"

I thought, do all pleasures involve a powerful sense of death, is that their explanation? I used an opener to detach the crown cap of a bottle of malt liquor; it fell among the toy sheep that the aforementioned corseted chickadee Armi had constructed out of fir cones and matches! The ashes whirled under the flames. Oh why couldn't I sustain a pleasure infinitely, as though forgetting myself; was the knowledge or sense of myself, the desire for possession, the cause of suffering? Was I somehow this cool air in late fall, this Indian-blue sky, did I somehow contain everything the north was all aglitter Corona Borealis the Plough the Dragon Cassiopeia?

I remembered how Jaacop had said how almost everyone suffers from Weltschmerz when they're young, when the interest in the self awakens in the form of questions about the Self awakening to its own death and how sometimes, looking at animals, he had wondered why he wasn't an animal himself.

For me, it was agony to stand in opaque telephone booths when the people in the street could only see my feet; I felt like my legs were on fire from the knee down even though my chrome-tanned calfskin shoes were reflecting the pedestrians into my view! The numbers spun, dimming under the rotary dial! Armi went apeshit. She lowered her fangs off her upper lip. "Damn! I'll hook the right number, even with this dead hand!" Her fingers worked with strings. The perforated, wobbling disk spun fiercely, circling. I wanted to sink beneath the horizon in shame. I asked Mom over to the neighbors', to tell her I was still alive. I was hanging out at Jaacop's because Dad still couldn't stand the sight of me. Unemployed, I disturbed the peace of his soul. He had no obligation to keep me. . . .

I was drafted into the landing troops on the Palm Coast (the southern coast of Finland); we surface divers shared the barracks with the peacoats.

Smokelike snow dribbled from the spruces I bumped into; I crawled in a snowdrift in the swinish drill, footcloths hanging from my boots. I gyrated in a self-conjured cloud of snow. I'd broken four teeth off my comb, marking four days of service, when my spleengraph blipped in the merry-go-round of the morning shower. I was imprisoned by the system! As I licked my catamount-pee-and-bromide in the canteen, my brain cells began to overheat. Why should I defend a country, when I didn't own an inch of its soil? Not even the part I occupied with my body. I was subordinated to a foreign authority! This Reeperbahn system was shamelessly exploiting my identity! I no longer even owned my wholesome physique, which was being ordered into line, left, right, left, right! Some morning horn would thrust his legs up close to mine, and my legs would meet the legs in front, and the detachment would pass the canteen in a cube-carpet of monkeymeat, singing lustily in one voice! Amidst the hubbub, spirals in my speech bubble! Forked lightning! But having enjoyed, for example, Armi's body (that is, enjoyed only my own) as her prosthetic fingers rubbed the scruff of my neck in lust, didn't the earth serve my needs? Ought I not defend it and the people who had been formed out of it, in my desire to live, should a sudden hail of salt shot lash at our buttocks from across the border? What was my freedom, what was freedom in general? It came from my autonomy, not coercion . . . and everyone had to find their own freedom. You can't dictate it to others. In the possibility of freedom lay my only salvation, comfort, joy, independence. I MYSELF. I reckoned.

I wanted to serve humankind VOLUNTARILY. To its and my best advantage, the way I wanted. Rattling a saber was not in my best interest! Someone absolutely had to take the initiative by stripping themselves of all the braids and swastikas and arms! Oh if that someone could be Finland and me! It made me sore to see those cows around me, willing to be milked, indeed, wishing to be milked for the benefit of this cattle co-op! Like whores they'd allowed the lard-asses to determine their morality and what was best for them—fuck, they entered this life like cattle and would leave the same way. Never one to be ordered about, I was nearly exploding! I wasn't a piece of state property! (And Christians shouldn't be either. Or how else can they employ their "freedom"?) I had to line up naked in front of the medicine man, who glanced at my balls, nor were they missing from the middle of that mighty wreath of hair, and in order to free myself from military service, I claimed I was suffering from androphobia. This word was INDEED found on the referral that took me, a former team athlete, to the military hospital for further examination. . . . As the doctor slate-penciled the papers to send me to Helsinki, I heard the medics and the warrant officers whispering that my blood pressure was exceptionally high! Which, years later, I was to attribute to my stifled aggressions, my internal boiling, I was born to be free, I reflected, inside the transport van, its sides thudding against the snowbanks as it hovered along the slippery road, I was in a cage, by what right? What justification? I hadn't considered myself mad at the military hospital. I thought I was only pretending to be mad! In striped pajamas and panting slippers, deliberately sucking my paunch against my spine! Panting fast, loudly, supposedly oblivious to my surroundings! The windows! The steel-tube bunks! The indolents! Bevies of girls festooning the sick with flowers! Girls who plugged cassette players into pig's nostrils in the walls, between the legs of the sickbeds, as bodies set to boogie; perhaps because of my loneliness, still ultimately vocationless, still searching for my place in society (how best to improve it), I craved attention and understanding! In the form of an examination and discussions of my prospects. I considered myself essentially a philosopher, who, with his rabbit-red eyes framed with freckle-rosettes that forced their white-blackhead-roots out of a snout bloated with red abscesses, did not envy those youths being licked by hot babes! Their freedom did not tempt me! So I imagined, when at night as I slept the cloud-gray pubes like flames around my stiff became soaked with come! Tadpoles! Latent idiots! Yet did all my expressions signal some genuine disease? I couldn't pretend to be something I wasn't! Wasn't the fear I had attributed to androphobia apparent, in my stomach, spotted with black moles, tremblingly affixing itself to my spine? I didn't want to receive or swallow anything external, brainwashing imposed on me by the system. In my brave and partly defiant independence, in my freedom from conformity to the values of the swastika? Therefore I was not only afraid that people would condemn me but also that they would somehow murder me, and by flaunting my fear in this way I was begging for pity—don't murder me (an unassuming guy, who's even reduced his belly so as to be as inconspicuous as possible! A wallflower driven into a corner, fleeing the ruthless Reeperbahnists!). I still farted noble thoughts! Thus my rapid breathing intensified my fear, without my knowing it! So "androphobia" was the key to my conduct after all?

Had I not been scared in some way, I would have invented some other way of playing sick! Nothing is invented by chance! One morning I was told I'd be released the following day and that my military service had been deferred two years, meaning that all my playacting and my entire bid to be free of saber-rattling was wasted. Besides, I no longer knew where I could slink off to, Dad having insisted on rent if I meant to reside at his dump. To Dad's chagrin, I was unable to kick coins into my pockets off the soccer field! Not even chalk stripes onto my suits! My red heart resounded in my brains in the smoking room where I sat squirting smoke out of my ears, my nostrils, the clock on the wall was almost half-past eight, and I should have been in bed by eight! Out of uniform tomorrow! Finally they found me by windmilling through the smoke I'd been spewing. I went behind bars without resisting, was put in the stocks and various leather straps throttled my physique! I sighed with relief when sleeping medicine was dribbled into my mouth—expecting a long incarceration! (I suppose it was insane to shorten cigarettes in the smoking room after eight!) I was now in the company of snorting, gargling crazies. One day the stethoscoped medicine man announced: "Your mother tells me you've painted pictures. Could we see some?" I nodded, the dumb leather bedstraps hanging loose on the floor, Mom had apparently been invited by letter to that charitable establishment, to discuss me, and now, protected by a gorilla, I was taken to see her, at the end of a long corridor; there were windows almost all the way up from the rubber floor to the ceiling. She in a dashing imitation mink coat (borrowed from the neighbor), a *canotier* hat, beige spike-heeled goatskin pumps, a hiddenite inflorescence in her semiloric ring! In the tears hanging from her lashes, her anarchist son, wonder! Thousands of questions! She said the medicine men had wanted to know whether I'd previously shown any signs of madness! Not in Mom's opinion! I said truthfully that I'd been calm throughout. We didn't discuss the motives that had brought me here. I kept them to myself. Out of fear.

I gave Mom permission to bring a few of my watercolors and one oil painting. Because the trepanners wanted to search for my possible disease in them. You don't need to be much of an expert to detect schizoid characteristics, psychoses, et cetera. I was sure my landscape paintings would bespeak my beautiful, balanced soul. The beauty of nature powerfully stimulated my aesthetic sense. I saluted the doctor in soldierly fashion, dressed in my striped wanker's nightie: "Doctor Lieutenant Colonel, sir, I am healthy!" Thus I managed to get my affairs rolling, by speeding up my illness!

In love with one of the nurses, I slouched off into a car, was hauled into another hospital for further examination. My character and my intelligence were tested. The psychiatrist chatted about Spinoza working as a lens cutter! I too should base my thoughts on some practical, alms-collecting profession, seeing as I lacked academic training. I would prosper with my ideas and my art. —But why I could hardly repeat any of the digits read out to me, the shrink didn't say. Perhaps he assumed it had something to do with my "anxiety" which he discovered in the womb I'd seen in one of the ink blots of the Rorschach test.

What with my lively imagination, I found it hard to concentrate (my head was filled with an endless cascade of images and thoughts, through which I barely realized I was in the loony bin), especially on matters that didn't interest me. And my love for that nurse at the soldier-repair-shop tormented me so hellishly that to free myself, apparently, I fell under the spell of another nurse in the closed ward, and when I was moved to the adjoining open ward, both being under the same roof, I was once more enchanted by the nurse who was looking after me. . . . I was now allowed home at weekends, on "holiday."

I glanced at the coltsfoots sprouting through the melting snow, white-hot laser beams bouncing off my face, branding it with hot freckles, and wrote to Mom asking for civilian clothes. We still didn't have a phone. Dad intercepted the letter from Mom; they came to see me, drunk. Mom fluttered yeast from her eyes, puzzled to wake up in the loony bin, she expected to be in a certain couple's apartment! Standing on his legs, Dad hysterically asserted his identity, showering me with clothes, my gabardine raincoat opened out as it flew through the air toward me, I was hit by anklets woolen gloves soccer shorts the binoculars Uncle Moose had given me landed on the bed a pointed shoe clanked against the radiator as Dad roared Of course it had to end like this, you choose your friends you choose your life, referring to Kant Lessing Novalis Hegel my hundreds of books as his flashing eyes already indicated, dressed in his turd-brown raglan-sleeved greatcoat, an astrakhan cap on his head, and a gay fly around his neck, black against a white elasticized nylon shirt, he was relieved, all agitation on my behalf was over Don't you dare come home he yanked Mom with him, having made her blind drunk, and here ended their flying visit I watched through the window, they mooned at me as they stuffed themselves into a taxi the weeping birches budding Dad no longer needing to worry about me, seeing his son tenanted in lunatic asylums had hurt his pride, whether I was a rationalist or not, upon a certain trepanner's announcement I had been freed of military service on the grounds of inaptitude and transferred among the idiots, militia Class E, irrevocably! As this spiritual repair shop was for acute cases only, the social adviser tried to nudge me in the direction of some building site and a rented dump until she concluded that I needed a lot of time to sort out my life and career and so I was carted to a funny farm outside Helsinki, in Nickby, in the country, white willows massaging the barred windows of the stone houses the color of dyer's greenweed; below, hunchbacks of Notre Dame were playing corona, anxiously cueing wooden counters into the reticulate pockets I laughed like a raven I was restless couldn't stay still asked the shaman for some tranquilizers which the nurse mixed into tap water in a measuring glass I was captivated by her and having thus in a short time eternally loved three white sisters transferring my love from one to the other, whoever happened to be serving the ward I was in except in the military hospital where I loved only one even in my leather straps, what abominable pain at parting, until a new nurse sprang to my assistance and now I was playing soccer on the hospital staff team in a cup competition between different businesses and workplaces only to stumble on my own genius which in my orphanage constituted my only remaining security and defense against external circumstance as I bumped into calf-headed lobster-clawed freaks juvenile anal-urotics idiots sodomites public masturbators sitting on benches against the hedge staring into the zenith of the swirling clouds gazing proudly with their nostrils at the passing ladies longing to seat themselves on their pleasure-beams as they sprayed out their sweet pee with dignity I laughed I cried not knowing which perhaps I was dreaming who would wake me I rubbed my eyes bubbles floated against the blue they were moving flies in the vitreous humor of the eye or vibrating grains of gravel in the sun the gravel road soared straight up if I was an idiot one night I used a crowbar to crack open a certain room and a cupboard door in the darkness the spot of light from the penlight slid over the letters enabling me to read the psychologist's report on my "anxiety" the lightspot crossed the following trills "occasionally capable of conceptual thought of an order that is beyond the reach of many college graduates." I wept! I sighed with relief! Such a fortune it REALLY caused a wave of relief I wasn't a dud after all I was a live round capable of anything you please as my lips tapered toward my ears in my huge sense of superiority I asked for an IQ test I was hungry for self-admiration through the eyes of others for discussions of my prospects I'd regarded myself as a philosopher and also a painter when I was murdered on the basis of a mere "inkblot test" what do these pictures remind you of they said it was no use going further hebephrenic schizophrenic REALLY I thought in panic I'd soon die a statistic of "youthful apathy" if the diagnosis was correct and again I sat being tested mainly however in order to be the object of discussion and again splinters of mahogany rattled and splattered in the dark room this time the crowbar was wielded by a fully charged psychopath unfeeling unable to empathize with others how then had I painted I reasoned how had I experienced aesthetic sensations and thus I saw that my mediocre IQ would never enable me to carry out my megalomaniacal designs in fact I was entirely discouraged when the psychologist who reached this conclusion could not on the second day of testing even be bothered to test me to look at my reactions but delegated the job and in the final session when, having such "vast intelligence" I had just praised myself, saying how people didn't understand me, misinterpreted me, in reply to the question What causes you anxiety, by the author of that report, without realizing that I was now being officially classified as a psychotic.

Translated by Philip Landon

Raija Siekkinen

Raija Siekkinen (b. 1953) specializes in the short story and has won a string of major literary awards, including the prestigious Runeberg Prize in 1993. A keen traveler, she has spent time in France and Italy, and translates fiction from French and other languages. Siekkinen is comfortable with the conventional short story, and her work can seem simpler than it is. Quiet, unadorned, and sharply observed, her narratives are slices of mundane middle-class life—internal monologues and banal social conversations that barely disguise underlying psychological strains. Siekkinen's characteristic mode is a Chekhovian blend of irony and sympathy, combined with an almost Pinteresque conception of dialogue as monologue. Katherine Mansfield and Raymond Carver would have appreciated Siekkinen's indirection and understatement: her brief, delicate stories suggest submerged volumes. With the utmost subtlety and tact, Siekkinen insists that humans speak mostly past one another and that the most ordinary and apparently balanced individuals are often engaged in a desperate fight to keep subjective horrors at bay.

Interview

PHILIP LANDON: Can you name any shared characteristics of contemporary Finnish fiction? Do you identify with any of your international or domestic contemporaries?

RAIJA SIEKKINEN: In my opinion Finnish fiction is in a state of ferment. The modernist tradition has continued with vigor, sustaining a high standard—on the other hand it seems also to provoke irritation. Our youngest authors are searching for new ways of writing, and I see this as an attitude of protest against the long-enduring modernist spirit. The old realist method of narration also seems to be making a comeback.

For my own part, I think I have a modernist lineage, insofar as the works of Antti Hyry, Veijo Meri, Paavo Haavikko, and Marja-Liisa Vartio made a lasting impression on me. In the seventies, when I began to write, I read the modernists in order to experience again and again the empowering feeling that individuality is a merit in literature, even though it is a fault in other parts of life. My upbringing stressed this latter perspective, and I needed literature because it strengthened my belief in the right to be myself. Modernism, specifically, seemed to grant me this right.

PL: How would you situate fiction in general and your own work in particular in relation to mass culture and the mass media?

RS: I think mass culture and the mass media are enemies of literature in that they simplify and constrict all that literature should expand: the emotions and the level of self-knowledge. As the term itself implies, mass culture entails the same dangers as all other mass phenomena.

PL: Kai Laitinen has written, "The traditional Finnish novel is close to nature. Nature features in the role of a friend or an enemy or both." Can we read your work as part of this tradition? Does nature require a new approach from writers?

RS: Nature obviously forms a part of my work; the sense that nature determines the rhythm of life is undoubtedly something that we Finns all share. On the other hand, in my own work, descriptions of nature have grown fewer over the years, and I don't consider that to be a bad thing.

PL: From the *Kalevala* to postwar fiction, much of Finnish literature has been intimately bound up with the question of national identity. Do you see yourself as a member of a more international generation?

RS: I certainly belong to a more international generation than those of my predecessors who were born in the thirties, and who spent much energy analyzing the causes and consequences of the war. On the other hand, the writers of the 1910s were an extremely international generation. Personally, I don't think I've ever directly explored the question of our national identity, although through my personality, it naturally enters each text in some way or other. I think questions of nationality are more topical elsewhere in Europe than in Finland. I am troubled by nationalistic ideologies in general.

PL: Contemporary Finnish writers frequently use autobiographical and mock-autobiographical forms. Why?

RS: I think writers always use their own lives as material. Some do it more overtly (for example, the Finnish writer Anja Kauranen), others are more oblique, even disguised. My own writings are not autobiographical insofar as none of the stories' events have actually happened to me. I combine fragments of life without caring about literal truth. My hope is that the end result might be closer to the truth than reality itself. I think writing is a search for truth—not for the meaning of life—and truth cannot be attained by copying life.

PL: You acknowledge the influence of Raymond Carver. His minimalist aesthetic has roots in modernism, Hemingway and Mansfield being important predecessors. Why does the understated, oblique short story still survive in countries like America and Finland, when interest in the form seems to have dwindled in many other parts of the world?

RS: Raymond Carver, of course, is only one of many authors whose short stories and formal innovations seem successful to me. He belongs to a tradition, as do all writers. In terms of my worldview and my idea of humanity, the writers who have influenced me range from Chekhov to Maupassant, from Hemingway to Bachmann. I am unable to say why the "oblique" short story is alive and well in Finland and America—perhaps because it makes it possible to talk about several phenomena at once, whereas a straightforward story or tale operates on a single level.

PL: A sense of isolation and emotional damage is never far from your fiction. Yet, on the surface, your narratives are usually poised, crafted, even serene. Is this a contradiction? Have you ever been tempted to experiment with disrupted forms?

RS: I think I am moving toward a more disrupted form. I have often described conflicts between the individual and the so-called world in which the individual has been damaged by the world. Nowadays I am more and more interested in describing the relationship between man and woman. This should also affect the form of my short stories, I'd say.

PL: You sometimes value implication more highly than direct statement. Dialogue is particularly sparse in your stories. Are you skeptical of the powers of language to order experience?

RS: I would say that indirect statements give readers the chance to exercise their own creativity and to avoid the feeling that the writer is spoonfeeding them certain ways of thinking and seeing.

PL: Many of your characters seem disoriented, vulnerable, and hollow, and appear to crave a sense of tangible order and security. Are you a chronicler of late-industrial alienation? Do you find the compact form of the short story at all limiting as a vehicle for studying, for example, history and the social environment?

RS: Through such characters, I think I can undertake more subtle and sensitive descriptions of experience; and, of course, my characters are like this because I am the same. The conflict between individual values and social values no doubt relates to late-industrial alienation. Society evaluates the individual according to social utility; the individual person, by contrast, feels worthy willy-nilly, regardless of utility, and suffers because society does not acknowledge such worth. This is particularly clear to a professional writer. It is a daily problem and thus something you tend to write about. Such literature is increasingly important in the contemporary world, when in Finland, for example, 20.5 percent of the working population has been left without jobs and has thus become worthless and even burdensome in the eyes of society.

The Black Sun

Life had set a trap, the existence of which did not become apparent before it was already too late: the trap had snapped shut, divided time. There now existed a before and an after, and all you could do was try to cope. The wind drove fallen leaves along the wet pavement, rain drizzled against the window every day, from one day to the next, and all around the world reverberated, growing more and more incomprehensible, blanching, like a patient making compulsive movements. Talk was out of the question, it was possible only to look the other in the eyes until the point when the eyes are closed; to intertwine in the darkness across which the gray afternoon coursed as a quivering stripe; to remain heavily clothed beneath the covers, but still shivering, seemingly naked and visible to all. At night, in dreams, strange people carried on as they wished; there was nothing to be done about them, and in the morning reality, increasingly distant, emitted its waning calls: leaves were raked, the lawn was mowed for the last time that autumn, the telephone rang for a long while before it went silent.

There was something around which thoughts revolved, startled, and which nevertheless bound them to itself: a radial image was formed; a black sun that illuminated all of life.

But the workmen had already been called in the springtime, and in the autumn they came. When they knocked on the door at seven in the morning, it was necessary to go, to stand at the chink in the door and to listen to what they had to say. They needed the key to the basement for the paint cans, they wanted to check the color of the doors, to measure the height of the fence and the size of the space between the boards and decide whether the yard should be terraced and whether bolts or screws should be used; it was necessary to begin to respond and to think. It was necessary to stand on the lawn barefoot, to shift from one foot to the other on the cold ground, to scrutinize the holes into which the fence posts would be set, and to know that, inside, the previous night's cigarette smoke was drifting slowly toward the recently opened windows and that there were coffee cups and unemptied ashtrays on the table and floor and, in the refrigerator, a great deal of food that no one had felt like eating and that already reeked, and that silence, like an odor, seemed to be everywhere, along with something that could not be said.

Outside the drawn curtains, scaffolding twenty feet high was erected for painting. In the mornings, you were now awakened by the sound of a circular saw. Loose paint was being scraped from the wall, the painters' conversations were audible through the windows, they discussed the promissory notes which would fall due, then the promissory notes that had already fallen due, and sometimes the carpenter came to tell the painters how a house was painted, and sometimes the painters told the carpenter how a fence was constructed.

The contractor came, a stout man with a loud voice, small feet, and the arms of a sumo wrestler, and he complained to the painters about expenses.

"Don't plaster so damn much, just start painting," he shouted up at the scaffolding, and from there came the response:

"There's no leaving it like this, you just go find that payroll."

"This is a landmark building, you hear?"

The contractor left. During lunch breaks, the painters sat in the park opposite and drank medium-strength beer and told passersby that the house was a landmark building and how it was to be painted and how long the paint would last on the walls: if it lasted two winters and a summer, then ten years. The carpenter ate his lunch on the grass in the yard; he drank spring water and talked about salmon nets. Was there a salmon thief or were there too few weights in the nets; there hadn't been any salmon for almost a week. We sat on grass warmed by the midmorning sun, but beneath the grass the soil was already cold; we planned a trap for the salmon thieves, aware the whole time that our own nets had yielded only a single salmon during the entire summer; even that had already been a month ago. The fish had been put into the freezer whole, now it was already frozen solid, a fish nearly a yard long; who would eat such a fish? We talked about the sea and the dangers involved in autumn fishing as though it were a previous life, knowing that meanwhile the nets were still in the sea and the algae had so coated them that there wasn't a clean line to be seen anywhere anymore; day by day the weight of the nets increased, and who would raise them, who would clean them, and when? We entered the home, opened the curtains and the windows, began to talk about raising the nets and about the salmon which we would yet catch.

When the facade had been painted, the painters began to drink. They sat in the park and drank cheap wine or vodka during lunch hours and after work, and the building was now being inspected from numerous park benches; the freshly painted facade gleamed, its lace patterns stood out prettily, but old gray paint flaked from the other walls. On paydays, the contractor came in search of them and so did the other painter's former wife. When the autumn rains and winds began, the painters came to say that it was impossible to paint; then came a long warm, dry spell, but they were out of paint and the contractor brought none. Now the painters came in search of the contractor on paydays; they sat in the yard beside the wall waiting, but the contractor didn't come.

"He lost ten thousand betting on the horses, he's not going to pay."

"He's not coming."

"No, he's not."

It became necessary to lend the painters money, to sit in the dimming kitchen and to listen to them talk. One had seen a man doing forest work cut his own leg off at the thigh and bleed to death before he had a chance to utter a sentence; another had gotten out of a car that had crashed into a traffic island at the very next intersection and everyone inside had been killed.

"The neighbor's son flew out of the windshield, his legs stayed in the car, he died there on the road."

Another had killed two men but it had been fair play, defending a legitimate cause: in other words, a woman; another's mother had died in childbirth. The painters were offered coffee or beer, the stack of dirty dishes on the draining board grew, and when the lights were switched on, everyone squinted. They heard about a man whose hand had been cut off but, because of the shock, no blood had flowed; when the man was brought out of shock by a slap on the ears, he bled to death. The beer began to run out, from outside came the sound of evening traffic, its acceleration and braking different from that of daytime traffic. The painters began to talk about women, what types they had had and the types they might have, and then they soon left.

There came a bright morning. Outside the window, the trees were bare, the previous night's wind had shorn them of all their leaves at once, scattering them about the park lawn and onto the street; there they were, like a golden carpet in some childhood fairy tale. Suddenly it seemed hilarious that people went on walking where they knew the sidewalk to be, wearing their coats and pants and shoes and, on their faces, expressions that suggested someone should come and rake immediately, restoring everything to how it had been before. It was necessary to get under the covers, to entangle oneself in another's hair and skin, to attack, to bite, to laugh or cry, knowing the whole time that outside the window a new page was already being turned.

That autumn, following two nights of downpour, the boat sank beside the jetty. It hung suspended beneath the water by its mooring ropes and prow chain, blue, beautiful. The wind and the small waves coursed over it, and the sides of the boat quivered. Its bottom grating and benches floated loosely alongside it. They were gathered onto the jetty. We stood watching.

"Oh hell."

"Right."

"Shit. Let's go."

The boat stayed like that for days. Meanwhile, there was talk of what would happen if one of the ropes were to break: the boat would then be left hanging by a single rope, perpendicular, pointing at the bottom, and finally even that last rope would give out. There were already frosts at night; each morning, the handrail and the roof of the neighbor's shed were covered with hoarfrost. At night one was awakened by the cold pressing in through cracks in the uncaulked windows and then lay there thinking about how the windows should have been caulked, and about the boat, which might be iced over any night now, and then there the boat would be, beneath a layer of ice growing thicker night by night, until it finally disappeared from sight, lost irrevocably, with a beautiful word on its side.

One weekend the boat was salvaged. Beams were used to prop up its sides, the water was bailed out, the boat was towed ashore by car and overturned at the base of a tree. A mixture of oil and water trickled from the forecabin and from beneath the sides of the boat, its wet underside turned white there as we watched and the following week the waters froze.

With the arrival of the cold weather, the painters stopped drinking and quickly finished painting the house. The contractor seldom came now, always explained when he'd be able to pay and quickly left again; then he stopped coming altogether. The painters said that he didn't have a new contract, that he had begun to drink, having squandered all his money on the horses; they came inside, tried to call him, and then sat in the kitchen talking about the types of women one of them had had but not the other. It was necessary to lend them money and to hear how paint was made from potato starch, how a pig was slaughtered, how an elk, caught between two trees by its horns, was set free, and how coffee grounds were turned into worm compost where worms lived and bred, which could then be sold.

"He promised us sauna and drink for a whole day once the job was finished."

"Then he promised us each a bottle of vodka."

"He gave us coffee and cake."

The first snow fell. The mornings were now long and dark, evening came early, the night was like a mass grave from which it was hard to exhume yourself in the morning. In the daytime there were black branches outside the window, behind them a gray sky, below, frozen grass. Sometimes flags hung on poles, sometimes candles burned on war veterans' graves; once we were awakened by singing and the laying of a wreath at the war memorial and, on Wednesdays, by funeral bells—if you listened carefully, it was possible to tell whether a man or a woman had died—or by an announcement that the siren which was about to sound did not signal real danger.

The painters were now painting the staircases of the building under a contract of their own. The contractor had deferred part of their pay; money was offered to them as a loan and they enumerated everything they could do and had done; they promised to get inexpensive firewood, to put topsoil on the yard, to put the doors on their hinges and to caulk the windows. They talked about their former wives and their former houses and the work they had done; they promised to repay everything with work, and left.

That is how the winter passed. At times, when the salmon was taken out of the freezer and portions were sawn off with a file, the previous summer and all that had happened came to mind: the sunken boat, the salmon nets retrieved from the water at the last moment, or the island with its rocks.

When you went out and saw the staircase, its newly painted walls reflecting the whiteness of the snow, or the fence that now encircled the house, you knew how near the end of everything was, and then you had to walk through the snow-covered city to the seashore and look at the islands visible far off in the distance like a different kind of land.

I did all sorts of things. I believed in time. I thought that it would ceaselessly carry me farther from what I wished to leave behind, in spirals, approaching occasionally but receding the whole time. And then some dead flower, or a fly from last year, found while cleaning, catapulted me back through the whole of that long journey.

Late one evening, during a snowstorm, when the streets were empty and blocked with snowdrifts and the wind blustered in chimneys, drawing stove flames upward, there was a knock at the door. A painter was standing on the steps, he said he had come to repay his debt with work, and although we protested and said it didn't matter and not to worry about it, he walked through the house and noticed that the lathes were still in the corner behind the door and the cupboard doors were still leaning against the corridor wall and that one particular tile was still missing from the fireplace; and so we set to work. Many evenings we worked, then drank coffee, and the painter described the occasions when he had been Santa Claus and what that had been like, and what he had received from his children for Christmas and what he had given. And one night I went outside, walked through the snow and looked at the house, its windows shining, illuminated in the midst of the darkness, and I thought about how I was within my own life from which I could go nowhere; I returned home along my own tracks and was met at the door by warmth.

In the spring the boat sank. We were on the island, we had just made love, we were alseep under the covers, I was dreaming of a land where not a single person had yet been. We were awakened by the wind. On the way to the beach we saw that two birches had fallen across the path. The sea roared against the rocky shore; beside the jetty, the boat lay under the water. We got the tackle, secured it to a tree and a cable to the boat, we towed the boat, moved the tackle farther; that's where that day went. Slowly, streaming with water, the boat rose onto the rock. I looked at it, and at the taut cable, and at the waves, and I felt as though I were already far away. A white sun stood above the sea and the rocks. When I closed my eyes, it looked black; when I opened my eyes, it was white again.

Translated by Ritva Poom

ROLF HAMILTON

Lars Sund

Lars Sund (b. 1953) combines solid historical research with consummate story-telling. *Colorado Avenue,* which won a number of prizes in Finland and Sweden, describes the life of Finland-Swedish immigrants in the United States at the beginning of the century. The narrator self-mockingly exposes the mechanics of narrative illusion by interrogating the characters in person, seating the reader in front of a silent film, and spinning the globe as he changes the scene from the New World back to Ostrobothnia, on the Finnish coast. Sund playfully questions the documentary powers of realism and underscores the fictional status of his history. Yet the fiction is more than just a game: Sund asserts the vital power of memory and the imagination. Light in its touch, generous in its spirit, and hospitable to the absurd and the improbable, Sund's work has a tragicomic, playful flavor.

Novels: *Natten är ännu ung* (The Night Is Still Young, 1975), *Vinter hamn* (Winter Harbor, 1983), *Colorado Avenue* (1991). Poems: *Ögonblick* (Moments, 1974).

Interview

PHILIP LANDON: Can you name any shared characteristics of contemporary Finnish fiction? Do you identify with any of your international or domestic contemporaries?

LARS SUND: Finnish fiction is no longer epic in the nineteenth-century sense; it is moving from the countryside to the cities and is rapidly becoming more urban, more modern.

Finland-Swedish fiction is another matter. We have always had great poets but fewer novelists. A change came about in the 1980s; suddenly we also had Finland-Swedish novels. Many of the best have been written by women—for example, Ulla-Leena Lundberg and Pirkko Lindberg. Their novels are epic and realistic but also modern; the "new" Finland-Swedish novel is no museum.

Identification with contemporaries? Perhaps novelists from Norway or Iceland who try to combine storytelling with irony and linguistic exploration—for example, Kjartan Flögstad or Einar Karason. The novels of Salman Rushdie have had a great influence on my writing, and the same may be said of some of the Latin American magic realists. Anglo-American writing, too.

PL: How would you situate fiction in general and your own work in particular in relation to mass culture and the mass media?

LS: Fiction will survive. I believe that people will continue to read books despite virtual reality and whatever else they come up with, because reading is great fun and the book is an ingenious invention. Fiction (that is, the novel) will hold out—as long as writers remember that their most important job is to tell stories and to tell them as well as possible.

As for my own work, I have no illusions. I write in an obscure language, Swedish. I belong to a very small minority, the Finland-Swedes, in a small European country that most people have barely heard of. The only thing I can do is try to tell my stories the best I can.

PL: From the *Kalevala* to postwar fiction, much of Finnish literature has been intimately bound up with the question of national identity. Do you see yourself as a member of a more international generation?

LS: Yes and no. I was born in the early fifties, and we are a generation devoted to international mass culture—the same rock music is known all over the world. We traveled the world in a way that no generation before us had. But then I found out that I knew virtually nothing about my own heritage, so I started digging for my roots. *Colorado Avenue* is the result of that search.

Hanna, one of the main characters in *Colorado Avenue*, goes to the U.S. and then returns to Finland. Perhaps it's symbolic. My first novel ends with the narrator dreaming about leaving his Ostrobothnian hometown, impatiently waiting to explore the world. He was voicing my own dreams. But whenever I return "home," I (like Hanna) carry my experience with me. I think the big wide world will always be a part of my writing. And I still like rock music, too.

PL: Despite its solid archival basis and putative commitment to historical authenticity, *Colorado Avenue* contains a lot of fantasy and play and is mediated through a manipulative, mischievous narrator. Are you averse to notions of objectivity and coherence and to the idea of a single controlling point of view? How important is deflationary irony in your novels?

LS: I don't believe fiction can ever achieve objectivity or a single controlling point of view; not if it's honest. But I believe in realism. In order to cope with a world that is hopelessly complicated, I as a writer must use every available trick of the trade. Irony tells me and the reader that all this is artifice and that you are reading a text and that someone (the writer) is trying to manipulate you. You shouldn't believe a word that person writes. By taking everything as a lie you might eventually reach truth—a statement about the world that has meaning. Lying is a back door to truth, somebody says somewhere in the novel.

Besides, I *like* playing around with a lot of irony and stuff. It's fun. Writing shouldn't be taken too seriously, as my wife always reminds me.

PL: *Colorado Avenue* largely deals with cultural cross-fertilization: migration and border crossings are central to its plot, and vernacular and even bilingual or hybrid speech provide some of its pleasures, along with details like the fresh Ostrobothnian metaphors that your immigrant-protagonist uses to describe America. Is the mixing of languages and cultures of particular interest to you as a Finland-Swedish writer?

LS: Yes. I think people who belong to a minority have a keener eye for these things than people belonging to the majority, especially in large countries. The effects of outside influence are, of course, easier to see if the size of your group is 300,000 instead of 30 million. But I think this issue concerns all writers and all people. Culture is always the product of disparate elements. It's an ongoing process; the mixture is always changing. And the changes can be seen very quickly and very clearly in language.

From Colorado Avenue

Hanna's great love had lain dormant within her like a she-bear in its winter lair for almost a quarter of a century, patiently waiting for Ed Ness to come walking up Colorado Avenue in Telluride one warm blue evening in the summer of 1897 when the air stank of dynamite.

Hanna's love was that rare sort that can be awakened only once in a lifetime, but is on the other hand so strong and genuine that it lasts for the whole of that life—and beyond. It was a love that, like the weather or epidemics, knew no frontiers. It lacked sense and judgment and proportion; it was also clear and completely logical. Its tenacity was derived from archipelago-bred Hanna's inherited stubbornness. My maternal grandfather's father stood little chance of avoiding it from the moment he stepped over Hanna's threshold.

He sought to flee on more than one occasion; but he never succeeded.

Yet Hanna's great love awoke in stages. It was driven by a power as strong as the machinery in those mighty steamers that had in recent years begun to cross the Atlantic in the improbably short time of ten days or fewer. And just as it took time to stoke up the pressure in the boilers of the Atlantic steamships, so did Hanna's love need time to build up to full strength. It was a painful process.

The atmosphere throughout the boardinghouse altered; the air became harsh and prickly, charged with static electricity as before an approaching thunderstorm. Her boys (as she was in the habit of calling the tenants of the boardinghouse) complained of headaches and poor sleep. Even inanimate objects were affected.

The morning after Ed Ness moved in, a windowpane on the first floor broke with a sharp crack, for no apparent reason. The pendulum clock in the dining room, which until now had kept time perfectly, began to behave very oddly—now the hands were in a furious hurry on their eternal journey around the clock face, now they were as tardy as sloths, and the striking apparatus rattled and chimed at the oddest times. Small objects disappeared, only to be discovered in the most unexpected places: a teaspoon fell out between the freshly mangled sheets in the linen cupboard; when Hanna lifted the lid of one of the large iron pots in the kitchen, she found a reel of woolen yarn she had been hunting for several days; one morning a rusty hammer suddenly lay in the middle of the dining room floor. The key to the outhouse disappeared from its nail beside the kitchen door and was never found again, no matter how hard Hanna searched.

At first, Hanna dismissed these incidents as irritating but irrelevant trivia, insoluble riddles of the kind life is full of. But when things continued in this way, she grew nervous and perturbed. She slept badly. For the first time since she had begun to menstruate, her period that month was very painful, the spasms contracting her abdomen to an aching knot and reaching high up into the small of her back; she felt dreadfully sick.

Her nausea was made worse by the sharp odor of dynamite that hung stubbornly on in the house. When she brought flowers in to deaden the odor, the result was merely that the scent of the flowers grew sickening in the motionless air—an unusually intense summer heat had settled over the valley—and in the end the whole house smelled like a funeral parlor. Angrily, Hanna threw the flowers out and locked herself in her room with a cushion pressed to her aching belly and an enamel basin on the bedside table to vomit into. She was half-dissolved in her own pouring sweat and felt like a wreck; she was ready to cry with desperation and shame.

One night the rain finally came, after several weeks of persistent drought.

Like everything else here in the Rocky Mountains, the rains have neither sense nor moderation. The rain flung itself down from the sky, roared against the boardinghouse roof; the gutter pipes could not swallow all the water but gurgled desperately like drowning men while the water cascaded off the edge of the roof. The dry earth heaved and crackled as it was inundated. Streams of water cut deep furrows in the slopes and dragged with them clods of earth and large quantities of gravel.

South of the San Juan Mountains a violent thunderstorm was raging, one which Telluride Valley was, however, spared; the rumbling sounded as though the steel-rimmed wheels of an immense wagon were rolling across a wooden bridge in a deep and narrow ravine.

For the first time in several nights, Hanna slept deeply and well, undisturbed by the storm.

She dreamed about my maternal grandfather's father and her dreams were naked and shameless, warm and damp as the air outside her bedroom window. At dawn she awoke, rested, warm and calm; her menstrual pains were gone. She smiled to herself as she got up. As she washed, the touch of the sponge against her skin grew into a pure and unfeigned delight—it was as if the topmost layer of her skin, even the small blond downy hairs on her arms and legs, had been charged with a sensitivity to even the lightest contact. Faint electric signals pulsed through her body, as if she were a switchboard in a telephone exchange.

She pulled the curtain open and saw the brief summer dawn penetrate behind Red Mountain Pass in the east and fill the valley with light. The sky changed from deep red to yellow and white and after that became bluer and bluer. During the latter part of the night the rainclouds had dispersed, the air now clear and pure like carefully polished glass, the valley and surrounding mountains looking as though they had been washed clean. Details and colors stood out with painful clarity: the green tops of the trees, the black roofs of the houses, the slate-gray slagheaps on the bottom of the valley, the yellow-scorched manioc grass that the rain had come too late to save, the gleaming dark-green scrub higher up, and finally the naked rock whose striations were a spectrum of colors: black, gray, brown, sepia, ocher, red, yellow, pink. The slopes were a network of ravines, crevices, and slip zones full of rubble; the snow on the highest peaks shone pure and white, as though they were covered by a freshly washed and bleached sheet. For the first time Hanna felt a desire to climb up into the mountains to see how the world appeared from that vantage point.

Sometime I'll ask him if he'll take me up there, she thought.

She stood for a long time by the window, naked, but for safety's sake concealed behind the curtain. The view changed gradually as the sun rose higher and the dampness began to evaporate. The sharp contours dissolved, the watery colors glimmered, soon the valley was filled with a shifting blue-white-yellow haze above which the highest peaks seemed to hover, weightless and trembling. Hanna thought about Ed Ness all the time. She was intensely conscious that he was there, a few rooms away. He had just woken up; he was still warm and heavy with sleep. She thought about his smell of sweat and dust, about his hands that were large and clean, and about them touching her. Waves of warmth billowed up from between her legs, slow as the swell on a calm late-summer morning in the archipelago back home in Ostrobothnia.

She closed her eyes and sighed.

For the first time in her life she explored herself, half-absentmindedly: she touched her breasts and felt their weight and the soft skin underneath and the nipples that contracted beneath her fingertips; she moved her hands around her thighs and over her bottom; she caressed her belly and felt the outermost strands of her pubic hair and marveled that these filaments could feel so rough. At last, carefully and almost fearfully, she placed two fingers over her labia: they were swollen and moist and parted beneath her touch.

It was Sunday, and there was no hurry about breakfast. The house was still asleep. It would sleep unusually late this morning. Naked and without shame she stepped out into the corridor that was resting in a quiet, pastel-colored dawn light and ran on light feet the few yards to his room and went inside. He was waiting, as she had known he would be.

With the sovereign power over time and space that is my due as narrator, I now hurl you, patient reader, thirty-one years forward in time, simultaneously giving the terrestrial globe a good half-turn eastward from Telluride, Colorado.

And so we find ourselves in the Siklax archipelago.

On Rödskär, to be more precise. In the large summer villa my grandfather Otto Näs built on the islet. Time: late autumn, 1928. The year the airship *Italia* crashed in the pack ice near the North Pole, Loukola, Nurmi, and Andersén brought Finland a triple victory in the steeplechase at the Olympics in Amsterdam, Nurmi turned professional, and the dockers went on strike. The summer was cold and wet. It was wet in other respects, too: in 1928 the Finnish people were reckoned to have drunk approximately two million gallons of illegal spirits.

But now it is a November night. A full gale is blowing. Lashing rain, howling wind. Klobbskat Bay is seething like a cauldron of saltpeter. The dwarf pines and the alders on Rödskär twist and sway in the gusts. The surf is thundering against the rocky slabs of the north point.

Otto's large villa lies abandoned, dark and silent. No, this last isn't quite true: the timber creaks and groans as the gusts of the gale hurl themselves against the walls. The wind leaps over the tin-plated roof. Somewhere a door is banging.

Restless phantoms wander through the rooms.

The cone of light from the narrator's flashlight reveals disorder in the villa. Furniture has been overturned, chairs broken, porcelain smashed to pieces on the kitchen floor. Clothes, paper, phonograph records, ornamental objects, fishing tackle lie strewn everywhere; the floors of the bedrooms in the upper story are covered in down and feathers from ripped mattresses. Fragments of glass crunch under the narrator's feet.

The police have, of course, searched the villa. Without finding anything: Otto was not so stupid as to keep his accounts here. But it can hardly have been the detectives who left behind such a mess, can it?

There is, however, no time to brood about it. We are here to look for a photograph. A picture of a man and a woman, yet not one of Otto's French postcards, brought home from Berlin, the capital of European sin; the couple in this photograph have their clothes on and are thoroughly respectable.

The narrator knows for certain that it is here somewhere. We must hurry, the night is passing.

At last we find it on the floor of the Brown Study, the room with the concealed door. Let's examine it in the bright light of epic realism.

So, then: an 8 x 10 photograph, originally sepia-toned, as the fashion of the 1890s prescribed, now faded to a lusterless brown-yellow. It is mounted in a broad maple frame with carved floral patterns, the style unmistakably American. In the lower left-hand corner it is disfigured by a large stain, tinged with lilac. Water, perhaps. Or spirits.

The photograph shows union organizer Ed Ness together with boarding-house manager Hanna Ostman. Or August Edvard Näs and Rödskärs Hanna. It was taken on their wedding day. The photographer's signature and the year are down at the right: *Byer's Studio, Telluride, Colorado. 1897.*

The narrator knows with certainty that Hanna sent the photograph to her mother. And that Hanna's mother put it away in a drawer. There it lay until Otto came across it in some connection.

The photographer Ebenezer Byer has done a good job—better than he himself probably realized. The background consists of a painted canvas depicting part of a Doric column, vines and spreading palm leaves. The bride is sitting on a chair; the bridegroom stands at an angle behind her.

Hanna is wearing a black muslin dress and her white veil leads one's thoughts to the snow-clad peaks of the Rocky Mountains. She has no bride's bouquet—they were not in vogue yet—but a flower is fastened to her bosom.

She is undoubtedly a most impressive bride. The first thing one notices is the great calm that she radiates: she seems to know that she is in control of the situation. She is smiling. The smile is, however, nothing more than an implied contraction of the corners of her broad mouth, controlled as if turned inward. As if she preferred to keep it to herself. Or is afraid of showing off: for thou shalt not tempt the Lord God with grand and lordly airs, pride goeth before a fall, and the proud shall be humbled; the proper thing to do before the camera is to comport oneself with dignity.

If one looks closely, however, one finds that this expression of calm and certainty of triumph is a little misleading. Hanna sits stiffly in her chair, obviously not leaning against the back of the chair; her head is pushed slightly forward, the muscles of her neck tensed. Her eyes have a gleam that is hard to define; perhaps it is nerves.

Her tension may perhaps be explained by the day's special significance. Yet I do not believe that is the whole story.

Hanna's gloved left hand rests, modest and controlled, on the armrest of the chair. She has, however, placed her right hand on top of Ed Ness's hand where it lies on her shoulder, probably in accordance with the photographer's direction. Her fingers clasp his lightly—almost as though she wants to be sure that he does not plan to withdraw his hand.

Ed Ness stands very stiff and straight behind his bride. He is dressed in a black serge suit, a detachable collar, and a carefully knotted bow tie. His free hand holds a white, broad-brimmed hat, his jacket is unbuttoned in order to let his watch chain gleam. On the lapel of his jacket is the union badge. It is an impressive emblem: a pair of crossed star-spangled banners on a large circle of cloth and the words "Miners' Union No. 63 of the WFM. Organized July 28th, 1897." Ed Ness looks very serious. He holds his chin slightly raised, as though he is on the point of nodding in response to something that has just been said in the cramped studio. He seems to be holding his breath, concentrating on standing stock-still while Ebenezer Byer makes his exposure. . . .

But Ed Ness lacks full control of his face. It is traversed by hairline cracks, invisible to those who glance only briefly at the photograph but very obvious to anyone who examines it under the strong lens of psychological realism: his face seems to be about to break into tiny pieces at any moment.

Unlike Hanna, he is not looking directly into the camera—no, his gaze slips away, as though he has a bad conscience. Or as though he is furtively trying to spot a door through which he can sneak away. His gaze reflects a chaos of emotions which, even on the photograph's surface of silver nitrate long since congealed, continue to live and swarm like Baltic herring in a freshly raised net. Love is undoubtedly present in his eyes: Ed Ness's love for the determined woman who sits on her chair in front of him is altogether obvious and positively steams around him. Pure and unfeigned pleasure glows in his eyes.

And fear.

My grandfather's father, the trade union organizer Ed Ness, is actually a bit afraid of Hanna!

And he stands and wonders how all this really happened. The boys at WFM's head office in San Francisco sent him here to Telluride in order to persuade all these mine workers of Scandinavian, German, Russian, southern European, and God knows what other extraction of the necessity for organization and solidarity, and also to campaign for the union's three basic demands: better safety in the mines, a wage increase of a dollar a day, and, most important, an eight-hour workday. Eight hours of work, eight hours of rest and recreation, eight hours of sleep. And what happens? Here he is getting married to this woman who makes him melt like wax in the warmth of her great, incomprehensible love. "How did this happen?" his eyes ask. "Why did she choose me?"

His hand on Hanna's shoulder. He feels the warmth of her body through the fabric of her dress. He breathes in her scent of eau de cologne and powder. And the even sweeter scent of her love, which makes his head giddy, tickles his groin. Her fingers close more firmly around his. His eyes glide around the walls of the studio; he is thinking about her, about the eight-hour workday, about nothing.

"Hold still, please!" the photographer Ebenezer Byer commands. His voice is muffled by the black velvet that covers his head and shoulders.

A long-fingered hand moves like a blind crab over the side of the camera. Finds the shutter's rubber glove.

The shutter's round mouth gapes wide-open behind the lens. It sucks Hanna and Ed Ness into the camera's angular belly. Silver nitrate and light react with each other; they stick to the glass plate in there like two flies to flypaper. Rustling faintly, the camera closes its mouth.

Ebenezer peeped out from under the cloth like Punch at a Punch and Judy show, the small head with its sparse tufts of hair nodding, satisfied. "Very good, very good indeed." Ed Ness exhaled with an audible sigh. Hanna got up from her chair, gathered her dress around her legs, smoothed out the fabric so that it wouldn't wrinkle. She looked up into Ed Ness's face, who could not stop smiling at her: she was pretty and warm and blushing, his smile made her weak in the knees. All the while, she continued to hold his hand. She is not going to let go of that.

Not till death us do part.

My maternal grandfather was the first of Hanna and Ed Ness's children to be born. He was not in any hurry to make his entrance into this world: Hanna was almost three weeks overdue when she finally gave birth. Otto was born with his eyes open; they had the same gray color as the sea in Ostrobothnia on a cold September morning. He was a large and robust baby.

With a quick prayer to the saints, the midwife severed the umbilical cord and slapped the baby on his bottom. He immediately screwed up his wrinkled, still damp eyelids and let out a powerful shriek.

"God bless you, boy. You've been born to live, I can see that," muttered the midwife, who was a pious Catholic from Ireland. "Only Heaven can tell if you'll be a bishop, a bandit, or a boozer—or all three at once."

She made the sign of the cross over him twice and touched the orifices of his body with the holy water she had brought with her in a special little bottle before washing and swaddling him. As an added protection against evil powers, she embedded a small pair of steel scissors in his feather mattress.

Thus, in January 1898, does my grandfather's long and varied life begin.

William McKinley has for barely a year now been the twenty-fifth president of the United States—a fervent advocate of protective tariffs and American imperialism, he will this year lead his country into a war against Spain that ends with the US acquiring the Philippines, Guam, and Puerto Rico, and occupying Cuba. In France Major Esterhazy is acquitted after a scandalous trial, and Émile Zola publishes his *J'accuse*. In Germany Admiral von Tirpitz pushes through the first bill concerning the building of a battleship fleet (which becomes a contributing factor to the outbreak of the First World War). The confrontation over Fashoda in the Sudan that same autumn leads France and Britain to the brink of war.

"Look at your son," Hanna said solemnly to her husband. It was two weeks later; Ed Ness had returned from a campaign trip to the coalfields of southern Colorado. And Hanna gave the child to Ed Ness.

Abruptly, Otto finds himself lying in a pair of arms that do not know how they should hold him. He feels this uncertainty with the whole of his small body. It is like lying on top of a couple of lengths of timber. He is going to roll off. He has been taken from Hanna's bosom, which is warm and large and infinitely secure, and now he is floating high in the cold air on a shaky foundation.

This is a first-class piece of treachery.

He opens his eyes. He looks into an immense face floating above him like a pink cloud. A rough mustache-end grazes his cheek, an ice-cold drop of water plummets down and lands on his face. The cloud breathes on him, a strong and incomprehensible smell.

Then Otto closed his eyes again, filled with terror. He shrieked for all he was worth.

When Otto was three or four years old, Sundays were the high point of the week.

Hanna and the maid ruled over him for six of the week's seven days. But on the seventh day the power of the womenfolk was inexorably broken. Then the otherwise calm and quiet boardinghouse was filled with men— large boisterous men resting after their work in the unknown and dangerous mines, men in striped shirts and work pants made of coarse cotton, men with creaking leather boots on their feet. There was a harsh smell of sweat and tobacco around them, and sometimes a trace of Saturday night's whiskey lingered on their breath.

The men's sheer presence dispatched the women to the periphery. Hanna and the maid were two shadows that imperceptibly vanished off to the church in the morning and, just as imperceptibly, returned to prepare and serve the Sunday dinner.

In summer the men spent the long afternoons of the day of rest on the veranda, where they dozed in chairs they tilted back against the wall. They had their hats pulled down on their foreheads and their feet up on the railings as they whittled their eternal round pieces of wood, smoked and contemplated with silent yearning the cloud-wrapped mountaintops that gleamed blue and distant in the heat-haze. Slowly they digested their food; their meager chat tottered between them like a lame mule. And the afternoon rolled slowly away, until the twilight came and filled the valley with its shadows and the evening concert of the crickets began. Then one by one they got up from their chairs and walked with heavy steps upstairs to their rooms; by seven or eight o'clock the veranda was empty.

Thus as a rule did the Sundays pass when Otto's father was away on his trips on behalf of the union.

On those occasions when he was at home, on the other hand, everything was different.

For Ed Ness possessed an invisible magic wand. When he moved his magic wand, a mysterious and wonderful change took place on the veranda.

Then all of a sudden there was no shortage of words. Great cartwheels of laughter rolled up and down the veranda's coarse planks. The men told stories. They wove narratives in intricate patterns and shimmering colors, and the resulting tapestry was immense; when one man stopped, the next took over at once. Yes, they told some whoppers and exaggerated like crazy, these men from Ostrobothnia. Then Otto loved them with all his little heart. And most of all he loved his father, who made this miracle of words possible.

On Men's Day Otto quickly wolfed down his dinner: steak with gravy, potatoes and string beans, meat pie or chicken—on Sundays Hanna always served up something extra. Otto was short for his age but powerful; a regular tree stump, his father would say proudly. His fair hair was allowed to grow long; it wasn't cut until his fourth birthday, when he also received his first pair of real short breeches.

His small lungs were capable of producing big sounds; his strong, short legs could, to Hanna's consternation, take him far away. He ate heartily; he was in every way a survivor.

As soon as he had finished eating and excused himself with a bow, he rushed out to the veranda. Big, calloused mine workers' hands were immediately ready to lift him high in the air—Otto shrieked, overjoyed and frightened at the same time—whereupon he was passed along the veranda in order finally to land on his father's knee.

Ed Ness is at home! He waves his magic wand—and the door to the treasure chamber of stories and whoppers opens wide!

First, however, a special ritual must be observed, as in church:

"Well," someone asks, "and what does Otto-boy know today, then?"

And Otto giggles delightedly into his small hands, which are still clean after their Saturday wash.

"You've been a good boy all week?" wonders another.

"Yes, sir!" Otto replies with deep earnestness, which provokes a cascade of laughter.

"Well, and what do you want to be when you grow up?"

Otto pretends to reflect. "A miner! Or a bandit!"

But now the talk is already in full swing; it runs light and free, as at a sharp trot. And should its tempo slacken, Otto's father is there at once to urge it on: he is no friend of long silences, Ed Ness. Of course they talk about the mines. About fronts and shafts that are driven into the hearts of the mountains, about hard work, about drills, ore-bearing veins and dynamite. About accidents. Almost every week they have fresh accidents to discuss. Otto does not like the mine talk. Neither, really, do they. It smacks too much of workdays, mine dust, noise. It arouses their fear, which they do not want to admit. For each of them knows that next week it may be the rockfall under which he himself has ended up that is discussed here on the veranda. Then as the talk stops of its own accord, each man ponders the vanity of his own life; Death leans for a moment against the veranda railing and looks attentively at the men. Then Ed Ness, the enemy of silence, says: "Did you hear about the guy from Perusbackan in Blaxnäs who came to New York?"

And that is the signal!

All inhibitions are released. The floodgates are opened wide. Words gush, foam, spurt from these normally taciturn men. They all seem to have a stock of stories and an unquenchable need to share them: it is as though the thin air up here at an altitude of 9,000 feet is going to their heads like sparkling wine from California and making them garrulous and full of whoppers.

But remember this: whoppers are truth's back door. If you tell enough whoppers, you will find that in the end you are telling the truth.

Most of them are young but have already been through a lot. The life of an emigrant takes its toll on a man. Once they get started, they never want to stop. They tell about prospectors who made incredible gold finds and became rich overnight. And about canny sharps who cheated the gold diggers of their mine at the poker table. And about grizzlies and wolves. And about human vultures, desperadoes and gunmen like the young Billy the Kid and Jesse James and Butch Cassidy, who once robbed the bank here in Telluride. And about the strange characters the mining districts swarm with. And about Italians and Poles and Mexicans, unreliable types. And about silent Indians who roam the mountains and can read the land like a book. And about glittering, fantastic cities like Chicago and New York, where the streets swarm with people and there are wagons that move all by themselves, without having to be drawn by horses, called automobiles. And about buildings so tall their roofs reach the clouds, and inside the buildings they have little rooms you get into and they take you up from floor to floor, they are called elevators. And about huge redwood trees in Oregon that are nine hundred years old. And about Mormons in Salt Lake City on the other side of the San Juan Mountains, Mormons who don't drink coffee or whiskey or play poker but who do on the other hand have two or more wives; this arouses speculation on the veranda: they must be pretty fit guys, Mormons—wonder if they sleep with all their wives at once or if they have them one by one. . . .

Then Ed Ness sends out a warning look: remember, the kid is listening!

The veranda has its rules. Some subjects are off-limits while Otto is around.

And the men clear their throats; someone sends a gob of tobacco into the brass spittoon. Another rolls himself a cigarette; fascinated, Otto watches as, apparently without effort, coarse fingers form a tight cylinder of paper and fragrant tobacco. A match is struck on the heel of a boot. Blue tobacco smoke eddies in the air.

The men talk about how well one can do for oneself here in this land, this mighty America, the promised land. On the veranda they like to talk about success. Immigrants who became big-time farmers in Dakota, where the land is black and rich and only a few years ago cost practically nothing. And about Sjöberg from Norrmark who went to the west coast in the eighties and began conserving fish, started a cannery, and had the whole town named after him. And the fellow from Blaxnäs who was in the mines and the lumber camps and now owns a big construction company, what was his name again. . . .

Yes, the opportunities are here, all right. As long as one's not afraid of work. But after all, they came here in order to work, didn't they? And one day they will have done so well for themselves that they can go back to the old country like lords and take a look at how they're getting on *over there*. In American suits, with watch chains over their bellies and five-cent cigars in their mouths. The dreams shine in their eyes.

As long as you keep fit and can stand the pace, a young man says softly; he is a greenhorn, of course.

They pretend not to notice the newcomer's comment but it makes them uneasy all the same. Their health and strength are the only capital they own. America is mighty in its lack of mercy, too; you have to manage on your own. No one wants to be reminded of that. A moment's silence descends over the veranda.

Then Ed Ness steps in, the king of yarns, the unsurpassed master of whoppers, the storyteller of storytellers. That guy from Perusbackan, do you want to know what happened to him when he arrived in New York and wanted to go and see his brother in Brooklyn?

They nod in relief. Otto sits up expectantly, now everything is all right again, laughter is already waiting in the corners of men's mouths.

Well. He knew no English, of course, the guy from Perusbackan, but he had his brother's address written down on a piece of paper. Now, as everyone knows, New York is a big, cruel town, and he soon got lost. So he started to ask the people on the street if they knew how he could get to his brother's place. In dialect, of course. They just shook their heads at him, of course, and he got dizzy from the crowd and from not having had anything to eat all day. Finally he decided to ask the first person who came around the next corner, and if he didn't get an answer he would lie down in the street and die.

Well, the next fellow who came along was a Chinaman, yellow and slant-eyed. Then the guy from Perusbackan decided he could finally count himself dead. But he thought he might as well ask one more time. So the Chinaman bowed and replied in the purest Siklax dialect: "Yes, I know fine where your brother lives, that I do."

At that point the guy from Perusbackan fainted. When he came to, he was at his brother's place in Brooklyn—the Chinaman had lugged him there. The fact was that the brother had done well in America and taken the Chinaman on as a manservant, and in order that they could talk to each other he had taught the Chinaman Siklax dialect; he thought that was simpler than him trying to learn China lingo. And that Chinaman must have been a clever guy, because he had learned the Siklax dialect so well that you would have thought he came from there, slant-eyed and yellow though he was, the damn fellow.

And the laughter booms out, yes, you can say that again, he must have been a clever guy, that Chinaman, yessiree, that was a sharp move and one day they'll probably take over the whole world, just you wait and see. . . .

Otto understood nothing at all of such yarns and tall stories, but he laughed along with the men; he pretended to agree with them and be one of them. Otto could hear the same yarns told as many times as he wanted. And on Monday he had imaginary brawls with grizzlies and gunfights with sheriffs and desperadoes and was an Indian who crept up on the maid when she was fetching water and let out a dreadful war cry so that the timid girl squealed with terror and spilled water all over herself.

Hanna boxed Otto on the ears a couple of times, making his head ring. To Ed Ness she said angrily: "You mustn't let the boy listen to all your talk, his head's spinning and you're teaching him to swear, too!"

But Ed Ness just laughed at her. "The boy's got to hear what men talk about if he's going to be a man himself."

Translated by David McDuff

Nils-Aslak Valkeapää

The musician, artist, and poet Nils-Aslak Valkeapää (b. 1943) is a leading figure in contemporary Sámi culture. A charismatic performer and ambassador of his people, he has nurtured and transfigured the artistic inheritance of the Sámi, combining the ancient monotone chant or *juoiggus* with electronic music and using traditional images and innovative book design to produce highly acclaimed verbal-visual poetry. The following extract is drawn from *Beaivi, áhčážan* (The Sun, My Father), a verbal-visual epic that was awarded the Literature Prize of the Nordic Council. The original work, written in Sámi, combines poems and photographs, many from archives, including the French explorer Prince Roland Bonaparte's (1858-1924) anthropological collections. Some of the more sinister images in that book are comparative charts produced by the Swedish State Institute for Race Biology during the 1920s. The intrusive and patronizing nature of such dated material is self-evident, and Valkeapää's pictorial record powerfully reconstructs a history of marginalization.

Like the celebrated "broken" epics of Tennyson and T. S. Eliot, *Beaivi, áhčážan* unfolds in fragments, in an ironic, elegiac, meditative mode that contrasts with the monumentality of more traditional epics. Valkeapää's poem interweaves the personal and the historical: as with *In Memoriam* and *The Waste Land*, a critical distance exists between the epic's speaker and the public realm he contemplates. However, Valkeapää is hardly haunted by Western-style cultural alienation. While avoiding the belligerent assertions of a nationalistic bard, he also shuns excessive self-preoccupation. Valkeapää takes pride in his nomadic ancestry and his close relationship with nature. The elements and the Arctic flora and fauna are viewed as part of a continuum with the social world. Births, deaths, arranged marriages, the rhythms and rituals of reindeer husbandry, the bustle of the marketplace, and the contemplative life of the nomad are all brought to life in freely structured stanzas, some only two words long. Valkeapää situates history in the context of an inexorable biological process, the "hoop of life" that circumscribes all cultures. He views impermanence with equanimity: the disappearance of an entire culture is a minor event in the cosmic flow. This poetry accepts and celebrates the ephemeral, earthbound role that humanity plays in the natural order, where truths, nations, and languages come and go like dreams. The consoling, pantheistic aspect of Valkeapää's cultural relativism is highlighted in dizzying glimpses of what it means to be defined by the physical world: when the poet perceives the sun, the sun swims inside him.

Selected books: *Terveisiä Lapista* (*Greetings from Lapland*, 1971), *Ruoktu váimmus* (Trekways of the Wind, 1985), *Beaivi, áhčážan* (The Sun, My Father, 1988), *Nu guhkkin dat mii lahka* (So Far, That Which Is Near, 1994), *Jus gassebiehtár bohkosivččii* (If a Siberian Tit Should Laugh, 1996). Selected recordings: *Joikuja* (Yoiks, 1968), *Vuoi Biret-Maaret, vuoi!* (Oh, Biret-Maaret, Oh! 1974), *Sámi eatnan duoddariid* (The Fells of Sámiland, 1978), *Beaivi, áhčážan* (The Sun, My Father, 1992), *Sámi luondu, gollerisku* (Sami Nature, Golden Brooch, 1992), *Dálveleaikkat* (Winter Games, 1994).

Interview

PHILIP LANDON: Can you name any shared characteristics of contemporary Finnish literature? Do you identify with any of your international or domestic contemporaries?

NILS-ASLAK VALKEAPÄÄ: Although I've read a lot of *Finnish* literature, I view it as an outsider and so am hardly the right person to answer your first question. As for *Sámi* literature, you must remember that its *written* form is extremely young compared to other written literatures. The beginning was really Johan Thuri's *Muittalus samiid birra,* published in 1906, and it was not until the 1960s and '70s that Sámi literature took off more widely (among ourselves). Sámi literature must build a foundation that is appropriate to our background. And our literary background is an *oral* one comprising "the reminiscence" (stories) and "the chant" (which contained lyrics).

No, I don't identify with other writers, neither Finnish nor foreign. I think my work is unique; as you know, I use both words and images, also music.

PL: How would you situate fiction in general and your own work in particular in relation to mass culture and the mass media?

NV: I can't—*don't want to*—start situating others. I myself don't write with an eye to the mass culture or media. Quite the opposite. For example, it was by no means a given that my work would be translated into major languages. It was not what *I* expected. (And in fact, what necessitated the first translations was the fact that the Sámi language itself comprises several mutually unintelligible dialects. Not all the Sámi can understand Fell-Sámi, the dialect in which I write. And it is for the Sámi people that I try to do what I do.)

PL: Kai Laitnen has written, "The traditional Finnish novel is close to nature. Nature features in the role of a friend or an enemy or both." Can we read your work as part of this tradition? Does nature require a new approach from writers?

NV: In answer to the first question, no, you can't. Because Finnish culture is ultimately informed by the Western ideology whereby HUMANITY IS MASTER OF NATURE. By contrast, the philosophy of indigenous peoples is that HUMANITY IS PART OF NATURE, NOT ITS MASTER. I think the latter attitude comes through strongly in all my books.

Globally, it seems that this philosophy is gaining ground; pollution has reached the point that it's high time the world heed the wisdom of indigenous peoples, particularly in relation to nature.

PL: From the *Kalevala* to postwar fiction, much of Finnish literature has been intimately bound up with the question of national identity. Could your work also be described as national Sámi literature? You have traveled widely—how much does being international mean to you?

NV: Yes—as I said above, building a foundation is important. You must first learn to respect yourself before you can respect others. I think this is also true of nations. Sámi literature has now taken this first step and can begin to express itself more freely, without having to inject national values into the text. I do believe my own work has also taken such a path. Consciously.

Indeed, I have been on the road for a quarter of a century. Naturally this has had an effect on my thinking, my work. Mind you, my travels have mainly been among indigenous people, which is something that has strengthened my own identity. After all, Sámi culture differs significantly in outlook from the culture of Western industrial countries. This despite the fact that the global media industry is rapidly homogenizing different life philosophies.

I am very grateful for having had the chance to travel and to get to know different cultures. It's been enriching, and perhaps it has helped me to understand different ways of thinking and acting—the existing diversity of cultures—and has broadened my philosophy.

PL: Contemporary Finnish writers frequently use autobiographical and mock-autobiographical forms. In your poetry book *Beaivi, áhčážan*, the personal and the cosmic are seamlessly joined. Can we see a cultural difference here between the Finns and the Sámi? Is it possible to write Sámi poetry in a city?

NV: *Beaivi, áhčážan* was six years in the making. (If you add the time spent on the recorded version, it was eight or nine years in all.) A vast amount of background information from a variety of fields was distilled into that one book. It contains a lot of prehistory, especially religion, as well as modern Sámi history. But I tried at least to write so that it could be understood in several ways: in a broad, almost cosmic sense; in a slightly narrower way, as the history of a people; and even more narrowly, as the history of a single person. It certainly also contains some of my own personal experience.

Now that the foundation of our literature has been written, urbanization is no longer an obstacle to Sámi poetry. It is time for Sámi literature to begin to produce texts that are universally human.

PL: Is oral tradition an important part of your work? Are you continuing Sámi traditions, or are you creating something new altogether?

NV: I think the oral element is particularly prominent in my work. I already mentioned the poetic tradition of the *juoiggus* chant. But music is also part of my work in another way: I always read my poems aloud before I accept them as being completed. If they *sing,* they are ready. I also use the *juoiggus* chant technique when I write; this explains why I might have several almost identical poems. The *juoiggus,* too, has neither a beginning nor an end, and the theme is always short, but it changes continually, over and over.

So yes: I am continuing the tradition—and creating something new all the time.

PL: You are a writer, a musician, and an artist, and you make free use of modern techniques in your creative work. How do you regard technology?

NV: I am very much part of nature, and in this respect, my relationship to technology is (in principle) fairly hostile. On the other hand, I recognize that technology is here to stay. So I favor and use the *most advanced* technology, which is less polluting and destructive. For example, I have a car— you couldn't survive without one *here*—and a DAT (digital recorder) and a PC. . . .

PL: Do you feel any cultural affinity with the indigenous peoples of, for example, America or Australia? Has literature or art from such sources had any influence on your work or outlook?

NV: What I'm most familiar with is the culture of North American Indians in the US and Canada. And yes, I have a number of soul mates among them. In some of my poems I have changed my style in their direction, so I have *allowed* them to influence my art a little. But this has always been deliberate. I also maintain a regular and fruitful dialogue with North American Indians. Beyond that, I nowadays have very little contact with other indigenous peoples, and therefore I absorb less influence as well.

PL: Your *Bird Symphony* is composed entirely from natural sounds: water, wind, birdsong, finally also human song. You said in a BBC interview that you wanted to record these disappearing sounds for future generations. Are you a pessimist? Do you believe that Sámi culture will survive?

NV: I am a pessimist. The world is being polluted and destroyed incessantly. The global population is exploding, and yet comparatively little is being said about it. I expect that these two factors and the situations they cause will impose enormous problems on the world.

Against this backdrop, Sámi culture is no worse off than any other. But *survival* is not the point; what has to be possible is *development.* The sign of a vital culture is that it develops all the time, and as long as that development continues, the culture is still alive. And so be it. If it fuses with something else, the culture can still be said to be fulfilling its purpose as long as the fusion takes place on the particular terms of *that* culture. On the other hand, if the culture *dies* (withers), it has still served its purpose, and it would not do to keep it alive *by force*. I see all cultures as part of nature and nature's cycle; they are born, they live, and they die. And this is as it should be. But of course, I can't accept it if cultures are stifled or killed, as also happens. But that is another matter.

At present, Sámi culture is quite vigorous—but I can't tell in what direction it will develop. However, I have a sense that it is nearing a more universal idiom, and if this were to happen on our own terms, through our own actions, I would have nothing against it.

Nevertheless, I will continue my own work on the basis of the convictions I have—and those are very closely bound up with traditional Sámi culture.

From The Sun, My Father

558. as if
I myself
inscribe

but often
I fly to the other side
and no longer
        know

life
turns
pushes
into action
      as if I
          myself

was doing it

and I draw

sometimes I believe
that this is me
        these images
              and
however I change
the images, images of me,
          or I myself
so many shapes of me, aspects, I could have been
so many, or almost anything
in another condition

      I find

                              readiness in me
to do everything that people do, and even more
simply wipe away a speck of dust, unfold an open human, naked
and when I draw myself, I suppose I draw others too
or is it just me, is it in me that people reveal themselves, modesty and greed
                        again I leave
                        fly away
                        to see
                        how I am

                        I feel fire
                        billowing

                        the mind's night
                        impure
                        the shame of deeds

                                        and nothing is strange
everything appears as if it was mine, and when they reveal their secrets
they are already present in me, in me too
        desire
            flesh
                    lust
                        urges
                            wishes
                                and even I

the animal keeping away from the others,
                  a world within me too, boundless, a universe
the wind
      time's restless infinitely unruly wind
over me
      and I disappear
with the gusts of wind
                to the sea of time
tomorrow is a new day
other animals
and I no longer see these visions

           time

           I flow in time
           with time
           in time
           in time's deep river
                    and the wind, time's restless
infinite wind
      nature
           the powerful ruler
I converse with the fire
                tomorrow
                  it too will have another language
new migration routes for tomorrow's reindeer, the stones will have different
      traditions
      an alien time within time
                alien
visions of wonders gradually reveal themselves
strange voices speak in my thoughts

ambiguous
      like an image, emblem, figure

with many meanings
      the symbols too
           more to choose from tomorrow

      time does not exist
      but fog does
      thought's fog

      time does not exist
      and not the river either with the same words
I have filled this vessel, this drum, I am filled
image on top of image, a door out, the desire to open
increasingly often
      it is not yesterday
      it is not tomorrow

      now, it is now

      if this too is not a dream

my vessel is filled, I, this semi dream, dream within dream
I open the door outward when I enter
what am I when I wake, what
who can see these dreams

        wind's wind
        infinite time
        timeless wind
        would light exist
        if there were no shadow
Rohpi Gahperus Stuora Njeaidán
Galbasuolu Cinkárássa Biellocohkka
Derpmesvárri Jollánoaivi Njamátvuopmi Goddoguoika
Luossacahca Dápmotoaivi Návdebuolza Bierdnamaras
Suohpat Sádgi Urttasvággi
                    I search for the track, interpret the visions
I stuff my shoes with grass, sitting on a pelt fur side down
I put on the red gákti
happiness rejoicing, boundless, an old demand
grief
    I heard
must get lost to be
die to live
        am I asleep when I dream
        dream that I am awake
I kiss these stones
embrace the twisted birches
the wind, my dear beloved, elated
and the star above Silbajávri
        lightens
        darkens
the river of loneliness
a path

> when will I complete
> when will I become whole

hitch up the draft reindeer
leave to arrive
a string of animals, the lead reindeer trots
no, no trail visible, no tracks left behind
> rain
> jaeger
> so black
> sea of demands
these lands, the stony cradle
I meander across the tundra
the belled reindeer
trots, the swans yoik
the yoikers
> the long fall
> the water
> shines the ice

> in the evening
> the ice roars
> breaks
> and wrestles the air

was it recently
I felt arms embracing, the warm lap, me too
the sun, in my eyes
no, in my head, in my mind
the sun,
your hair, rays, gold flowers, swans
blue throats
yoik in my ears
in my breast, the yoiking
sea rises, falls
advances, withdraws
coastal avalanches

        fog

        along the peaks
        could have climbed
        into heaven

these dreams, could have been
these images, the yoiks of the images, the images of the yoiks
and if they are left behind
              anyone ever, for some reason
someone that silly
inscribed in stone on the drum in the air to itself
yoiks, powerful words, word power
image, the symbolic
imagery

snow
the white snow
the snow-whiteness

the sea's ocean
blackens
becomes harder
tightens
loosens
roars

the cold
sneaks under the skin

the sky glows
I'm coming,
     the Sun, my father

               I am coming, I come
I remember
I roped the young white doe
    a white thread in the right ear
      a path
         to the sun

        night bird

        life
        over us

        without asking

Translated by Lars Nordström, Harald Gaski, and Ralph Salisbury

Book Reviews

Evan Dara. *The Lost Scrapbook.* FC2, 1995. 476 pp. $21.95.

The first thing the reader of Evan Dara's *The Lost Scrapbook* sees are two mottoes: from Kierkegaard, "To honor every man, absolutely every man, is the truth"; and from Blake, "O let me teach you how to knit again / This scattered corn into one mutual sheaf, / These broken limbs again into one body." We are tuned in, then, to the need to respect the individual and the need to "knit" the individuals together as a community. The first motto, we might suggest, underscores Dara's practice of letting his characters speak; the second the fact that one character speaking is not sufficient. What the characters share is speech. And so, speaking is the first way in which Dara's people are "knit again": indeed, one voice morphs into another. And we cannot always be sure when the switch has occurred. Thus, the second way the people are "knit again" is through content (i.e., shared concerns).

The book begins in dialogue form, although it seems to be an imagined dialogue. A nineteen-year-old is faced with the question of what he wants to be. (The other side of this dialogue represents a high school guidance counselor.) The youth resists the straits of a career choice. He is interested in many things and abhors the narrowing of interest into an occupation. (In terms of the range of interests, I must say that Dara presents us with an impressive range—from composer Harry Partch to linguist/political activist Noam Chomsky, from archeologist Richard Leakey to photographer Eadweard Muybridge, among many others.) But community must be made. Witness how few eligible voters register to vote. And not even the young are immune: the difficulties faced by the first character have led him to run away from home. Unfortunately, what this action teaches him is unpalatable: "Now my sole function in this world is to serve as receptacle for the proof that I am inconsequential." Only an eviscerated community could come from such realizations.

He may feel inconsequential, but he is hardly alone. Indeed, this character soon becomes another character, late for an appointment. The appointment becomes an opportunity to catch fireflies to be filmed later for a commercial. Thence a return to Dave's house (one of the firefly-catchers), where Dave talks about his son Michael and his interest in drumming. And so on. And so on.

Indeed, what is most striking about Dara's ambitious novel is that the narrative voice keeps changing. One narrator gives way to another with few rhetorical clues and no outward flourish. This can be a little off-putting—to find the situation one has been immersed in suddenly jettisoned for another. Moreover, not all situations are likely to strike a reader as equally interesting. Still, once the reader learns that the narrative voice is constantly morphing, the practice should not throw her. After all, the morphing of voices is a daring way for Dara

153

to involve the reader with his concerns for differences and community. We might recall Bruno Latour's point in his recent *We Have Never Been Modern:* "Reason today has more in common with a cable television network than with Platonic ideas." Perhaps that is why the model of channel-surfing comes so readily to mind.

Yet, rather than dispersal, there is a strong impulse toward gathering in Dara. In other words, the channels should add up to something. We might take a clue from Dara's words on Chomsky and suggest that what *The Lost Scrapbook* attempts is the "reconstruct[ion of] the crystal"; putting the shards of community back together. Thus, if so many voices—voices that register their gender differences, age differences, political differences, etc.—are transmitted through a common source, the materiality of that source augurs sharing. Still, one voice may directly oppose the views of another. Yet they are transmitted (if we may put it that way) over a common source.

Though there are many incidents in the book, the last hundred-plus pages are concerned with one principal event: the dumping of pollutants into the environment by Ozark Corporation. This provides an occasion for the views to differ— principally, as to whether the danger of pollution is as great as some think, and whether Ozark has been aware of the dangers. It is hard not to read the pollution of the environment as referring to the pollution of the communication environment as well as pollution of the ground of the community. As such, this pollution comes down to a binarization that blocks both communication and community. (In this way, *The Lost Scrapbook* can be seen as one of our more timely books, considering the recent budget stalemate in Washington, D.C.) To speak out against the corporation is to risk one's livelihood. To remain silent is to risk one's health. Given the entrenched positions, where else can we go but silence? "Yes this definitive reclamation, this grand extreme regathering and reclamation into silence, for where else could this go but silence, yes silence: silence. Silence," as the book ends.

And yet the end is perhaps not as important as the journey. For it is a journey into the individuality and commonality of people living in contemporary America. As such, it is a book raising significant questions for our day—and, one suspects, beyond. [Bruce Campbell]

*

William T. Vollmann. *The Atlas.* Viking, 1996. 461 pp. $27.95.

I admit to being a Vollmann addict. I can never get enough of his work. It almost borders on obsession, and sometimes worries me. What a joy, though, to get my hands on *The Atlas,* which I'd been hearing of for the past two years, and parts of which I've read in various magazines and journals. *The Atlas* is not just a chronicle of Vollmann's world travels over the last five years, but a revue selection of many Vollmann obsessions, recurrent themes, fetishes, and concerns: prostitutes, early North American history, crack, prostitutes, Cambodia, Bosnia, prostitutes, love, and prostitutes, as well as the love of prostitutes. From his very first novel, *You Bright and Risen Angels* (where the real-life whore

Brandi makes several appearances) to *Fathers and Crows* (whores in the streets of Montreal) to more focused novels as *Whores for Gloria* and *Butterfly Stories,* to his collections *Rainbow Stories* and *Thirteen Stories and Thirteen Epitaphs,* Vollmann doesn't conceal the fact that he holds dear the image of the prostitute, American and foreign alike. Many, if not all, Vollmann heroes (real and make-believe) tend to fall hopelessly in love with these women time after time.

One aspect of Vollmann's work that has always struck a chord in me is the groping search and need for human connection amidst bleak decrepitude, which permeates his work like freshly discharged semen on dirty bedsheets. The search for connection, and love, is the unifying theme of the many pieces in this book. Old Vollmann and new Vollmann alike share space, as we are given pieces with titles from his books, like "Fathers and Crows," "The Butterfly Stories I & II," and "The Rifles," which enlighten the already published works with these addendum words and sentences. The stronger pieces, however, are recent Vollmann fixations, such as Bosnia, Somalia, and the death of his sister at a young age. As many followers of Vollmann's work know, he was nearly killed in Bosnia when the jeep he was in ran over a land mine. His two companions, one a longtime friend, died. He took pictures of them. While Vollmann, like any good narcissistic writer, strips naked and spreads his ass for the public, he never confronts this part of his life face to face, unlike other events. There are only two pieces, "That's Nice" and "A Vision," where the experience is mentioned. In "That's Nice," Vollmann deals with the insensitive car dealer who wants to know who's going to pay for the land mine-damaged vehicle; in "A Vision," Vollmann takes hallucinogenic mushrooms and remembers his friends who died in a foreign country.

When I refer to Vollmann as the protagonist, he is. These works are not fiction, but essays, or news broadcasts from hell—yet intermixed with obvious works of fiction where the Vollmann hero is not Vollmann himself, but some runt appendage from the crux.

Jaded am I, for my favorite works in *The Atlas* have to be the "Best Way" series: "The Best Way to Smoke Crack," "The Best Way to Chew Khat," "The Best Way to Drink Beer," and "The Best Way to Shoot H," each one filled with heartbreaking longings and images that'll make you cringe and sob simultaneously. The people in these pieces are hopeless, helpless, and disgusting, yet with low glimmering nuances of humanity and solicitude that cause us to wish them well and hope for the best. The piece that finally pulls the hardest at my heart is "Under the Grass," as the Vollmann hero wanders the world trying to save the souls of orphaned girls and wayward whores to atone for the death of his little sister, which he'll forever blame on himself.

Look at *The Atlas* texts as guidelines to a black heart wishing for purification, a blackness existing in us all. Vollmann is a brave, and often cocky, Vergil, and for all the pain splayed across his pages—and there's plenty—we're all the better for it. At least I am, anyway. [Michael Hemmingson]

*

Péter Esterházy. *A Little Hungarian Pornography.* Trans. Judith Sollosy. Northwestern Univ. Press, 1995. 215 pp. $24.95.

Routinely placed among Hungarian literature's postmodern defiers of a traditionalism that since 1948 often meant schematic socialist realism, Péter Esterházy has been in Hungary a popular and controversial voice since the 1970s, when his first collections of short fiction and his first major novel, *Temelésiregény* (Productional Novel), appeared. Americans for the most part came to know him through Judith Sollosy's 1994 translation of his novel *The Book of Hrabal.*

Self-described as his "most East-European book" in which "pornography should be understood as meaning lies, the lies of the body, the lies of the soul," *A Little Hungarian Pornography* romps through thirty or so years of the accumulating personal and social wreckage that was life in communist Hungary— from the days of Mátyás Rákosi through the "overripe period of the [János] Kádár era." Like a hyperventilating Washington Irving, Esterházy offers a collage of vignettes, jokes, conundrums, anecdotes, asides, and plagiarized passages ("You might call this a . . . flotsam and jetsam medley of memoir fragments") whose collective purpose is to denounce those state-sponsored "terrors and apprehensions of the people [that] led them into a thousand weak, foolish, and wicked things, which they wanted not a sort of people really wicked to encourage them to." Or it might be said that, by focusing on the duplicities of politics, language, and sex (this last as both metaphor and synecdoche of corrupt lives), the author wishes to plumb the question, "does the dictatorship of the proletariat *happen* to you, so to speak, or, conversely, are you making *it* happen?"

As Esterházy compiles his miscellany of stories otherwise "relegated to oblivion, because they are not sufficiently *official,*" he also asks what literature should do in the face of such horrors and humiliations. His answer, that the writer must "provide a clear description of the situation," is not what this densely national (and legitimately experimental) novel will seem to be doing for many reading it in translation today. (Nor, since forewarned is forearmed, will many find the novel as humorous as it was meant to be and doubtless once was, save in the way old Lenny Bruce bits are still "funny" today.) But Esterházy is nobody's fool, and he knows what many of the most important writers of this century have known: that "he who does not feel himself truly lost will be lost without reprieve, he will never find himself, will never discover his own reality." Consider *A Little Hungarian Pornography,* then, a way of getting productively lost. [Brooke Horvath]

*

Ilan Stavans. *The One-Handed Pianist and Other Stories.* Trans. David Unger, Harry Morales, the author, and others. Univ. of New Mexico Press, 1996. 196 pp. $22.50.

Long-time readers of *RCF* will recognize the name Ilan Stavans: he has written for our special issues on Barth, Gass, Puig, and Kiš, and guest-edited our Felipe Alfau issue, in addition to contributing numerous book reviews and (most recently) interviewing Mexican writer Fernando del Paso. All of these authors are cosmopolitan by nature, in outlook if not in actual circumstances, as is Stavans himself: born in Mexico of Russian-Polish Jewish descent—his complete name is Ilan Stavchansky Slomianski—he has traveled widely and now teaches at Amherst College. (An autobiographical essay, "Lost in Translation," concludes the volume, a fascinating account of Stavans's multicultural upbringing and its influence on his writings.)

In this first collection in English of Stavans's fiction, Kafka, rather than any of the above, is the presiding influence. The first story, "A Heaven without Crows," takes the form of a letter from Kafka to Max Brod, explaining his decision to have his writings destroyed. ("Because I am an imposter who has invented a dark reality. Because I've made a career out of being a victim.") Kafka is evoked in the second story, "The Invention of Memory," where a Czech man moves to his mother's neighborhood in Mexico City to lose his memory and die under the voyeuristic eye of a neighbor. "The Death of Yankos" is a brief tale in Kafka's lighter, more absurdist vein, while "The One-Handed Pianist" concerns a woman whose inexplicable defects recall Kafka's sense of the incomprehensibility of God. (In the first story, Stavans's Kafka writes: "My idea of God is of a distant warden in a state of alertness, always ready to punish.") The centerpiece of the book is "Talia in Heaven," a metafictional novella that is both the most Kafkaesque (in the general sense of the term) story in the book and the one most concerned with the Jewish heritage. Filled with anecdotes from the Talmud and written in a racier tone than the others, "Talia" is a tour de force, the most difficult but the most impressive fiction in the collection. "House Repossessed," like a surprising number of the other stories here, is narrated from a woman's point of view, and the final story, "Three Nightmares," brings us back to Kafka territory, where dream and reality are blurred.

Stavans has already distinguished himself as a critic and essayist; this volume of his brooding, erudite fiction places him in that small circle of writers who are as accomplished at fiction as they are nonfiction. [Steven Moore]

*

Eva Figes. *The Knot.* Sinclair-Stevenson, 1996. 170 pp. £14.99.

This novel explores the life of its protagonist, Anna, from her birth to her own motherhood. While a number of novels by contemporary women writers have investigated such a trajectory of female experience, *The Knot* is distinctly unlike any other feminist coming-of-age story I have ever read. What distinguishes Figes's experiment from others is that her novel frames Anna's life in terms of her experience of language. The novel begins before Anna can speak and concludes with scenes in which she teaches her young son to talk.

Because the novel is told from Anna's point of view, we directly witness her own language-learning, her struggles to develop language skills and her questioning of the purpose of words. Each of the five parts of the book depicts a different phase of her life. It opens with her birth, described in terms of sounds because Anna does not yet know the words to describe the experience. We then see Anna as a baby lying in the grass of her family's backyard and observing the sky, the trees, and the earth without knowing the names for the objects in the natural world. During Anna's rebellious teenage years, Figes shows Anna's attempt to understand what it means to be "Anna" within her own family. The novel describes her experience as a student of linguistic theory and concludes with her romance, marriage, and the birth of her own child.

In my favorite section of the book—which depicts the courtship between Anna and Daniel, the man she will eventually marry—she tells him about her desire to write poetry and her conflict about the ways in which language functions as currency within daily life: "It's like passing a coin around day by day. It gets worn down, loses definition, its hard edges. And half the time people don't even notice, they're so busy shopping, putting it in slot machines, whatever."

Eva Figes was born in Germany and moved with her family to England just before World War II began; after the move, the family never again spoke German. This linguistic dislocation no doubt allowed her to question the function of language in the formation of identity. Her exploration of that relationship is at the center of this evocative and compelling novel. [Nicole Cooley]

*

Diamela Eltit. *The Fourth World.* Trans. Dick Gerdes. Nebraska, 1995. 114 pp. Paper: $10.00; *Sacred Cow.* Trans. Amanda Hopkinson. Serpent's Tail, 1995. 106 pp. Paper: $12.99.

Diamela Eltit is a performance and video artist known for her work with the poor in Santiago; she is also a professor of literary theory, and a committed activist who refused to leave Chile, or to remain there quietly, when the military dictatorship was established in 1973. She is one of a group of writers whom Raymond Leslie Williams identifies as emergent in the 1980s, when a "direct questioning of dominant ideologies" of Latin American literature and/as politics was inflected, for the first time, with feminist consciousness and theoretical knowledge of the social construction of gender and subjectivity.

These texts are "matters under stress, on which [are] woven the threads of a story"; they both "end" with tropes of their own production, but to say that Eltit has written a pair of "self-begetting novels" would be utterly misleading. The conditions under which first-person narratives become (in)conceivable are the focus of her writing, a focus that comprises a novel and almost inarticulable subject. The language is de- and re-formed, poised obsessively (as in a Valenzuela creation) at the skins of its own characters, the physical tissues marked or lacerated by pressures from without as well as within. The voice speaks: "Exasperated, I tried to find techniques, *formulae in the process of failing, to thereby negate that space where the payment of debts crosses over into inflicting wounds in those areas of greatest vulnerability.*" Eltit's books speak with pain, difficulty, and rage from these areas, recording a political landscape with sharpest visual acuity and engendering a new novel by implication.

In *Sacred Cow,* the primary narrator is not named; her lover, Manuel, has "disappeared," and the reason for that is not quite named either. There is her friend Ana, who carries on a sexual affair with Sergio, shared by the narrator; Sergio was also a lover of Francisca, who seems at intervals to be nursing a dying parent, and who is physically battered and abandoned by, possibly, Sergio. The book proceeds to gather characters toward a kind of climax, when the narrator attends a "fiesta" which is also a politically produced decoy of a spectacle, a pretext for the gathering of workers who formulate a demand for "living space" and whose activity seems alternately promising and cruelly farcical to the narrator.

Writing from the vantage of the anarchic, victimized, and radically creative female body authorizes the "view fugues" at work in both novels. The narrative distortions trade legibility for radical sympathy and promise to reinvent readerly attention profoundly. The first person gives way to the third person in the fourth world . . . and it doesn't finally require that much political intelligence to understand why the compatriots of self-same are so divided. "And although I would rather forget, for ever after I have imprinted on my mind the image of the narrow stretcher and her body half covered by a sheet." Here the narrative shifts violently, for the first time in the text, from "I" to "she," and thus accounts for the rape incompletely figured in the passage before. The text raises the question of autobiography in an era of violence and dissociation.

This certification of narrative as the production of an otherwise unidentifiable position is the technique of the very brilliant *Fourth World,* a split narrative that begins in the womb (the fraternal half of a pair of twins begins to tell the story as a fetus) and is also triggered by the incestuous violation of the sister twin by the brother (the point at which she begins, in effect, to produce the text at hand). Inevitably, someone with more historical and intuitive understanding of political forces at work in Chile before and after Pinochet's dictatorship will explicate the Oresteian aspect of *The Fourth World:* the social codes embedded in the incestuous family romance which explicitly prefigures the narrative. The purposive obscenity and ambiguity of Greenaway's film *The Cook, the Thief, His Wife, and Her Lover* come to mind.

When North American critics write about "the Latin American novel," they do not typically mean this succession of ideologically constituted hieroglyphs which, in a very particular place and time, define access to the language of dreaming. Eltit delivers. [Marisa Januzzi]

*

Peter Høeg. *The History of Danish Dreams.* Trans. Barbara Haveland. Farrar, Straus & Giroux, 1995. 356 pp. $24.00.

I admire this intriguing novel. It is a challenging text because it apparently questions the very notion of its form. If we look closely at the title we are startled by the concepts of "history" and "dreams." Some of the questions the title suggests are the following: Is "history"—or the past—a "dream"? How can one write a "history of dreams" in chronological order? Is the historian *dreaming* the Danish dreams? The text begins with a foreword written by a narrator, a historian who claims that he made his text as "simple" as he could. He then mentions two mysterious, cryptic incidents. One describes Carsten and his father in 1929. The father, Carl, is assembling a machine gun in his living room. "The weapon pointed, with the most liberating determination, into the hazy future." The historian notes the enigmatic scene. Why does Carl *construct* a gun in the room? The historian then goes on to describe a scene occurring at *the same time*. Anna watches her mother's obsessive cleaning of the room, trying to attack all the dirt.

We are puzzled by these events for several reasons. Why is the "coincidence" mentioned? Is there some metaphorical or symbolic linkage? The historian suggests that he has heard about these events from Carsten and Anna, but he cannot understand why, of all the events he has been told, he remembers these. Thus he forces us to *interpret* the events, to *understand* their significance. We are placed in an awkward situation because we don't know yet anything about the characters, the meaning of the odd incidents. But the suggestion that we must help the historian is made. We must help him interpret history. Already, before we read the history, we are "lost."

The text itself consists of various events involving several people; it follows a chronological order but at the same "time," it seems to undermine the idea of logical reconstruction. The historian now and again speaks to us and to the characters. There is a kind of rupture because we are irritated by the comments of the meddling historian. For most of the first two sections of the text (which cover the years 1520-1939) we read about bizarre events, events which are, to say the least, "unreal." When we finally get to the third section—the years between 1939-1989—we notice that the subtitle of this long section is "A Longing for Order." This section seems to be less "magical," less hallucinatory, than the previous ones. At first we believe that the text is cracked, that the modern events are not as wonderful (in all senses) as the first two. And we are especially disturbed by the interruptions of the historian who speaks obsessively to the characters. But after we begin to feel that the text has, in a sense, fallen— that it has become a mere series of commonplaces—we suddenly realize that the historian himself sees the rupture. He says: "there will be no future to face up to. . . ." He calls out to the past for help. And in the last sentence of the text the historian is "lonely"; he muses that perhaps he has dreamed the entire text.

The text, in effect, "ends" with a whimper. It does not ultimately commit itself to any stable continuity. It "overwhelms" the historian. And thus Høeg apparently implies that history itself is a dream, that "reality" is hallucination, that the historian is our "dream." [Irving Malin]

*

Antoine Volodine. *Naming the Jungle*. Trans. Linda Coverdale. The New Press, 1995. 167 pp. $18.95.

The rain forest of Antoine Volodine's *Naming the Jungle* is a far cry from Longfellow's "forest primeval"; nor does it resemble Tarzan's vines and waterways, or Rima's green mansions. Rather, it is all phantasmagoria, hallucination, with rotting flora and fauna, huge bats, crocodiles twenty feet long, tarantulas as big as your fist, waterways muddy, shallow, and undefined. This is the world of indigenous Indian tribes who have been involved in civil war for years. The capital city of Volodine's unnamed country, Puesto Libertad, "could be any Latin American city torn by the strife of civil war." The very first sentence plunges the reader into this South American "heart of darkness": "Once again the revolution was dead." Once again, winners and losers. One of the losers, Fabian Golpiez, feigns madness to avoid interrogation and torture by the secret police. The form of his rehabilitation requires that he consult regularly with Dr. Fabian Gonçalves, a psychiatrist/shaman who is, like Golpiez, a Jucapira or Tupi Indian. His sessions take place in a dilapidated office, formerly used by an executed dentist who left behind a dental chair which now functions as a Freudian couch. With the aid of an old slide projector and a plentiful supply of pictures from the past, Gonçalves involves Golpiez in a talking cure reminiscent of Pinget's inquisitive interviewer in *The Inquisitory:* "Tell me something concrete instead of whining, he said. Instead of wallowing in stupid abstractions. You know perfectly well that death has no reality for us. Primeval inexistence, yes. Mud, yes. But not death." After a number of such sessions, Golpiez feels himself "slipping back into my true nature. . . . I was becoming an Indian again." "Becoming an Indian again" requires that he remember or learn all of the Indian terms for the world of the jungle.

The ending has many of the elements of magic realism; Golpiez, Gonçalves, Manda (an Indian woman), and Rui Gutiérrez, another Indian, set out for the headwaters of the Abacau to "establish Juaupes, an egalitarian commune governed by a shamanistic and revolutionary administration, and to set up a clinic for the surviving Cocambos and Jaboanas in the area." Manda dies from poison darts fired by local Indians, Rui dies jabbering about equality to an audience of large spiders, Golpiez drifts into the upriver maze of channels, and Gonçalves drifts back to the environs of Puesto Libertad. The ending, like Golpiez's quest for his identity, is buried somewhere in the jungle, along with the Indian nomenclature for every creature, every object. As Gonçalves had put it earlier to Golpiez: "Give us something more substantial. . . . You're just spinning out your old traumas! There's no plot, no structure to your stories!" Yet there is method in Volodine's jungle madness—an alternative picture of life in the rain forest. [Jack Byrne]

*

Vassilis Vassilikos. *And Dreams Are Dreams.* Seven Stories Press, 1996. 261 pp. $18.95.

Vassilikos interweaves seven fictions into a novel that is partly magic realism, partly metafiction, and wholly concerned with transformations. His narrator is a writer who, under the pressure of a deadline, has squirreled himself away to complete a novel. This writer's self-avowed preoccupation is with women "in transit" and such "transit zones" as airports, railway stations, or other places of exchange. What emerges is a novel/collection of stories that is far superior to his typical "romance" novels because he has extended his preoccupation both literally and figuratively to other aspects of life.

The collection opens with the narrator and his colleagues founding a journal devoted to dreams and the belief that dreams complement reality. The journal is immediately transformed, however, not by its editors but by its environment—a sociopolitical atmosphere that fosters the reading of everything in terms of oppositions. Dreams are swiftly identified as rivals of reality in the competition for followers and resources. The second story juxtaposes classical Greek mythology (with the figurative personification of gods and goddesses by passengers on a cruise) against the evolution of the modern Greek state in the nineteenth and twentieth centuries. A further concern Vassilikos addresses is that between history and story—displayed to some effect by the intrusion of the narrator into this story.

These somewhat static juxtapositions (dream/reality, ancient mythology/modern history, and history/fiction) provide the background against which subsequent stories play. More dynamic is the great love story of the book—that between Doña Rosita and Don Pacifico. Trading on the ambiguity of whether Rosita is dream or dreamer and the various manifestations of the writer/narrator's own love affair with Doña Rosita, Vassilikos activates a series of transformations, including one wherein magic realism slides into metafiction. There are occasional disappointments, including the uninspired story that recounts the transformation of a tiger into a woman. More typical, however, are the delightful ways in which events and themes developed in one story reemerge in later stories and twist against these new contexts until they themselves are transformed into other concerns, other threads. [Rick Henry]

*

Augusto Monterroso. *Complete Works and Other Stories.* Trans. Edith Grossman. Univ. of Texas Press, 1995. 152 pp. Paper: $12.95.

Monterroso is one of a handful of consistently strong Latin American experimenters who have had almost no attention in the United States. Since the 1950s he has been publishing, among other things, quirky short-short fiction that tends to make a great many American short-shorts seem simple or old hat. *Complete Works and Other Stories* contains some of the best of these pieces.

Through the course of the volume Monterroso carefully constructs stories that challenge our notions of narrative discourse. They slide through transitions of scene and voice, fizzling or crackling, turning on themselves to break into a polyphony of voices when least expected. Monterroso is constantly reinventing himself. Many of the characters and narrators are presented ironically though subtly, and this is coupled with an accuracy of language that bleeds through even in translation.

The forty-five stories range from one line—"When he awoke, the dinosaur was still there"—to ten pages. Many are metafictional, the storytellers unable to stop themselves from poking their heads in, the stories themselves falling apart to reveal a narrator trying to sew together scraps of different narratives, but the interruptions are fluid and convincing rather than irritating. Others, such as "Mister Taylor," a story about the exportation of shrunken heads, are more straightforward, more immediately involved in social satire. The characters and narrators are often blind to their own weaknesses, and one of the great pleasures of the stories is Monterroso's ability to make the reader feel privy to a view of the narrator that the narrator himself will never have.

There is also an obsession with flies here, the eccentric implied author of the second half of the book taking great joy in collecting passages from literature that mention flies (each story is given an epigraph in which flies are mentioned), declaring that in literature "There are three themes: love, death, and flies" and speaking of his desire to assemble "a world anthology of the fly."

The pieces feel contemporary. Fully cognizant of the short-short's relationship to anecdote, aphorism, poem, vignette, fable, parable, and epitaph, Monterroso offers a wide range of short fiction that is at once entertaining and scintillating. [Brian Evenson]

*

Michael Martone. *Seeing Eye.* Zoland, 1995. 192 pp. $20.95.

A writer of historical fiction faces a choice: Emphasize the historically important or what was relevant day to day? Lincoln or Lincoln Logs? Michael Martone, happily, writes out of the Lincoln Logs tradition. This is not history as you know it, but you'll wish Michael Martone had been your history teacher in high school. The stories in *Seeing Eye* form a history of common things and daily ways. A reader will find in these stories Nehi bottles and a Chatty Cathy doll, a woman playing Barbie and lice checks at public schools. In "Blue Hair" a woman remembers when she was a child and had her hair volunteered for the war effort, to be used in fashioning the crosshairs for bomb sights. In Martone's hands these moments provide more than setting and nostalgia; for him they are golden opportunities for metaphor, chances to open up a time and see how it worked.

These are stories that piece the time together from what's left and what's remembered, "the whole imagined from a few bits." A farmer in "Outside Peru" stores the wreckage of a plane in his barn. "The wingtip, dented and discolored . . . implies the missing wing." There are also bits of dinner-table stories, about the chalk signs left by tramps or the Dish Nights sponsored by movie theaters. Martone's stories are like antique shops. He browses countless shelves for evidence of the past. The wing of a model plane, an old wristwatch with the minutes marked by radium paint, a gravy boat orphaned from its pattern—things start to fall into place. A woman in "Fidel" listens to her father's radio and his favorite station: "After midnight scratchy recordings of big bands were introduced by Listo Fisher, who pretended the broadcast still came from the ballrooms of the Hotel Indiana. Alfonse Bott, Tyrone Denig and the Draft Sisters, the brothers Melvin and Merv LeClair. . . ." The list in Martone's story reels on, a broadcast without break, until the narrator punctuates it with this thought:

"It was as if I had tuned into my father's era."

Many of the stories in Martone's collection are set in the era of the father. Many are monologues, speakers who come through as clear as callers to AM stations. Many of them are set in Indiana, which should not surprise readers of *Fort Wayne Is Seventh on Hitler's List*. Many, however, are also contemporary, as are all the stories in the second section, narrated by former Vice President Dan Quayle. The same specificity and popular sense of history is here too, and joined by a wonderful sense of humor. In fifty years these will be read by people for whom Carson, Arsenio, and Letterman are names as suggestive but finally mysterious as Listo Fisher is for me today. These readers will know Dan Quayle, maybe, from BUSH-QUAYLE campaign pins in the glass cases of the antique stores of our future. They will find they can tell the time from the stories in Martone's book. [Paul Maliszewski]

*

Michael Hemmingson. *Crack Hotel.* Permeable Press, 1996. 55 pp. Paper: $3.50.

Hemmingson has provided a good study of corruption in *Crack Hotel.* He begins with a drifter, Mudd, with no real past other than what can be guessed from a leather jacket from Morocco. Mudd begins by emphasizing his whiteness and separateness from the world of the crack hotel. Then he works there. Then he smokes crack there. Then he threatens violence. Then he fucks a TV hooker. And so forth and so on, farther and farther into the realm of murder. This descent is told in very spare prose, in short numbered sections often only a paragraph long. Mudd's own emotions are hidden from us, as they apparently are from Mudd. With each descent, the forces of the world provide him some form of anesthesia, usually crack or sex or both.

Mudd fantasizes about corrupting a young woman named Tara, a reader of postmodern fiction who is a symbol for all of Hemmingson's readers, but her slumming in and near the crack hotel simply makes it too much trouble. It would take an effort to corrupt her, so he just lets the natural world do it.

The overriding word concerning corruption is *ease.* It's easy to take a little money from the whores working the hotel at night; it's easy to fuck Marie, the TV hooker; it's easy to screw the unconscious Irish girl. Eventually it's easy to kill—the whore he kills even gives him the idea. Corruption is just a winding down. Mudd isn't the only one we see fall into the quick decline of corruption. The whores, the cops, the visitors to the hotel all wind down into lower and lower realms. Eventually Mudd can't even say his "Vignette about wishing to be something else." He glimpses that a whole story belongs only to people who visit the crack hotel for a season and get the fuck away.

Hemmingson's work is read since he writes about sex and drugs. This is good, but it would be better if his work was read since it explains how corruption works—how quickly, and with what ease we all can sink into the depths. [Don Webb]

António Lobo Antunes. *Act of the Damned.* Trans. Richard Zenith. Grove, 1995. 246 pp. $22.00.

Portuguese author Lobo Antunes, among the world's best and least appreciated novelists, seems incapable of writing less than brilliantly. He sets this work first in Lisbon, then almost due east, in towns along the Spanish border. It's 1975, a time of social upheaval in Portugal, during which a communist revolution seems possible.

Lobo Antunes deals here with greed, cruelty, and decadence. The family patriarch, Diogo, after suffering a stroke, has little time left. Relatives gather at his home waiting for him to expire. Almost all are exasperated, there out of a sense of duty. Simultaneously they're petrified by fear of a communist takeover, poised to cross into Spain. Diogo's son-in-law, Rodrigo, who has had a child by his own bastard daughter, waits for the old man to croak so that he can gobble up his estate. It turns out, though, that Diogo has spent or mortgaged everything he possesses, leaving only debts. Poetic justice does not reign, however, in this novel.

The author describes the philandering and corruption of his major characters in considerable detail, and sometimes with a good deal of humor, for example when discussing the adventures of Nuno, the amorous and spiteful dentist.

The group of people Lobo Antunes has created here, including the depraved and the retarded, resembles a William Faulkner cast of characters. In fact, the similarities between *The Sound and the Fury, As I Lay Dying,* and *Act of the Damned* suggest that Faulkner's novels may have inspired or influenced Lobo Antunes. As these works evolve, both writers shift the focus from character to character and employ interior monologues and reveries during their first-person narratives.

There's considerable emphasis in *Act of the Damned* on describing a crumbling, rotting physical environment, something Lobo Antunes has done skillfully throughout his career. His novel also contains nightmarish, hallucinatory portions. Though certainly not a pleasant or easy read, it ranks among the more powerful and evocative prose fiction volumes published recently. [Harvey Pekar]

*

Brooks Hansen. *The Chess Garden, or The Twilight Letters of Gustav Uyterhoeven.* Farrar, Straus & Giroux, 1995. 480 pp. $22.00.

The title of this startling text is strange. What is a "chess garden"? Is it a "place" in which we play chess? Or is chess itself a garden? Or, conversely, can chess, a "game" of war, ever become natural? Thus the title works in an odd way; it forces us to explore, to see things in a slanted, unusual way. And we recognize that the title is a clue, an omen, to the curious text that follows.

Once we enter the text—or the world?—we are disoriented by all descriptions. We are told that Mrs. Uyterhoeven is dying—the time is "near dawn on March 25, 1912"; the place is her home in the "Dayton View section of Dayton,

Ohio." A Mrs. Conover sits as caretaker near the bed, but she seems to be interested in wading through some text concerning the revelations of Hildegard of Bingen. The entire text is even announced (or hinted at) by the "con" of Mrs. Conover—the "bridge," the connection between language and mortality. And these connections between "letter" (spirit) and body (matter) continue to plague us as we enter the "commotion" of the future text.

The "text within the text" is repeated throughout *The Chess Garden*. We read about Dr. Uyterhoeven, who is in a distant place called "the Antipodes." He describes extraordinary adventures in which he meets knights, kings, rooks. He is, if you will, on a chessboard that has become transformed into a three-dimensional world. The "letters" describe his movements. And, of course, the book itself consists of movements of time and space so that we are in some supernatural world.

Swedenborg is mentioned as the messenger of truth: he "claimed to have led a basically dual existence, traversing comfortably between the realms of nature and spirit, conversing with angels as openly and easily as with humans." Swedenborg's texts guide the letters of Uyterhoeven, whose letters from the Antipodes are read by the Dayton citizens on ritualistic days.

Although Hansen's book is at times "philosophical"—in the bad way—it resembles *Alice in Wonderland*—another text that is "fantastic" and partly played on a chessboard; it questions its own existence. It plays itself. [Irving Malin]

*

Steve Katz. *Swanny's Ways.* Sun & Moon, 1995. 550 pp. $22.95.

These are the memoirs of William Swanson (Swanny), introduced by entomologist Jackson Ryan as "confessions, or narrations, or barely controlled fits of imagination." The novel consists of a series of these narrations, overlapping episodes in Swanny's life, punctuated by Ryan's comments. Swanny writes from his perspective in the 1990s, but is mostly concerned with his obsession in the early 1970s with events of the late 1940s, particularly the murder of his friend Florry O'Neill.

This novel is the third in a trilogy; the previous two are *Wier & Pouce* (1984) and *Florry of Washington Heights* (1987). Katz is a talented writer both as stylist and storyteller. His William Swanson is a funny and engaging narrator. Like Katz, Swanny grew up in the Washington Heights neighborhood of New York. His roots are Jewish Irish—"Jewish mom, Irish dad. Avoid it if you can, like mating an anteater and a penguin."

In almost every episode Swanny is hung up on a man named Kutzer who he thinks murdered Florry O'Neill. In one episode Kutzer is a fake guru; in another he is a gangster; in another, a businessman. Also in most episodes Swanny is involved in a love/sex relationship that turns sour because of his obsession. His lover is Lucinda, Kyrie, Tasha, Adrienne, Joanie; they become interchangeable. The overall effect, which brings to mind Robert Anton Wilson's use of parallel universes, can be frustrating for the reader at the same time that it is enlightening. Our lives are revealed as fictions that we constantly create and re-create. But at times the reader's indulgence is strained by this undermining of the fictional "reality."

It is the recurring theme of Florry O'Neill's murder that gives the novel coherence. Swanny loves to talk about Florry and use the phrase "Florry of Washington Heights." It becomes his mantra, his key to understanding his own life and all the strange events and happenings of the late twentieth century.

As the novel progresses Jackson Ryan is revealed as a boyhood nemesis of Swanny's, a rival gang leader. He becomes more central to the story, and more confused and Swanny-like as his entomological certainties are shaken by problematic human relationships. ("O to be chitinous," he laments.) He too begins to look to the past to try to comprehend and cope with the present. Like Swanny's narratives this relates to the Proust referent of the title. *Swanny's Ways* certainly deals with time and memory, and like a postmodern American bebop version of *Remembrance of Things Past.* [Daniel Barth]

*

Dennis Barone. *Abusing the Telephone.* Drogue Press (P.O. Box 1157, Cooper Station, New York, NY 10276), 1994. 81 pp. Paper: $10.00.

In *Abusing the Telephone* Dennis Barone offers fictions that do not operate according to principles of linear progression or to the accrual of meaning through a sense of developing character. Rather, the ten fictions gathered in this book present voices which, while only inching forward linearly, digress in intriguing ways into realms cobbled together of different speech genres and different selves. Each paragraph both provides a means for moving on and for a fizzling of progression, the paragraphs serving as nexus points, as crossroads for paths of discourse leading in several directions. In that sense, Barone's text is rhizomatic, operating with a logic that refuses to be profitably understood through standard measures of narrative.

Where Barone seems most accomplished is in several of the shorter one- or two-page pieces. "Let's Play," for instance, is the collision of a voice discussing music and a pseudoscientific discourse with other concerns. "Philosophy" offers a rhetorician's stance to a philosophical discussion of aesthetics that threatens to collapse. Many of Barone's sentences have hints of the speech genres of theoretical explanation or scientific proof, Barone sharing something with Ben Marcus's mock-science, though the drive here is not toward the formal completeness of Marcus but rather toward a maddened and unresolved formal conflict.

The danger is that the pieces, employing many of the same formal strategies, will sound too much alike. In that regard, one or two of the pieces seem less dynamic, such as "Willie Master's Niece," which is a skewed salute to both David Markson and William H. Gass, though the connections are less interesting than the disjunctions. Here, as elsewhere, Barone uses a scheme of allusive referral that seems to dead-end. Which suits well the broader challenges of narrative that he offers.

Most successful is "Bus Trip to Dresden," the longest piece in the volume. Its initial narrator, a man researching a photograph, is intriguing, the voice more continuous and revealing than in the other stories. The second narrator, a woman obsessed with him, is strong as well. Possessing more of a narrative than the shorter pieces, it provides a kind of satisfaction that is lacking (though not necessarily needed) in the shorter pieces, and reveals that Barone's literary strengths are more extensive than the rest of the volume suggests. Generally promising, *Abusing the Telephone* is an interesting effort by an author willing to provide a new twist to the more usual experiments in language. [Brian Evenson]

*

Shelley Berc. *The Shape of Wilderness.* Coffee House, 1995. 279 pp. Paper: $12.95.

The Shape of Wilderness is a strange and somewhat exhaustively panoramic novel whose prose has a Whitmanesque yawp to it, a nineteenth-century "Can Do! Give Me Your Destitute! All of America is a boomtown!" feel. Anything can happen within the shape of Shelley Berc's wilderness—one does not slap a genre on this terrain. It's fairy tale, farmer's almanac, folklore, fabula, historical chronicle, allegory. There are even pretenses here toward a realistic story concerning twin sisters raised in a Spruce Goose of a hotel built by their South American—and one gathers indio—father and a northern mother, but any reader holding onto these shreds of realism will soon enough be KO'd; this is a Wile E. Coyote of a book and it makes liberal and tendentious use of Native American creation myths and trickster or transformer legends.

The Hotel—always capitalized within the novel—is built in the middle of nowhere, except it's in the middle of the American wilderness which is very definitely and significantly *not* nowhere. Everything in *The Shape of Wilderness* is hugely and ingenuously allegorical and sometimes carried off with a layering that fascinates by its sheer audacity. There is an Emmanuel here and he is everything—and more—that that name would imply. He has no father but rather a mother who roams the world in search of him. He is father of the twins, and by various twists and turns, destroyer of them both in that he represents variously Judeo-Christian religion, patriarchy, and the rapacious brutalization of a new land by the gross materialism of capitalism. Emmanuel is on stage through most of the novel as Trapper, an old and skillful taxidermist who rationalizes his ravaging of the American wilderness's fauna with Native American notions of an animal and his soul and with more Christian claims of a knowledge of the secrets of immortality. He shoulders this signification fairly well, but late in the novel he becomes almost a caricature of patriarchy reminiscent of those deeply paranoid cartoonish depictions of blacks during Reconstruction. Unfortunately much within the story feels suddenly very gratuitous.

A great deal about this book is excellent and there is some terrific and smart writing. It needs some sensitive editing to allow its strategies to come off polished and timely rather than haphazard, but one can't deny a certain brazenness within the storytelling which is compelling and ambitious and ultimately very seductive. [Michelle Latiolais]

*

Eugene K. Garber. *The Historian: Six Fantasies of the American Experience.* TriQuarterly Books, 1995. 233 pp. Paper: $14.95.

Winner of the William Goyen Prize for Fiction, *The Historian* is a meditation on the nature of history as well as a work of fiction. It consists of character-linked stories stretching, in rearranged temporal order, from 1807 to 1912. The characters themselves, often amalgams of several figures from several different times, seem ultimately very little bound by age or by time: Simms, for instance, can flit from 1870s New Mexico in one story to appear next in 1807 in the Connecticut River Valley, and then later on a train in 1911. The historian, the other primary character, seems fully a manifestation of the spirit of his time, and as notions of people's relationship to events change, he changes as well, becoming involved in journalism and sociology in an attempt to capture the nature of a time. Indeed, he is hardly the same man from story to story, seems in fact to have a progression of selves.

The strength of the book results largely from the sorts of meditations it makes on history, the breadth of its exploration. There are strengths as well in terms of the language, Garber's handling of English being both elegant and accurate, his use of the language finely crafted. Garber is a metafictionalist but has a sense of finesse that metafiction too often lacks: a measure of unreality creeps into his work so casually and quietly that it seems fully necessary and integrated. The shifts in time are not jarring, and the fiction is convincing enough that we quickly suspend our disbelief.

Though at times not as strong as some of the stories in Garber's earlier book, *Metaphysical Tales* (1981), *The Historian* has a great deal of strength and interest. It is a worthwhile book, very carefully controlled and highly inventive, and makes one hope that there won't be another twelve-year wait before Garber produces his next book. [Brian Evenson]

*

Raymond Roussel. *How I Wrote Certain of My Books.* Ed. Trevor Winkfield. Trans. by the editor, John Ashbery, Harry Mathews, and others. Exact Change, 1995. 264 pp. Paper: $15.95.

You need to know the work of Raymond Roussel (1877-1933) to make sense not only of many contemporary French writers—for this reason, Leon Roudiez's survey *French Fiction Revisited* begins with a chapter on Roussel before jumping ahead to Duras, Robbe-Grillet, *et Cie*—but also contemporary American novelists like Harry Mathews and Gilbert Sorrentino and poets like John Ashbery and Kenneth Koch. This new anthology from Exact Change—not to be confused with the book of the same name published by SUN in 1977—is an ideal Roussel reader. It opens with an introduction by Ashbery (a longtime Roussel scholar), which is followed by Roussel's eye-opening title essay, and then selections from his major works: the novels *Impressions of Africa* and *Locus Solus,* the play *The Dust of Suns,* the long poem *New Impressions of Africa,* and all the surviving fragments of his unfinished novel, *Documents to Serve as an Outline.* Also included are the fifty-nine drawings Roussel commissioned to pad out *New Impressions of Africa*—one look at them and you'll understand how Sorrentino's *Under the Shadow* works—and an annotated bibliography by the editor that doesn't mince words. (Rayner Heppenstal's critical study of Roussel is described as a "Simpering apologia, not worth the paper it's printed on.")

Roussel's writings themselves are exotic and quirky. In his lifetime they attracted Dadaists and Surrealists—though Roussel was unaware of their aesthetics—and there's a superficial resemblance between some of them and the novels of Ronald Firbank written at the same time, but they more closely resemble the works of his followers, like Mathews's early novels, Kenneth Koch's novel *The Red Robins* and his narrative poems, and Sorrentino's recent novels. In France, the *nouveaux romanciers* adapted his tendency to give long, detailed descriptions of inanimate objects and to allow the imaginative manipulation of language to generate form and content, a practice later followed by the OuLiPo school. For his influence alone Roussel deserves to be read, and this nicely designed anthology is the perfect introduction to his work. [Steven Moore]

*

Joanna Scott. *The Manikin.* Holt, 1996. 276 pp. $22.50.

Shrieking "Worship me," a snowy owl wings its way southward—to be shot down by a young hunter's rifle. Once stuffed and mounted, the owl becomes the brooding animus of *The Manikin,* the latest novel by Joanna Scott (whose previous works include *Arrogance* and *Various Antidotes,* both finalists for PEN/Faulkner awards). The year is 1927, and the manikin in question is not a mannequin but a house, a rambling Edwardian monstrosity in the wilds near Rochester, New York. Here a widow, heir to a taxidermist's empire, lives "alone" with a host of stuffed animals and a staff of servants, including the virtuous housekeeper, Ellen, and her adolescent daughter, Peg, whose relationship forms the spiritual heart of the novel.

Like a manikin—a taxidermist's dummy made of excelsior and clay, over which an animal's skin is sewn and posed—the mansion provides the structure over which the novel is stretched. And that structure not only upholds but also oppresses: "the dense silence of a country house in winter crushes against the ears with the deafening pressure of many fathoms of water." The house is the object of financial disputes, the apparent cause of madness, the site of romance; it pushes and pulls at its inhabitants, inexorably drawing them back.

A large cast of characters live varied but claustrophobic lives here, amid an atmosphere of Gothic gloom and mystery. The estate abounds with devils:

Boggio, the aging taxidermist and resident Mephistopheles; Lily, the China-doll flapper who entices Peg into an "unnatural" affair; and a mysterious man who lurks on the fringes of the estate, threatening young girls and other fragile creatures. There are also more sympathetic spirits: Sylva and Peter, the black cook and handyman whose marriage makes their scenes an idyll; Lore, the taciturn and nobly animistic groundskeeper; and Ellen and Peg themselves, who certainly have their flaws (most appreciably in their dysfunctional dealings with each other) but manage to claim equal portions of the reader's sympathy.

We have to ask what all these characters, all this mystery, add up to—do we have a living, breathing community, or merely a collection? Early on, Scott gives future taxidermists a few rules for posing: "Combine motion and danger, and you have a cruel realism, with one story told over and over: the story of the hunt." Occasionally she heeds her own advice and lets motion and danger work together—as in the girls' first love scene, which constitutes one of the book's few hunts: one in which Lily and Peg are mutually prey and predator. Here the language soars into life: "for a split second paranoia subsumes pleasure, and Peg pulls away and looks toward the door, certain that someone is watching . . . when she looks down again she sees fear—Lily's, or the reflection of her own fear in Lily's eyes." Unfortunately for some readers, such scenes are as few and far between as houses are upstate; like the Saturnalian revel positioned at the book's climax, these moments seem to struggle against the power of the decaying house, but they don't quite succeed in overturning it. The book is, finally, a study of a pose rather than of motion—a manikin rather than a living creature. [Susann Cokal]

*

William O'Rourke. *Notts.* Marlowe, 1996. 241 pp. Cloth: $22.95.

This novel describes the journeys of two young Irish-Americans around Britain during the 1984-85 miners strike. Michael meets Jessica on the flight over, starts a sexual relationship, and the two then travel to Nottinghamshire (the "Notts" of the title) where Michael delivers a conference paper on Orwell. This, however, marks only a brief time-out for him from what has become his over-riding priority: to visit the Midlands coal fields and witness the pickets and marchers in action. Michael focalizes the novel throughout, filtering all sights through his perceptions of culture. "I'm a professor of stereotypes," he declares to Jessica, with only a small degree of self-mockery; but this supposed awareness does not grant him any special insights into the situations he encounters. On the contrary, O'Rourke's use of present-tense narration conveys a moment-by-moment immediacy to all descriptions which curiously encode everything Michael sees as spectacle.

The novel brilliantly captures the circumstantial estrangement of a young American in Britain not at all prepared for the persistent cultural differences that are going to strike him at every turn. Everything from the London subway to details of food is sharply focused; but everything is seen, as it were, through glass. And this effect persists even when the two visit the mining district where they are either introduced as minor celebrities (two "American supporters") or attacked because conditions in U.S. mines are felt to be worse than in England. Apart from his visit to the conference, Jessica takes the initiative throughout as the mover, taking Michael from one picket line to another, introducing him to a medley of English socialists whose politics he can never quite pin down. The miners strike in fact screens another, more sinister political situation—that of the IRA bombings. In between the narrative segments of the novel O'Rourke inserts brief excerpts from a secret British government report on the shooting of two young people in London—obviously Jessica and Michael. The reader is thus drawn into searching the text for signs of this impending outcome. This impressively austere novel closes on a note of "officialese" when the report concludes that the shooting was committed by "unknown assailants" in a failed attempt to provoke an international incident. [David Seed]

*

Douglas Messerli. *The Walls Come True: An Opera for Spoken Voices.* Littoral Books, 1995. 99 pp. Paper: $12.95.

Messerli's *The Walls Come True,* the second part of *The Structure of Destruction* trilogy, is only an opera in the loosest sense of the word—no rotund men and women singing here. Rather, Messerli's assumption is that voices, in the way they speak and interact with one another, in the cadences they create, can create their own music. Whether this is the case or not is difficult to know from the words on the page—the work demands performance to be fully realized— but what is clear is that Messerli is carving for himself a space between genres, creating a work of performance art that is difficult to classify either as play or as opera.

The Walls Come True consists of several speaking voices that recount various events and engage in verbal acts of all kinds. Backing up the words, letters are flashed on a lightboard, short (sometimes artsy, sometimes mildly disturbing) films and slides are shown, and a few sound effects are added for good measure. The filmic segments are perhaps the most suggestive. The piece as a whole is very concept-oriented, plot attenuated to the point of nonexistence, bits and pieces offered in the place of a solid whole, the action accruing through a sort of buildup of discrete moments. Though there is a sense that somehow this is a sort of detective/mystery novel, and though there are moments in which things seem to coalesce, the failure to coalesce is as important as the fumblings toward unity. It is ritual rather than narrative drama, a summoning and dispersing, a clearing of the memory.

Despite the piece's strengths, there are occasional weaknesses. There are moments perhaps reminiscent of other stage art (a scene for instance reminiscent of Beckett's *Happy Days*), but generally Messerli explores territory that is very much his own. The language is at times too conscious of itself, too purposefully heightened without a concomitant sense of awareness or irony. Most disturbing, perhaps, is a voiceover read at the end of the play which provides a certain amount of explanation for a work whose thrust precisely desires to resist explanation. Still, there is much to be offered here, reflections on what makes us inhuman and human, obscure but nonetheless revealing. [Brian Evenson]

*

Julieta Campos. *Celina or the Cats.* Trans. Leland H. Chambers. Latin American Literary Review Press, 1995. 140 pp. Paper: $15.95.

This is the third of Cuban-born Mexican writer Julieta Campos's books to be translated into English, after *The Fear of Losing Eurydice* and *She Has Reddish Hair and Her Name Is Sabina* (both 1993, and likewise translated by Leland H. Chambers). Those two novels are experimental, metafictional works dating from the 1970s; *Celina or the Cats* is a collection of five stories dating from the 1960s, and thus may be a less daunting introduction to this wonderful writer.

The book's title, and the author's introductory essay on the place of cats in mythology and symbolism, is somewhat misleading, for cats figure only in the title story. "Cats are those soft, rippling, cruel, delicate beings, those solitary, always unpredictable beings that inject our everyday world with the sphere of the unknown," Campos writes in her introduction. The other four stories, then, could be said to focus on catlike humans whose feline sense of "the sphere of the unknown" makes their life in the everyday world problematic. It is appropriate that one of these stories, "All the Roses," first appeared in *Anaïs,* a journal devoted to publishing fiction in the tradition of Anaïs Nin, for that's the writer most readers will be reminded of, along with something of the languid lyricism of early Marguerite Duras. (Campos was educated in France and studied the *nouveaux romanciers.*) The final two stories, "The House" and "The City," evoke her birthplace, Havana, by way of a fragmented treatment of memory and the passage of time.

With three of Campos's four works of fiction now available in English, it is high time that North American readers acquaint themselves with Mexico's most innovative female writer. [Steven Moore]

*

Dorien Ross. *Returning to A.* City Lights, 1995. 178 pp. Paper: $9.95.

This first novel by Dorien Ross is a rare literary event that marks the emergence of a gifted writer. Set in Andalusia and the United States, *Returning to A* recounts the love affair of a young American woman, Loren, with the Gypsy culture of Andalusia. Disrupting geographical and temporal boundaries, the narrative mimics the rhythms of flamenco music. Thus the three parts into which *Returning to A* is divided—"*Soleares/*Song of Loneliness," "*Bulerias/* Song of Sensuality," and "*Siguiriyas/*Song of Weeping"—signal the changing stages and moods of Loren's journey. "I was not stolen by the Gypsies as a child. / I stole the Gypsies as my own," Ross writes in the epigraph to the book, capturing her protagonist's relationship to the flamenco artists she encounters: Diego del Gastor, a father figure of mythological proportions yet rooted in the unquestionable earthiness of the world of Bar Pepe, Ansonini—whom Loren does not know whether to regard as a "Zen master or an oblivious old fool"— the generous Rafael, and Manuel, both teacher and lover. Loren does not want to be a dancer like the other women; she wants to play the guitar and conquer the secrets of flamenco, jealously guarded by the male artists who are her models and teachers.

The story of Loren's initiation into flamenco art unfolds in a fragmentary fashion that translates the movements of Loren's soul, rather than those of historical development. Throughout the story looms the suicide of Aaron, Loren's brother, addressed in a second-person narrative through which Loren explores the "geography of grief." Her search for a language that will articulate her sadness is fulfilled in Andalusia, where "it is all right to be sad," where the roads, the fountains, the churches, the trees, all weep with the rain, embracing Loren and allowing her to give voice to her unspeakable sorrow. Through the cadences of flamenco music, Loren transforms her loss and despair into poetry.

At once novel, memoir, essay on flamenco music, and cultural document, *Returning to A* testifies to the vitality and beauty of Gypsy culture as seen through the eyes of a displaced Jewish American woman who finds her home among the Gypsies who, renaming her "Lorea," welcome her as one of their own.

A 45-minute tape of flamenco, *Homage to Diego del Gastor* by Christopher Carnes, a companion to *Returning to A,* is also available through City Lights. [Edvige Giunta]

*

A. Manette Ansay. *Read This and Tell Me What It Says.* Univ. of Massachusetts Press, 1995. 142 pp. $22.95.

Each of A. Manette Ansay's endearingly expressed stories is filled with burdens. It is up to Ansay's humorously entrenched souls to locate an individual integrity that is not necessarily God-given. The struggle for salvation is indeed one of the themes running through the collection, whether religion plays a part or not. The ones who transcend discover that there is more to being alive than any fundamentalism. Full of unrecognized pain, the stories also emit quiet and louder triumphs that provide characters with some inner freedom or transparency.

The Midwestern landscape is meant to be seen in its parked parameters, but characters are terrifically unsettled. The crux of their situational difficulties often parades around them until some turn of events is evident. It is often the initial failure to realize their plights or drives that makes these young to elderly characters so appealing. Ultimately they must reach some clearer view or stay in the mire. In "Evolution of Dreams, North of Sheboygan, 1986," the ungainly young Pip (Dickens aside) is forced out of a violent trailer existence with his sister and her overwrought boyfriend, his only prospects being his own personal ad and a janitorial job offering. In "Silk," an observant woman desires greater intimacy between herself, her repressed husband, and her cross-dressing son.

The title story concerns an anxious young woman's trials to retain her sanity in an overreliant family and the risks she manages to take, however unlike her fatally daredevil best friend. "July" entails a woman's self-independence in the face of various oppressions, and sixty-year-old protagonist of "Sybil" must rely on a neglectful daughter-in-law to get her own desires met.

Immediately engaging, these stories last just long enough to peer through to the very edge of troublesome circumstances, relationships, and character flaws. Ansay leads you in and takes you to the center before dropping you off somewhere that may stun you. Sometimes her departure point is that there is none. There are no flights of fancy here, only heartfelt deliverances that inspire compassion. What these characters know and do not know about themselves works to *tell* the reader *what it says:* "But Adelaide knew how to reach beneath the glassy surface of silences and words, select a few careful details and, from these bald scraps, piece out the complex tapestry of a story" (from "Neighbor"). Ansay delves into the peculiar complexities of people's deepest needs and unlocks our humanity toward them. She mines this all too uncertain good/bad territory and with the real story hinted somewhere in between. Explosive ironies can be found there in italics. [Alystyre Julian]

*

Gary Eberle. *Angel Strings*. Coffee House, 1995. 315 pp. Paper: $12.95.

Gary Eberle's *Angel Strings* is a road novel, though less a Kerouacian road narrative than a Fielding-style picaresque adventure through contemporary America. It is both a satiric look at Americans' searches for something monetary or metaphysical that will make their lives better and a story of the self-discovery that comes from being open to the random events of one's life.

The novel's narrator, Joe Findlay, came to show business early as assistant to his magician father, straddling a cynicism that all of life is like a magic trick, explainable in terms of behind-the-scenes systems, and a nervous suspicion that he is at the mercy of incomprehensible forces, that someday his father might *really* make his head disappear. Having spent several years in a dead-end marriage and a dead-end job (playing backup guitar for a Vegas casino's "Dead Superstars Review" [*sic*]), Joe finally snaps and heads off in his van to seek his destiny, which he thinks is a New York audition to play for Sclapped, an up-and-coming hard rock band. But in Ohio he meets Violet Tansy, a not-quite-twenty-year-old woman with a baby (who may or may not be kidnapped) in a cardboard box and a plan to meet and marry her sailor boyfriend when his submarine docks in San Diego. Before long, Joe is traveling not to New York but to Toledo (where his guitar is stolen), Detroit (where Tansy's grandfather replaces it with one, he says, once owned by an angel), the Midwest Pagan Convention (where he discovers that his wife has added electronic music to a song he wrote and made a New Age hit), a Nebraska tent meeting (where his new guitar has a hypnotic effect on the congregation during the collection), Denver (where the guitar's angel first appears to him with a message), Las Vegas (where his father and wife beg him to become Zak Bendzi, the supposed author of his own song), and San Diego for the reunion with Tansy's boyfriend. Joe remarks at one point that death is like "a rude interruption, like hacking off a rope," but his story makes clear that that's what life is too: a series of interruptions that divert us from where we think we're going.

The novel's humorous depiction of the overlapping worlds of show business and religion is accomplished through characters exaggerated enough to be satiric targets but human enough to be real: the beer-swilling Fagan the Pagan, the vertically challenged Rev. Lenny Laird, the Lord's Littlest Laborer, a lama addicted to french fries, a smarmy New Age talk show host, and, especially, Violet, who is appealing, annoying, pathetic, and stubborn enough to motivate Joe's transformations. The novel is less satisfying in its metaphysics. Joe is on a journey to the discovery of real magic, "what happens inside, between a man and a woman when the fates step in and make them fall in love, and nobody can explain it." But this payoff doesn't support the build up: the speculation that Joe is a "conduit for a divine message" and the angel's climactic, apocalyptic return.

Still, if *Angel Strings* falls short in its philosophizing, its characters, its engaging narrative voice, and the eye it casts on America make it an enjoyable read. [Robert L. McLaughlin]

*

David Shields. *Remote.* Knopf, 1996. 206 pp. $22.00.

David Shields's imagination has always locked on the idea of remoteness. In his first novel, *Heroes* (1984), a cerebral sportswriter named Al Biederman longs to possess the urgent vitality of a very physical basketball player named Belvyn Menkus. In his second, *Dead Languages* (1989), self-conscious stutterer Jeremy Zorn obsesses on the magic of fluent words that might somehow connect him to the world. The protagonist of Shields's short story collection *A Handbook for Drowning* (1991), Walter Jaffe, a geekish young man who carries a bright innocent belligerence within him, perceives himself cut off from his lovers, his fellow students at college, his parents, anything much beyond his own whirring consciousness.

It's small surprise, then, to open this addictive mosaic of fifty-two flash critifictions, most just a few pages in length, several comprised from a series of even shorter pieces, and discover Shields announce in the third sentence of the prologue: "I'm reading my life as if it were an allegory, an allegory about remoteness, and finding evidence wherever I can." He finds evidence in a taping of Oprah Winfrey's show in Seattle and the distance between humdrum existence and celebrity; his need to organize the information—electronic and tactile—of his life; an entire essay built from nothing but bumpersticker, license plate, and T-shirt slogans; a report of his chance semi-encounter with O. J. at a Häagen-Dazs in Brentwood, California; his intellectual journey to determine if he's related to Joseph Schildkraut, the man who played Otto Frank in *The Diary of Anne Frank;* his contemplation on the erotic power of glasses; the pastiche he creates of fans' dreams about Kurt Cobain after his suicide.

Every verbal skit, many ending in pithy punch lines, connects with every other through linguistic sleights-of-hand, leitmotifs, and repeated chapter titles, creating the impression of symphonic structure, or, more appropriate, channel-surfing infoglints retrieved from the late-millennium mediascape. By inserting himself into the data-storm as a character, Shields raises questions about where memory and meditation hemorrhage into fiction, where the flesh ends and the cathode-ray tube begins.

Some of his literary gestures work less well than others here—the plot-heavy take on character actor Bob Balaban's repetitious roles is repetitious, for instance, and the photos that speckle the book are less interesting aesthetically and thematically than they might be (with the exception of one very funny collage-text)—but in large part this is a breathtakingly intelligent project of confession and appropriation textured with electric insights, glassy prose, and a cool, dry, arch irony about David Shields's favorite subject, David Shields, a character at once stingingly self-aware and painfully forlorn: "I don't know what's the matter with me—why I'm an adept only at distance, why I feel so remote from things, why life feels like a rumor."

With *Remote*, Shields has dropped the pretense of pure fabrication in his inventions and colonized the twilight space between fiction and fact. In that nexus he flourishes. [Lance Olsen]

*

Mark Kharitonov. *Lines of Fate.* Trans. Helena Goscilo. The New Press, 1996. 332 pp. $25.00.

Tolstoi's comment about families reminds us of a similar connection between utopias and dystopias. Utopias create happy families based on sameness or commonality; dystopias deconstruct and disrupt families in an effort to re-create social order. The very best descriptions of the latter have been about modern Russia: *We, Doctor Zhivago, One Day in the Life of Ivan Denisovich, Darkness at Noon, The Gulag Archipelago.* . . . Now we have Mark Kharitonov's *Lines of Fate,* the second volume of his trilogy, *A Provincial Philosophy.* In order to create his own picture of life in Soviet Russia, Kharitonov resorts to the well-known literary device of the discovered diary or manuscript. In this case, his contemporary hero, a young graduate student, Anton Lizavin, crosses the decades of Soviet tyranny to rediscover and write a biography of a turn-of-the-century writer and philosopher, Simeon Milashevich, who becomes his alter ego. His sources are the numerous *fantiki*—candy wrappers used by Milashevich and others as writing paper during the early Soviet period—left by the provincial writer. These scraps of "slogans, poems, songs, aphorisms, stream-of-consciousness meditation, and extracts from a writer's notebook" provide Kharitonov with his almost fifty characters: "artists, criminals, drug addicts, sorcerers, suicides, and half-wits." Kharitonov's major theme in this mystery novel is the "persistent 'melody of destruction and loss'—bloodshed, hunger, separations, clandestine organizations and incarcerations, the wholesale demolition of an entire way of life." History is mystery, to be retrieved subjectively by investigators with the passion of Tolstoi and the poetic vision of Pasternak. The truth about Mother Russia is discovered by a careful observation of life in the provinces where "banality of the everyday is the inevitable stuff of life." From this view we are given the novel's central existential revelation: "There is no meaning besides that which you yourself create." Kharitonov's search for meaning helps us to better understand the Soviet debauch, remnants of which are still with us. [Jack Byrne]

*

Nick Hornby. *High Fidelity.* Riverhead Books, 1995. 326 pp. $21.95.

Even punks grow up sooner or later. That's the message of Nick Hornby's hilarious and moving novel about an ordinary bloke who reconciles himself to his extraordinary ordinariness. Something of a cult figure in England, Hornby was associated with *The Modern Review,* Julie Burchill's immensely readable but short-lived journal. Hornby went on to publish *Fever Pitch,* a book about his obsession with a soccer team. But this first novel ushers Hornby into the league of Martin Amis and Julian Barnes, writers who continually return to an appealing adolescent worldview despite their inexorable drift toward dotage.

Hornby's hero is Rob Fleming, who describes himself as "average. A middleweight. Not the brightest bloke in the world, but certainly not the dimmest. . . . My genius, if I can call it that, is to combine a whole load of averageness into one compact frame." He has settled into the modest career of running a record store, called Championship Vinyl, from which perch he tries to find true love. A fanatical record collector, he has a tendency to make lists of everything ("Top five American movies, and therefore the best films ever made: *The Godfather, The Godfather Part II, Taxi Driver, Goodfellas,* and *Reservoir Dogs*"). The novel begins with his list of top five heartbreaks, which he annotates, thus giving the reader a thumbnail sketch of Rob's life. Not included is his last girlfriend, Laura, who doesn't quite make the list. He spends the rest of the book either trying to forget her or trying to get her back.

Like Amis and Barnes, Hornby has a proclivity toward mini essays on various aspects of contemporary life. These dissertations tend to be witty and insightful, and fit in perfectly with Rob's chatty persona. "People worry about kids playing with guns, and teenagers watching violent videos; we are scared that some sort of culture of violence will take them over. Nobody worries about kids listening to thousands—literally thousands—of songs about broken hearts and rejection and pain and misery and loss. The unhappiest people I know, romantically speaking, are the ones who like pop music the most; I don't know whether pop music has caused this unhappiness, but I do know that they've been listening to sad songs longer than they've been living the unhappy lives."

Unlike Barnes and Amis, Hornby has a less bitter view of life. Rob is a recognizable "type," but under Hornby's deft hand, Rob moves from list-making Tarantino fan to pained adult, embracing a fuller "adult" life without necessarily abandoning his passions for music and movies. Hornby makes it clear that Rob's highest fidelity is to Laura as well as to his music. [D. K. Holm]

Eileen Drew. *The Ivory Crocodile.* Coffee House, 1996. 288 pp. $21.95.

A man I once met in Kenya, the son of missionary parents, told me that there was no place he could call his own. Like Nicole, the narrator of Eileen Drew's fine first novel, Africa pulled at him whenever he left, but upon his return, all he had to do was look in the mirror at his startling whiteness to realize that no matter how African his soul might become, his skin would always set him apart. Drew's gift in this and her earlier collection of stories, *Blue Taxis,* is to illuminate not just the cultural differences separating Africans and Americans, but to reveal the seductive and sometimes dangerous pull of the continent's rootedness and tradition.

After a childhood following her father to various African diplomatic posts, Nicole has come to the fictional Central African country of Tambala to teach in a rural village and to step outside the fence that in her privileged childhood separated her from the real Africa. Arriving in her village of Mampungu, Nicole makes the acquaintance of a magnetic radical Angolan, Bwadi, who teaches at her school, befriends a beautiful young student named Diabelle, and attempts to forget what everyone around her cannot: that she is a white-skinned American.

However close she may come to African-ness—whether that means respecting the communal ethic rather than penalizing students for helping each other with their work, wearing the traditional *pagne,* falling for the brooding Bwadi, or cooking corn and squash and manioc instead of consuming the American delicacies proffered by Mitch, doctor for the nearby bridge-building project—she is still more fairy godmother than good mother. And it is here that Drew most perfectly captures the experience of even the most well-intentioned Westerner in Africa; he or she may be most valuable not for anything personal and intrinsic, but for what he or she can provide: a camera, sugar, birth control pills. By the novel's end, Nicole has faced a startling and depressing fact; when events in her village take a tragic turn, she is caught between blaming herself for not preventing what happened and recognizing that taking on the blame will make her into what she most wanted not to be—the paternal Westerner. Where does that leave her? The same place the novel leaves the reader: in sadness and resignation.

Although the political discussions may wax a bit long for some readers, *The Ivory Crocodile* is an eye-opening immersion into the life of the African continent. Drew writes with sensitivity, with skill, and with assurance; this is a worthy first novel, both for its style and its subject. [Greg Garrett]

*

Diane Schoemperlen. *In the Language of Love: A Novel in 100 Chapters.* Viking, 1996. 358 pp. $23.95.

The 100 small chapters of *In the Language of Love* are based on the 100 words of the Kent-Rosanoff Word Association Test. Beginning with *table* and ending with *afraid,* the novel's course subverts the direction these words seem to promise. Through a series of flashbacks, the novel details the growth and maturation of Joanna, who was raised in a small Canadian town. She ends up relatively happy, with a husband, child, and an indeterminate career as an artist. She has a bossy, fearful mother, an indifferent father, two lovers—one below her in class and one married. As a child she steals something or other from the local five and dime. We read about her teachers, her childhood friends, and her first sexual experience.

In fact, the novel is all detail but in the end we have very little information. The detail is generous, but unrevealing and ordinary. The novel strangely draws one in by its unwillingness to surprise. Each small segment flows to the next until suddenly the reader is on the last page. Perhaps that is the point: to document the way that ordinary details take you from one day to the next until you find yourself grown up and in the middle of a not-so-bad life. [Ellen G. Friedman]

*

George Saunders. *CivilWarLand in bad decline: stories & a novella.* Random, 1996. 179 pp. $22.00.

In the future setting of many of these stories, the most unique desire is now commonplace—in fact it would be impossible to have a desire so autonomous it couldn't be turned into a theme park. The gimmick of the Burn'n'Learn, for example, "is a fully stocked library on the premises and as you tan you call out the name of any book you want to these high-school girls on roller skates." It's not a far-fetched future—when they pass out costumes for a historical theme ride, a man sues over the emotional distress which ensued after his stint as hangman. Violence is frequent and nonchalant, though most of the characters are understandably bothered after they've killed someone (which does seem to be one of the standard plot points on which these stories hinge). Perhaps death is not so horrifying because the dead feel free to keep occupying the landscape after they've died. One little boy who visits his accidental murderer (negligent, he crushed him in a wave machine) doesn't quite get the hang of being a ghost: "when he tries to be scary he gets it all wrong. He can't moan for beans. He's scariest when he does real kid things, like picking his nose and wiping it on the side of his sneaker."

Saunders's voice is strong, funny, and unique. The novella *Bounty,* in which one of the Flawed goes out into the world of the Normal to find his sister, also Flawed, goes on too long in its unrelenting portrayal of various types of cruelty masquerading under the same shallow inhumane impulse, but the best stories of this collection, "Isabelle" and "The 400-Pound C.E.O.," are redemptive in their humanity. They speak to and of people beaten down who come again and again, against all odds, to faith and love. They are stories that can break your heart and lift you up at the same time and they are the type of stories that are proof to me of the necessity of literature in a world that isn't trying hard enough to avoid the bleak future of Saunders's other stories. [Gale Walden]

*

Cydney Chadwick. *Oeuvres* and *Persistent Disturbances*. Texture, 1995. 21 and 39 pp. Paper: $5.00 each.

Chadwick is the editor of *Avec,* one of the more consistently interesting journals of creative writing. In these two chapbooks, Chadwick again demonstrates (as she did in *Enemy Clothing*) she's as good a writer of short fiction as she is an editor. *Oeuvres* is a story about a woman who links herself with a man obsessed by the mysterious Arthur Cravan (1887-1920?), Dadaist poet, boxer, and husband of the more talented Mina Loy. Against her better judgment, the narrator moves in with the Cravan wannabe. Chadwick's affectless prose perfectly captures the despair of a lonely woman who links herself to a man merely because his life seems more interesting than hers, even if the man neglects her.

Persistent Disturbances consists of seven brief stories, each a study in anomie: a recital of a couple's tense visit to their parents, a hair-raising encounter between a woman and a friend of her lover's at the London Zoo, an increasingly involuted account of a violin-and-piano recital, mostly written in the present tense. They are not epiphanic, like most stories, but instead convey a history of loneliness or depression—hence the title. What is most striking about Chadwick's stories is their silence: there is no dialogue in any of them, and the effect is like watching a black and white movie with the sound off. Many of Chadwick's characters are bookish types, who assuage their anomie with a book because "print is such a comfort, even when what is written is not pleasant, not pretty." Chadwick's chapbooks offer a similar dour comfort. [Steven Moore]

*

Dale Peck. *The Law of Enclosures.* Farrar, Straus & Giroux, 1995. 306 pp. $23.00.

I must write a few words about this haunting novel. Although it is, on the surface, a deeply moving, grim work—a work about the loss of youth, the repetitiousness of married life; the cruelties of noncommunications—it is also an attempt to convey that "law of enclosures" which rules our lives.

The novel contains three parts: "The Bough Breaks," "Lamentations," and "Red Deer." Each part is a variation on the metaphor of *enclosure.* The first, for example, begins with an italicized passage in which the child, Beatrice, believes that she is separated from her parents: *"she sensed that if she somehow managed to penetrate the thin membrane which separated her body from theirs she would drown, and so she never poked too hard, just sat and watched, listened, silently."* The child is trapped in her body and mind; she doesn't have the *words* to describe her parents' lovemaking. The pattern begins: the entire novel is a body work (a work about the decaying body). Beatrice eventually meets Henry (in college) and falls in "love"—if that's the word—with his deformed head, the brain tumor he calls "Candy" (can die). Henry's body is linked to words. Death is "a word which meant nothing more than its definition." But what is the definition? The novel, then, becomes a meditation, a lamentation about the inadequacies of matter (body) and language. It is reflexive. It is obsessive to the point that Peck's words are more "alive" than the "bodies" they describe. And thus he makes us feel *pain:* "She concentrated on her physical pain and did nothing to relieve it. . . ." And the pain encloses us so that we fear it, fear our own skin.

Part 2 suddenly becomes a memoir. Peck writes about his early years. He realizes that his pain has created Beatrice and Henry, that art does not free him from his own *enclosures*, from the prison of his consciousness. Part 3 links the "red deer"—the redness of blood—to Henry in an unnerving manner. Henry is a red deer shot by hunters. And although at first we begin to worry that Peck is overdoing things, that he is thrusting his words (his metaphors, his painful puns—read deer) at us, he somehow captivates us. And in the final count-down—the prose poems move from ten to one—Peck redeems himself. Despite the fact that he insists at one point that "Beatrice" and "Henry" are merely words, he has made them live, bleed, die. [Irving Malin]

*

Shusaku Endo. *Deep River*. Trans. Van C. Gessel. New Directions, 1995. 216 pp. Paper: $10.95.

Deep River explores isolation, loneliness, and the possibilities of rebirth and reincarnation, or what one character calls the "transport to another realm." As in his earlier fiction, Endo evinces a deep concern with the intersection of Christianity and Eastern pantheisms as well as a continued challenge to Chris-tianity in his belief that the kernel of the sin also contains the seed for redemp-tion.

The novel interweaves the stories of four disaffected Japanese who have al-legedly come to India to tour the Buddhist temples, but who are, unbeknownst to themselves, on personal quests for reconciliation and/or redemption. Isobe, a Japanese businessman, searches for his reincarnated wife, having so promised as she slid into a coma. Kiguchi is a veteran of World War II and the Highway of Death in Burma, an experience so profound that he is unable to empathize with those who have not. Numada is a writer of children's stories and is miracu-lously recovering from a terminal illness. His retreat from the world is such that his primary social engagements are with birds, dogs, and cats. Finally, there is Mitsuko, who lives the life of Thérèse Desqueyroux, a character from the nov-els of François Mauriac, rather than risk herself in sincere interactions with the men she encounters.

For varying reasons they remain in the city of Varanasi while the tour con-tinues without them. Here, with the waters of the Ganges teeming with living and dead, with bathers and funereal processions, is the site of their possible redemptions. A bitter tour guide, a pair of carping newlyweds, an old friend/ victim of Mitsuko's who has become Christ-like, and the assassination of Indira Gandhi (for bringing too much harmony to the fractional Hindus, Sikhs, and Buddhists) provide a gross background against which we can measure loneli-ness and despair.

Readers familiar with Endo have probably encountered him through *Silence* (1966), a dark and deeply disturbing rendering of the persecution of Christians in seventeenth-century Japan, or *The Samurai* (1980), his novel depicting squabbles between the Jesuits and Franciscans as they vie for the souls of the Japanese. While *Deep River* shares these earlier concerns, Endo has turned inward; the questions have taken a decidedly personal turn, as have the possibilities of reconciliation and rebirth. In this way, *Deep River* complements his masterpiece, *Scandal* (1988), which concerns the multiple aspects of identity and sin as they are revealed in the disengaged live(s) of an elderly writer and his dopplegänger. [Rick Henry]

*

Marcel Cohen. *The Peacock Emperor Moth.* Trans. Cid Corman. Burning Deck, 1995. 106 pp. Paper: $8.00.

I find that I keep returning to Burning Deck, the press that dares to publish odd, noncommercial books printed in beautiful typefaces. The texts are selected by the distinguished Rosmarie and Keith Waldrop; they recognize outrageous, transgressive talent. Thus I am not surprised to admire their latest offering. Cohen's texts—short stories? prose poems?—are translated by Cid Corman. The texts haunt me.

Perhaps all of these texts deal with the problematics of identity, interpretation, writing itself. Cohen manages to write a few lines that say more than long novels dealing with similar themes. (And Corman, an excellent poet in his own language, is able to capture the tentative, probing, and final smash of Cohen's lines).

I'll select just one of Cohen's texts—which, by the way, remind me of the aphorisms of Kafka, Jabès, and Edson. Here it is: "In his bedroom a child avenges a humiliation by ripping off fifteen centimetres of wallpaper above the dado, then, feeling this isn't payment enough, empties half the contents of his pen upon the carpeting." The one sentence is about the relationship between guilt (or revenge) and writing. How much can writing save him and us from the wounds we bare? How much can we create by destroying the self? What is the linkage between art and pain? These questions are not answered. The style itself is elliptical: I notice that the (in?)action takes place in a "bedroom," a hallucinatory chamber. I see that, in a way, the child humiliates himself to avenge a humiliation by others. Art is produced by such paradoxical, ironic circular "knowledge."

So is criticism. I am "ripping off" Cohen's text. My explication tries to account for its power; but my account, by necessity, "empties" the fullness of his text. The total effect becomes reflexive and duplicitous. It, therefore, suggests there is *never enough* humiliation, "ripping off," to capture the "figures in the carpet." [Irving Malin]

*

Kirk Hampton. *The Moonhare.* York, 1996. 222 pp. Paper: $19.95.

Austin has more than its share of good science fiction writers: Chad Oliver, Bruce Sterling, Howard Waldrop, William Browning Spencer, and now a new member of the club, Kirk Hampton. Hampton's work may not come as easily to the average fan's notice because he has broken the rule (broken by the others on the list, though not as severely) of not following the mode of that most reactionary of all genres. Hampton has gone where few have gone before into the range of the Etym, and written an SF novel in the wake of the *Wake*. *The Moonhare* follows the quest of "deatective" Dann Quuluyr for his wayward daughter lost on the planet Wemm. Wemm is a hallucinatory landscape/mindscape controlled by the alien Hophounds, who have not only removed the great number of techno-goodies that Wemmites once enjoyed—they have removed the ability of anyone to make planned overt actions that are not suitably concealed as art. If you don't act in a sufficiently suprarational manner they'll come along and swallow you in a Moonhare.

Dann had run away while a teenager, setting the mythic pattern for his daughter's run. Dann's own description shows the instability of Wemm—not only as alien landscape but also as alien wordscape: "So as a teenager I ran away. You have to understand Wemm and the strange, disembulpeird weirld that we lived in then, to conceive how shocking that was." Dann has to be deatective, you have to look for the goddess Etym while looking for her daughter and your daughter. Can any man know what Wemm want? Can he manage to get the planet disembulped? Can he bring the plethora of machines out of their state of xembulpkt?

Hampton manages the adventure tale, the wonder tale, the meditation on reality and language tale all at once. The energy and playfulness of this novel, which you have to read aloud (or Dann won't sound any cooler than any other detective), will slow its reception, but guarantee its survival. [Don Webb]

*

Richard Meltzer. *The Night (alone).* Little, Brown, 1995. 304 pp. $22.95.

Richard Meltzer is most famous, or notorious, for *The Aesthetics of Rock,* a seriocomic exploration of philosophical themes in rock and roll first published in 1970. That was a landmark volume that influenced and encouraged a generation of rock critics—and a book that Meltzer says (in the introduction to the recent reprinting) that he is tired of people bringing up at the expense of his more recent efforts. These efforts include poetry, architecture criticism, and autobiography, as well as *L.A. Is the Capital of Kansas,* perhaps the best book ever written on the myriad tangents that comprise Los Angeles. Like his other prose and poetry, *The Night (alone)* eschews conventional novelistic storytelling for a patchwork of impressions, experiences, and moments of transition in the life of its multimoniker narrator, presented in a breathtakingly fertile prose style that is part William Burroughs in its sexual frankness and part James Joyce in its verbal fluidity, as in the passage titled "I Never Fucked My Sister," which starts out "normally"—"I inched close, crept close with my brains pounding and my blood pounding and I reached 'round and found / felt her titnotyet, cupped cloth of titnotyet, but I can't lie, I won't lie, I probed not between (not beneath) (not behind) for her fawn warm particular"—and descends into a long passage of ecstasy and madness describing the girl's sexual parts ("sour calm sheet hot gumthumbed thighhigh rumpplump footloose shoeleathersquidsatin"). Though Meltzer has been toiling in relative obscurity in recent years, *The Night (alone)* confirms that he is not letting anonymity prevent him from exploring the (uncommercial) possibilities of the novel form. [D. K. Holm]

*

Abigail Stone. *Recipes from the Dump.* Norton, 1995. 271 pp. $18.00.

I read this novel the way I ate leftover stuffing after Thanksgiving—in furtive guilty intervals, marveling at its melded variety of textures and flavors, and never quite shedding the feeling I should have been doing something else. Its narrator, Gabby Fulbriten, is a single jack-Mormon mother in her thirties. She has a hard time paying her bills. Her obsessions include her weight and her ambivalent hunger for a man. She lives on the outskirts of a town called Leadbelly, Vermont, and her house sits by the dump. She quilts and cooks and listens to Shakespeare on tape, hunting (as the book jacket flap indicates) for "the essential ingredients in a cluttered world."

Gabby is sharply observant, and the novel is quirky and true enough to have spared her author the expected murder-by-blurbs: invidious comparisons with that toxic commercial classic, *How to Make an American Quilt,* for instance. This book dramatizes the material and spiritual quotidian challenges faced by its narrator very succinctly: "When J.D. wanted me to sew him a Ninja Turtle suit for Halloween," Gabby (his mother) tells us, "all I said was 'I can't. We don't have enough money for the shell part.' " Like many in the book, this line seems nonessential, a complete throwaway—but the detail-oriented rendering is just right, and it makes you stop to consider: a lesser writer would have stopped the sentence after "enough money." Patched into the narrative are imaginary texts of personal ads ("WANTED TO RENT. LARGE SUNNY MAN WITH VIEW OF THE INTERIOR.") and recipes that tend to reflect the surrealism of domestic circumstance and the narrator's ability to make something out of an immediate preoccupation. Sometimes, as with the recipe for "Amish Friendship Bread" ("you get the starter, called the 'mother,' from a friend. . . . Day 1: put mother in a large bowl"), the narrative landscape conjures successfully in an American Gothic mode.

Gabby is offered to us as a sort of polyphonic flea market, which is unsettling at times. None of the other characters seem to have much reality, even when their dialogues or letters or actions are reported directly by Gabby. On the other hand, when she considers a news photo of a bird covered with crude oil somewhere in the Middle East, its misery-sickened gaze makes direct contact, an almost unbelievable reminder to narrator and reader alike that we live in such a world. Gabby is a gabby female equivalent of Stevens's "Man on the Dump" insofar as she "beats and beats for that which [she] believes." Yet her prose portrait is also an unstructured grab bag of smart lines and self-absorption. I grazed right on through, and finished feeling stuffed yet still hungry. But PS: the author photo at the end is funky and confrontational, just like the book in its better moments. [Marisa Januzzi]

*

Arnold Skemer. *D.* Phyrgian Press, 1995. 66 pp. Paper: $6.00.

D uses the experience of looking at photographs (family photographs) to meditate upon time. But, of course, it's not just time that's the focus of this meditation: it concerns, as well, people and objects—life and death. As the novella unfolds, we learn the narrator's mother, Dora (hence, the "D"), has died. Looking over the photographs, the unnamed narrator finds "the only grist for speculation for the musing melancholic." He is (to pun on Olson's phrase) "an archeologist of mourning." This means that he is left to read the material traces of existences that preceded his. But here, the fact that he is a family archeologist introduces a distinction. The material traces speak of those who had to precede him in order for him to be here at all: "the totality of events leading up to his conception." Totality is always staggering but, in this case, it cannot hide the subtext of mourning: he too will die. He is, thus, a "profound tragic cognizant of the continuum."

Yet the continuum does something else as well. Much as it gives the sense of a totality, it undermines it. If there were totality it would not include him; where he is included, there is no totality. This gives us the second reason why the cognizant is "tragic." The best position for understanding is not the best position for living. It takes death to reveal the life: "It is only then [i.e., after death] that dimensions and nuances of decades fall into place, forming a complete picture of sad regrets and mental burdens." Consequently, living involves a measure of meaninglessness, as well as a measure of secrecy. Of course, we can also see this as a metaphysical reason for the continuum. Someone else is needed in order to understand the life. Perhaps this mirrors the relation of book to reader. And, in that, let me say that *D* is a short but full book, displaying Skemer's fluid density and philosophical probing, in need of a reader who will think her way through. [Bruce Campbell]

*

Delia Poey, ed. *Out of the Mirrored Garden: New Fiction by Latin American Women.* Anchor Books, 1996. 222 pp. Paper: $12.00.

Like dangling études. . . . The Latina writers in Delia Poey's pristine anthology, many worldly and accomplished, introduce shapes and shadings of cultural irony, ruptures, outpourings, and myths. Her title for this work, *Out of the Mirrored Garden,* is meant to be interpreted by readers, as Poey points out in her introduction, which also emphasizes the significance of the soil underlying these fictions. The stories gathered here puncture wounds and wiles ranging from the otherworldly to the domestic. The reader is invited to look through one window after another at the lapses between traditional boundaries and the urgent necessity to foresee a break in the glass.

Each writer is piercing through some mold, injustice, or timeless scenery. A few simply construct pathways to explore a recurrence such as Elena Castedo's carriage horse for a narrator in "Ice Cream." When the setting is the Latin American family, whether a tribe of sisters in Carmen Naranjo's "Over and Over," or the *Auntesque* of Barbara Jacob's "Aunt Luisita," one sees a large cast of connected characters that can both delight and suffocate.

Particularly memorable is Carmen Boullosa's animated consciousness in "So Disappear"; her exasperated narrator is impassioned by an unliteral bunch of "children" whom she is utterly fond of, not knowing what she would do without their incessant wildness to provoke her. Fans of Julieta Campos will enjoy her moody "Allegories," which begins, "There are stage sets which by themselves tell a story. Places that, on being described, narrate themselves." Symbolic discord animates Rosario Ferré's transformative doll "Amalia," Algina Lubitch Domenco's mother obsessed with "Bottles," and Angela Hernandez's water-crystal-loving "Teresa Irene." To counterbalance these surreal tales, "A Family Man" is Vlady Kogiangich's earthy incidental love story turned tragic; a contemporary woman on horse and a city man with car cross each other's seemingly vast paths on Sunday escapades yet consistently misunderstand their inevitable attraction. In "Aunt Elvira," Angeles Mastretta becomes a rebellious and clever heroine in spite of a framed abduction. The most jarring and realistic is Rosa Maria Britton's "Death Lies on the Cots"; Ana Berta fades in and out of her recent past, which becomes her bloody trail of tears while she reels in a hospital waiting room with impassive attendants.

Poey's selections imprint unusual essences, whether fidgety, fleeting, or inflamed. Narrators speak *out* of their own reflections and so create worlds in which to mirror them. The storytellers here have given them the reigns and the rites to captivate. [Alystyre Julian]

*

Staszek. *Three-Hand Jax and Other Spells*. Permeable Press, 1996. 176 pp. Paper: $9.95.

Mellifluent and often possessed writing by someone named Staszek ("Stan" in Polish, we're told) about one gay man's activity and thoughts in the pomo condition; five prose pieces and one play that has to be some of the finest queer writing I've come across in a long time. What I like best is that Staszek doesn't deconstruct his childhood and avow his first love and coming-out awakening like too much work I've come across lately. Instead, we dive into his world headfirst—a plunge that for me, being straight, makes Staszek's community like a foreign land that's attractive to explore. I'm sure this book will have no problem being embraced by its target audience as distinct and piquant, bringing the author scores of devout readers. The title piece, "Three-Hand Jax," concerns the book's cover photo of a model's perfect buttocks, more photos of which appear within the text; the narrator happens to meet and connect, occasionally, with the actual model of the famous photographs by Paul Dahlquist. In a time of AIDS, the lovers are conscious of the necessity of latex, but find mutual masturbation much more stimulating than plain old sex. It *is* an AIDS story, as this model discovers he is infected and has fewer T-cells than fingers to count on; this is not, however, your usual, sappy "My Story of a Lover Who Died of AIDS" brand of prose that has been polluting the print media for the past few years. The final piece, a novella-length prose poem, "Weird Daddy," is a monologue over a phone conversation between two men—again, that distance (phone sex) being much more preferable than a tangible, physical connection. The heart of this humanity is explored in the unapproachable fear of true coupling. [Michael Hemmingson]

*

Joseph Roth. *The Radetzky March*. Trans. Joachim Neugroschel. Overlook, 1995. 331 pp. Paper: $13.95.

With NATO troops now encamped in Bosnia to enforce the peace plan, it is fitting that a new translation of Joseph Roth's *The Radetzky March* has recently been published (with a foreword by Nadine Gordimer). Roth's novel traces four generations of the Trotta family from a young Slovenian peasant, who quite by accident saves Emperor Franz Joseph's life, through his male descendants that include a rigid district captain and his son, Carl Joseph, on whom most of the action centers.

This is a novel, first issued in 1932, about Slovenians, Croats, Hungarians, Germans, Russians, and Austrians; about the dissolution of the Austro-Hungarian empire and its glorious Franz-Joseph, pictured, finally, as a doddering oaf with a "drop hanging from his nose." It is about history, memory, forgetfulness, and the foolishness of "honor" and politics.

And, in perhaps a primary sense, it is a novel about the inability of men to either know enough about their own emotions or to say what needs to be said to each other. The rigidity of the conventions that determine the links between fathers and sons—one Trotta after another writes family letters that are strictly by the book and therefore say nothing—is especially poignant, although male friendships also founder on an incapacity to convey love. Men, in the Trotta clan, are to be "pale, terse, and resolute." It is not that the Trotta males have nothing circulating in their hearts; they do. But it is an inchoate, inarticulated mass of feeling usually hidden by the strict etiquette of military and family, institutions that none of the Trottas, try as they might, are able to escape.

Roth's novel weaves a detailed tapestry of the Trotta clan as a kind of emblem of the Empire, but the story also transcends the immediate historical circumstances and gestures toward the even deeper changes wrought by modernity. "If a life was snuffed out from the host of the living," he writes, "another life did not instantly replace it and make people forget the deceased. . . . But everything that had once existed left its traces, and people lived on memories just as they now live on the ability to forget quickly and emphatically." This attention to the disappearance of the object reminds me of Cézanne, Rilke, and Benjamin, and reading *The Radetzky March* recalls the fragility of individual lives, the childish senility of grand designs of Empire, and the necessity to make the attempt to remember. [Gray Kochhar-Lindgren]

*

Norman Conquest, ed. *By Any Means: An Avant-Pop Anthology.* HOB Press (P.O. Box 180158, Coronado, CA 92178-0158), 1995. 80 pp. Paper: $12.00.

OK, since everyone seems to be so quick to hop on this Avant-Pop bandwagon, social satirist Norman Conquest has released a limited artist's edition of what may be the definitive Avant-Pop anthology: a collection of photocopied copyright pages of various books by authors known and unknown, famous and obscure. Conquest defies the law of "no part of this book may be reproduced in any form" by reproducing the very pages that deny him this act. There's Kathy Acker, Stephen Wright, Derek Pell, Susan Daitch, Lance Olsen, William Vollmann, Thomas Pynchon, Eurudice, and even (gulp!) myself, and that's just a small sample. The mock introduction is dedicated to Larry McCaffery, infested with dozens of footnotes, even a reference to a fictitious book, *The Collected Footnotes of Larry McCaffery,* supposedly published in 1993 by Osford University Press. This is certainly quite the novelty and a fine addition to collectors of rare, limited editions. [Michael Hemmingson]

*

Caradoc Evans. *Nothing to Pay.* New Directions, 1995. 237 pp. Paper: $11.95.

New Directions's Revived Modern Classics series has largely tended to stick with some of the safer, more marketable choices—authors who are relatively well known, critically current, or who are likely to be accessible to readers. This, however, is not the case with Caradoc Evans's *Nothing to Pay.* Evans was never terribly well known outside of Wales (where he was hated), and the little attention he received fell to his stories, in which religion is seen as vicious and the Welsh as thick and scheming. *Nothing to Pay* and his other novels have been unavailable in America since the 1930s.

Nothing to Pay is the story of Amos Morgan's life in the drapier trade. Amos is hardly the sort of person that one would care to identify with, and indeed the rest of the world seems little better. Amos is greedy to extremes, sees religion as a tool to justify love of money, and cares only about amassing as much money as possible. Though he keeps a fortune pinned to the pages of his Bible, he lives on scraps so as to amass more.

Most of the book is spent with Amos in the drapier trade, trying to be a perfect cringer, always willing to turn on his fellow employees if to do so will improve his lot. The drapiery industry is shown in a scathing light as well, as a destroyer of the human will, and Evans draws in merciless detail the conditions for shop assistants.

The strength of the book comes not so much in the social critique or in the exposure of religion as in the personal extravagance of Evans's language. Evans has created an almost private language made of Welsh transliterated into English and mixed and warped with biblical phrases. The blunt language naturally meshes with the harshness and brutality of the world Evans portrays. There is not an ounce of emotion wasted, everything falling to Evans's unblinking eye. A book surprisingly modern and challenging, Evans's *Nothing to Pay* is well worth a second look. [Brian Evenson]

*

Wayne Karlin, Le Minh Khue, and Truong Vu, eds. *The Other Side of Heaven: Post-War Fiction by Vietnamese and American Writers.* Curbstone Press, 1995. xvii + 411 pp. Paper: $17.95.

The Other Side of Heaven collects thirty-eight stories and novel excerpts from as many Vietnamese, Vietnamese-American, and American writers, many of them veterans. As the collection's subtitle reveals, these stories concern war's aftermath, the way war lingers on in those who fought and for those who loved or knew those who fought. Published on the twentieth anniversary of the end of the Vietnam War (what in Vietnam is known as the American War), these are stories that, as Wayne Karlin explains in his introduction, chart the continuing "cost of the war to both countries" even while helping former enemies "suddenly become human beings to each other."

Working mostly with varieties of realism, including magic realism, but offering as well a couple of forays into Gothic horror and allegory, the writers gathered here do much to achieve the reconciliation that can come, again in Karlin's words, "from a mutual recognition of pain and loss." Toward that end, for American readers the stories by Vietnamese writers are essential reading, and if I do not set down their names, it is only because I doubt the exercise would be terribly meaningful although most are, in Vietnam, much-admired writers with long lists of publications and honors. American contributors include many familiar names—Tim O'Brien, Robert Stone, Philip Caputo, Bobbie Ann Mason—as well as some less familiar but equally striking voices. Yet what strikes me is how often I came upon a story that, superficial details aside, could have been written by someone on either side of the conflict. Whose sentiments, friend or foe, for instance, are these: "He had found a life beyond the war after all, but in it he was still sitting in darkness, armed, enraged, waiting"; "none of us displayed our citations on the wall or pinned our medals on our chests"; "that was a tranquil afternoon, when the war was only a blur far outside the feeling of a heart in love"?

Gloria Emerson observes in her epilogue that this is an anthology that allows us a close look at "the men and women who would not submit to our fearful technology and firepower," and this is true. It is equally true that *The Other Side of Heaven* may perform a similar service for American veterans, providing a corrective vision not so much for Vietnamese readers (how many Vietnamese readers of this book are there likely to be?) as for the rest of us with our many and often ugly preconceptions about Vietnam and those, on our side, who fought there. [Brooke Horvath]

*

Robert Weninger. *Framing a Novelist: Arno Schmidt Criticism 1970-1994.* Camden House, 1995. 148 pp. $52.95.

In Germany, critical activity on Arno Schmidt (1914-79) has been running at industrial levels for several decades now, comparable to the Anglo-American Joyce industry, and for much the same reason: Schmidt is often called the German Joyce because of the lexical density, range of reference, and experimentation in his works, and he has attracted a core following that supports a good deal of publication. Schmidt's achievement, if not as great as Joyce's, is certainly more prodigious: twenty novels and novellas, dozens of short stories, two literary biographies, nearly two dozen translations of authors ranging from James Fenimore Cooper and Wilkie Collins to William Faulkner and mystery writer Stanley Ellin, and six volumes of some of the liveliest and most innovative literary criticism I've ever read (which exists in translation in manuscript only at this time). *Caveat lector:* these remarks are hardly impartial, for I have been Schmidt's American editor and consider him to be the best thing to come out of Germany since Christa Päffgen changed her name to Nico and joined the Velvet Underground.

While Schmidt has attracted some critical attention in the U.S. and England —most notably Michael Minden's book-length study (Cambridge, 1982) and our spring 1988 issue—the bulk of the criticism has understandably been written in German, all of which is intelligently analyzed in Weninger's splendid new book. Writing for an Anglo-American audience that knows no German and that knows Schmidt only from the handful of translations that have appeared so far, Weninger first provides an informative overview of Schmidt's life and works before breaking down Schmidt criticism into various categories. Before 1970, most of this was limited to book reviews and occasional essays and followed typical approaches of the time. Everything changed in 1970, the year Schmidt published *Zettel's Traum,* a massive Übernovel (1300 pages, 13" x 17") that immediately became Germany's *Finnegans Wake* (the nonstandard apostrophe in Schmidt's title imitates the nonstandard absence of one in Joyce's) and attracted the kind of specialist who contributed to the old *A Wake Newslitter*—which, in fact, is where I first learned of Schmidt. (Schmidt's newsletter is playfully called the *Bargfelder Bote*—the "Bargfeld Bugle," after the town Schmidt lived in during the last twenty years of his life). After 1970, Schmidt criticism proliferated, and even critics who hated his work felt compelled to deal with him. Weninger guides the reader through the secondary literature in an evenhanded manner, pointing out the inadequacies of some criticism and the insights of others, and in the process provides a fine introduction to Schmidt's work itself. A separate chapter focuses on the critical reception of two novels, an early one called *The Stony Heart* (1956; scheduled for English publication in 1997) and his last completed novel, translated as *Evening Edged in Gold* (1975; 1980). Even if you don't have a particular interest in Schmidt, Weninger's book is an instructive account of how scholarship develops around an author, how it builds on previous scholarship, gets sidetracked by critical fads and trends, or (more recently) takes what Stanley Fish has called an anti-professionalist stance—that is, denigrating previous scholarship as inadequate and/or biased.

As Schmidt's works become available to Anglo-American readers—the third in Dalkey Archive's four-volume edition of his collected early fiction will appear this fall—critical appetites are sure to be whetted over this fascinating author. For anyone writing on Schmidt in the future, Weninger's *Framing the Novelist* will be an indispensable tool. [Steven Moore]

*

Phillip Herring. *Djuna: The Life and Work of Djuna Barnes.* Viking, 1995. 386 pp. $29.95.

Djuna Barnes has taken scholars of modernism to their knees, in both senses of the expression. Enough biographical material has circulated to confirm its importance for students of her allusive and elusive work, but much of it is informally conceived and, in the case of Andrew Field's gossipy biography, poorly documented. Thus Herring has performed a great service for Barnes readers, supplementing Hank O'Neal's engrossing memoir and the reminiscences gathered in Mary Lynn Broe's essential collection with the first scholarly account of her turbulent life.

From many angles, this could not have been an easy book to write. Herring gives us a vivid picture of Djuna's childhood in the unconventional and sexually eccentric Barnes ménage, allowing us to see something beyond mere lunacy in the bigamous extended family she so obsessively revisited with hyperliterate bitterness. As a young girl Barnes was probably subjected to sexual violation at her father's behest. She found a degree of refuge in her relations with her grandmother Zadel Barnes, the sexual subcurrents of which seem to have carried her into passionate adult liaisons with individuals (most notably Thelma Wood) who reminded her of Zadel. Like Louisa May Alcott, Djuna was forced to harness her writerly energies at an extremely tender age in order to fill the financial breach occasioned by her father's choices (inactivity, except in fertile beds). Yet these circumstances made Barnes into a writer, and Herring's meticulously researched sketch of her resourceful, magnetic, and widely published grandmother is particularly helpful in showing us how this came to be.

Knowing that Barnes was reared in upstate New York does not begin to hint at the literary connections with which the poet and journalist Zadel Barnes constructed her career (and awakened her granddaughter's vocation). Zadel had ties to the radical salon of Lady Wilde (Oscar's mother), was friendly with Eleanor Marx, Robert Browning, and some of the pre-Raphaelites, and also managed to elicit literary and financial support from established American writers like John

Greenleaf Whittier and Jack London. This part of the biography succeeds at situating the creative efforts of the Barneses in a political as well as social context. I missed this textured approach somewhat in consideration of Barnes's later writings; though excellent on the subject of her journalism, the book offers very little analysis of Barnes as bisexual homophobe, allowing her to stand as an enigmatic character among eccentric acquaintances without assessing her literary and personal debts (acknowledged and unacknowledged) to the broader social forces that fanned modernist aesthetic flames. (A laconic index entry reads: "Feminist movement, xviii, 12.") And although Barnes's affinities for Jacobean tragedy and the plays of Synge are explored, we get very little sense of Barnes as a reader. Herring links her ably with Joyce and Eliot, but does not give any indication of the impact of the *Journal of Marie Bashkirtseff* on the young Barnes, nor does he pursue her literary affinities with two of her closest friends, Mina Loy and Emily Holmes Coleman, influential but unsung writers who turned out their best work during the *Nightwood* years.

Nevertheless, Herring's biographical readings of the major novels and plays are skillfully handled. I expect he will be criticized for the acknowledgment that he has occasionally drawn biographical evidence from the writings, but I think it is an entirely defensible strategy, and very carefully done. If anything, he may draw too broadly from the Barnes–Coleman correspondence, but this serves to suggest that the figure of Emily Coleman (secretary to Emma Goldman, experimental prose writer, later a convert to the Catholic Worker Movement) deserves a hearing and a biography of her own. *Djuna*'s notes are a trove of little-known archival resources, and it should provoke renewed consideration of the doings of the Baroness Elsa von Freytag Loringhoven and Charles Henri Ford, among others. This book is a valuable and much-needed scholarly biography of a brilliant writer who was said not to be on "speaking terms" with her own psyche. No one should be surprised if it is not the last. [Marisa Januzzi]

*

Djuna Barnes. *Poe's Mother: Selected Drawings.* Edited with an introduction by Douglas Messerli. Sun & Moon, 1995. 241 pp. $29.95. Carolyn Allen. *Following Djuna: Women Lovers and the Erotics of Loss.* Indiana Univ. Press, 1996. 142 pp. $35.00; paper: $13.95.

Sun & Moon continues its invaluable restoration work on Barnes's oeuvre with an extensive collection of her drawings. Although she illustrated many of her works, this is the first time they have been gathered for separate publication. The earliest date from Barnes's newspaper days, where her witty, Beardsleyesque sketches accompanied her even wittier profiles, interviews, and stories. (Many of these newspapers are disintegrating, and many of the drawings here come from microfilmed versions; given the situation, most look remarkably crisp.) The visual element is strong in all of Barnes's work, even in the non-illustrated *Nightwood,* so these drawings are an essential part of her artistic vision and it is useful to have them reproduced in such a handsome volume, accompanied, like most of Sun & Moon's Barnes books, with an informative introduction by Douglas Messerli.

Barnes scholars will also want to pick up Carolyn Allen's new book, for it not only offers perceptive readings of *Nightwood* and the "Little Girl" stories ("Cassation," "The Grande Malade," and the little-known "Dusie"), but traces the example of Barnes's exploration of lesbian power and loss in the fiction of Jeanette Winterson, Rebecca Brown, and the underrated Bertha Harris. [Steven Moore]

*

Michel Butor. *Improvisations on Butor: Transformations of Writing.* Ed. Lois Oppenheim. Trans. Elinor S. Miller. Univ. Press of Florida, 1996. 214 pp. $34.95.

During the 1980s the French novelist Michel Butor published three books of literary criticism called *Improvisations*, each one focused on a particular writer (Flaubert, Michaux, Rimbaud); in this fourth volume in the series he turns his attention to his own large body of writings. Based on a series of lectures he gave at the University of Geneva in 1991 before retiring, it functions as his intellectual autobiography. He has had quite a life: enduring World War II, the postwar excitement of French intellectual life, the development of the nouveau roman in the 1950s (of which Butor is a leading exemplar), the multimedia experiments encouraged by the 1960s, travels all across the world. But as the subtitle indicates, it is also a meditation on the way writing has changed in his lifetime because of new technologies, transcultural influences, and the example of other media. (Butor has worked extensively with musicians and visual artists.) It's as much a book of cultural studies as a study of his own writings, and for that reason it should appeal to a wider audience than Butor specialists. The translation is very supple, maintaining the conversational tone of the original lectures. [Steven Moore]

*

Richard Walsh. *Novel Arguments: Reading Innovative American Fiction.* Cambridge Univ. Press. 1995. 179 pp. No price given.

This dissertation, written for Tony Tanner, is a lucid, graceful, thoughtful study (in a distinguished series). It is a close reading of five texts: *The Dead Father, Flight to Canada, The Public Burning, How German Is It,* and Acker's *Don Quixote.* The readings are wonderfully acute; they are decidedly "new."

In his introduction Walsh notes his dissatisfaction with postmodernist jargon. He writes about his strategy and position: "The term 'argument,' then, contains both formal and substantial senses in exactly the right relation, that of complementary *aspects* of the same phenomenon." The statement gains greater clarity when Walsh explains in his first chapter that his texts, although apparently possessing linguistic "autonomy," somehow manage as well to lead readers into the "giddy void of . . . solipsism." He offers several versions of critical discussion—blaming the critics (the usual suspects) for not realizing that "post-modernism" is *about something*. The question, in effect, is *what is it about?* Criticism, itself, has obscured the answer to the questions—the question which, in effect, goes back to ancient times. For example, there is "history" in Abish's text—the World War II is in the text. There is "history" in Coover's text. But the emphasis in both novels lies somehow in my *consciousness*. Although he published his study before encountering *The Tunnel*—perhaps the most complex meditation on "evil"— he would have a rather difficult time coping with questions about "history" raised by a philosopher who has brooded his entire life on the *possible meanings* of self, memory, and so forth.

I'm still not convinced that Walsh has solved the questions raised. But I know that his book is profound. [Irving Malin]

*

Bin Ramke. *Massacre of the Innocents*. Univ. of Iowa Press, 1994. 83 pp. Paper: $10.95.

Bin Ramke is a collagist; inspired by Max Ernst and Joseph Cornell, he creates virtual worlds out of scraps of poetry and images lifted from glossy magazines, trash, and family albums. Like his collages, his poetry proposes a species of impossible optics—simultaneously microscopic and telescopic (and anamorphic, too). Ramke is not a "clever miniaturist" but invariably moves from finite cipher to cosmic equation, e.g.: "what harms us makes us mean." If the poet is a collagist, he is also a mathematician. And he is master of irreconcilables. Unique for their tender ironies and thoughtful sorrows, the poems are also apocalyptic. As though memory and the act of poetry were caustic, causing the poet and the world to dissolve. I can think of no writer who manages to convey *aware*—the fleetingness of things—as well as Ramke does, except for the great Murasaki Shikibu herself.

Acknowledging the darkest of dreams, the unholiest of terrors, and daring to name and number them, his gift is the gift of clairvoyance and sadness. The conjunction is engaging, utterly, and illuminating always. If Ramke is a consummate poet of despair, his themes the swiftly vanishing world, the terrible weight of being, the weight of history, of oblivion, of lovelessness—the poetry is invariably informed by self-irony and unceasing tenderness: life-giving, generous, and kind. This is not to say that Ramke is sentimental—a thing he *never* is:

> . . . and beauty is so lovely and nice
> hollowing out a nest of nerve
> while you live on air and ice.

Watcher and lover—if at a distance—the poet, fighting for air as the world disarticulates, offers his most precious things: his heart and his eyes on the altar of endings. If with an articulate gaze one could both reveal the wounds of the world and heal them, Ramke's poems would save us. [Rikki Ducornet]

The Diaries of Dawn Powell, 1931-1965. Edited by Tim Page. Steerforth, 1995. 513 pp. $32.00.

Almost forgotten until Gore Vidal "rediscovered" her in the eighties, Dawn Powell is enjoying an enviable posthumous career: most of her novels have been reprinted—Steerforth just reissued *The Locusts Have No King*—a biography is in the works (by Tim Page), and now her diaries have been published. The book will appeal to Powell fans, of course, and to those interested in the New York literary world of the 1930s through the sixties (she died in 1965). For readers of this journal, the book is valuable for its material on Felipe Alfau (subject of our spring 1993 issue), for whom so little biographical material exists that one is grateful for anything. Like many of the figures depicted in the *Diaries,* Alfau doesn't appear at his best here: he is described in an entry for 1938 as pro-fascist and anti-Semitic—not a word about his great novel *Locos,* published two years earlier—but he is also quoted on differences between Spain and America, the theme of his even greater novel, *Chromos,* which would be written ten years later. Nevertheless, Powell respected him: "Felipe Alfau, brilliant, dazzling mind, witty, Jesuitical, a mental performance similar only to Cummings, but a scholar—erudite, fascinating, above all a romantic about his Spain, fiercely patriotic, a figure out of a medieval romance, a lover of Toledo, of old Spain, valuable surely to his country—talked so brilliantly of Totalitarianism that is based on human weakness, human error, human conduct, that it almost convinced me."

I first heard of Dawn Powell as one of the reviewers of Gaddis's 1955 novel *The Recognitions,* one of those whom Jack Green designated a "bastard" for her condescending review. There's no mention of Gaddis here—perhaps he was left on the cutting-room floor (this book represents about three-fourths of the extant diaries)—but almost every other writer of the time is mentioned in one way or another, making *The Diaries of Dawn Powell* a valuable resource for students of the first half of twentieth-century American literature. [Steven Moore]

*

Harvey Pekar and Joyce Brabner. *Our Cancer Year.* Illustrated by Frank Stack. Four Walls Eight Windows, 1994. Paper: $17.95.

Readers of Harvey Pekar's influential autobiographical comic book, the ironically titled *American Splendor,* are used to hearing the irascible author gripe about the little things in life: we've heard him kvetching as he serves on jury duty, wheedles his magazine editors, and hassles his co-workers at the Cleveland Veterans Administration hospital. One long story details his travails when he loses an Italo Svevo book, another the calamity of a pair of lost glasses; as Pekar says in one story, "I consistently get shook up over nothing, over less than nothing." In 1990 Pekar finally got something to complain about: a lump in his leg was diagnosed as cancerous lymphoma. Sometimes harrowing, sometimes lyrical, and always deeply affecting, the resulting graphic novel, *Our Cancer Year,* is the story of how Pekar and his wife, Joyce Brabner, struggled with the physical and psychological stresses of the disease and its (so far) successful treatment.

Our Cancer Year is structured around two intertwining plot threads, Harvey's illness and Joyce's friendship with a group of young peace activists (*Our Cancer Year* is as much Brabner's story as Pekar's). Brabner, author of the documentary comic books *Brought to Light* and *Real War Stories,* attempts to keep her sanity and her connections to the world outside of Harvey's cancer by helping her young friends (some of whom live in Israel and the Occupied Territories) cope with the escalation of the Gulf War. The theme of the limits of self-sacrifice runs through both plot lines: as Harvey becomes increasingly debilitated from chemotherapy, Joyce eventually realizes that her Cambodian friend Kimmie's desire to make everything all right for the teenagers mirrors her own longtime caregiving instincts, and that both of them need to accept help from a larger community.

Pekar has spent nearly two decades showing what a frustrating and aggravating person he can be, and *Our Cancer Year* is not a story of the ennobling effects of suffering; in a mortal crisis as in his daily routine Pekar is resolutely himself. Harvey characteristically chooses a short but harsh course of therapy that leaves him prone to episodes of psychosomatic paralysis and bouts of excruciating pain. The same honesty that *American Splendor* routinely brings to the mundane happenings of daily life permeates *Our Cancer Year* as Harvey considers committing suicide, Joyce mourns the loss of her husband's body hair to chemotherapy, and Joyce slaps the prostrate Harvey in rage and frustration at the helplessness of them both. These scenes are depicted vividly in Frank Stack's versatile and evocative drawings; readers accustomed to the solid lines and straightforward realism of many of *American Splendor's* regular artists may be startled at first by the impressionistic style of Stack's art, but the densely textured, sometimes highly stylized pictures create the powerful effect of pages from a diary or first-person journal. *Our Cancer Year* displays the graphic novel medium at its sophisticated best, and, eschewing the uplifting clichés of "the disease novel," Pekar, Brabner, and Stack have demonstrated that comics created with intelligence and unflinching candor can be deeply moving literature. [Joseph Witek]

Reference Books

We rarely review reference books, but several have appeared recently that can be recommended to the student of contemporary literature. (And believe me, after eight years of editing a scholarly journal, I can tell you that critics don't use reference books nearly enough—to verify names, spelling, dates, etc.—and would be well-advised to pick up one of the following books instead of some newfangled excursion in literary theory.) The reference book having the greatest use is Merriam-Webster's new *Encyclopedia of Literature* (1,236 pp., $39.95). This has everything: concise, intelligent entries on authors, titles, characters, critics, literary terms, mythology, movements, prizes—everyone and everything from Jeppe Aakjær to the *Zuo zhuan*, with an impressive number of contemporary writers (e.g., Sorrentino, Mosley, Brophy). It also gives the proper pronunciation of names, so if you've always wondered how to pronounce Kazantzakis or Saint-Exupéry, this will set you straight. The book is nicely illustrated—there's a pretty photo of Nancy Mitford, for example, and one of Pirandello typing with one finger—and beautifully designed. This should be on every critic's bookshelf, and in every literature major's working library, right next to that compact edition of the *OED*.

As comprehensive but focused on a single subject, *The New Oxford Companion to French Literature* (865 pp., $49.95) is an authoritative guide to every aspect of French literature, including francophone writing from outside France. Contemporary authors are well represented: Jacques Roubaud has an entry as long as Dumas *fils*. There are numerous extraliterary entries as well, such as cinema and painting. Edited by Peter France, this is an invaluable aid to studying French literature.

More specialized yet is HarperCollins's *Reader's Encyclopedia of Eastern European Literature* (605 pp., $50.00). Consisting almost entirely of author entries, the book ranges from medieval Bulgarian authors to contemporary postmodernists like Péter Esterházy. Authors who have been translated into English have separate bibliographies at the end of their entries, which also lists anthologies and any critical studies. Following the authors is a section devoted to anonymous works, and three indexes. A pronunciation guide would have been useful, but anyone interested in Eastern European literature will find this book essential.

The reference book with perhaps the most relevance to readers of this journal is Peter Parker's *Reader's Guide to the Twentieth-Century Novel* (748 pp., $35.00, Oxford Univ. Press). The book is organized chronologically, with 500- to 1500-word entries for the most interesting novels written in English published in a given year (up to 1993). It can be enlightening to have certain books set in a context of what else was being published at the time. The year 1955, for example, has entries for Beckett's *Molloy*, Bowen's *A World of Love*, Donleavy's *Ginger Man*, Gaddis's *Recognitions*, Greene's *Quiet American*, Lewis's *Magician's Nephew*, Mitchison's *To the Chapel Perilous*, Moore's *Lonely Passion of Judith Hearne*, Nabokov's *Lolita*, Powell's *Acceptance World*, Tolkien's *Lord of the Rings*, and Waugh's *Officers and Gentlemen*. The entries are critical as well as informative, giving proper due to innovators like Firbank, and while one could carp about omissions of certain favorite writers or books—especially American writers, given the British bias of the editor—there are enough unfamiliar titles here to keep one reading for a lifetime. [Steven Moore]

Back in Print

Alexander Theroux's 1981 masterpiece *Darconville's Cat* has just been reissued in paperback (Holt, $16.00). I've exhausted my superlatives on this book—see my introduction to our Theroux/West issue (Spring 1991); it's a Gothic cathedral of a novel, unparalleled in contemporary fiction. This edition has the added attraction of a few revisions by the author. [Steven Moore]

Books Received

Abiel, Rami. *You and No Other.* JKSM Publications (Norway), 1996. Paper: no price given. (F)

Abram, David. *The Spell of the Sensuous: Perception and Language in a More-Than-Human World.* Pantheon, 1996. $25.00. (NF)

Acker, Kathy. *Pussy, King of the Pirates.* Grove, 1996. $21.00. (F)

Aidoo, Ama Ata. *No Sweetness Here and Other Stories.* Feminist, 1995. Paper: $10.95. (F)

Aldiss, Brian W. *Common Clay: 20 Odd Stories.* St. Martin's, 1996. $24.95. (F)

Artaud, Antonin. *Watchfiends and Rack Screams: Works from the Final Period.* Ed. and trans. Clayton Eshleman with Bernard Bador. Exact Change, 1996. Paper: $15.95. (F/Poetry)

Bajema, Don. *Reach.* 2.13.61, 1996. Paper: $11.00. (F)

Baker, Peter. *Deconstruction and the Ethical Turn.* Univ. Press of Florida, 1995. $34.95. (NF)

Balaban, John, and Nguyen Qui Duc, eds. *Vietnam: A Traveler's Literary Companion.* Whereabouts, 1996. Paper: $12.95. (F)

Baratham, Gopal. *Moonrise, Sunset.* Serpent's Tail, 1996. Paper: $13.99. (F)

Barber, David. *The Spirit Level.* TriQuarterly, 1995. Paper: $12.95 (Poetry)

Barker, Stephen, ed. *Signs of Change: Premodern → Modern → Postmodern.* SUNY, 1996. Paper: $24.95. (NF)

Barone, Dennis. *The Returns.* Sun & Moon, 1996. Paper: $10.95. (F)

Barrett, Andrea. *Ship Fever and Other Stories.* Norton, 1996. $21.00. (F)

Beasley, Conger, Jr. *The Blood of Dead Poets.* Wordcraft of Oregon, 1996. Paper: $9.95. (F)

Becker, Jurek. *Jacob the Liar.* Trans. Leila Vennewitz. Arcade, 1996. $21.95. (F)

Birbalsingh, Frank, ed. *Frontiers of Caribbean Literature in English.* St. Martin's, 1996. Paper: $18.95. (NF)

Blanchot, Maurice. *The Most High.* Trans. Allan Stoekl. Nebraska, 1996. $35.00. (F)

Bobrowski, Johannes. *Levin's Mill.* Trans. Janet Cropper. New Directions, 1996. Paper: $12.00. (F)

Bolger, Dermot, ed. *The Vintage Book of Contemporary Irish Fiction.* Vintage, 1995. Paper: $14.00. (F)

Booker, M. Keith. *A Practical Introduction to Literary Theory and Criticism.* Longman, 1996. Paper: no price given. (NF)

Bosquet, Alain. *A Russian Mother.* Trans. Barbara Bray. Holmes & Meier, 1996. No price given. (F)

Bowering, George. *Shoot!* St. Martin's, 1996. $22.95. (F)

Breton, André. *Free Rein.* Trans. Michel Parmentier and Jacqueline d'Amboise.

Nebraska, 1996. $35.00. (NF)

Bruccoli, Matthew J., and Judith S. Baughman. *Reader's Companion to F. Scott Fitzgerald's "Tender Is the Night."* South Carolina, 1996. $29.95. (NF)

Bristow, Joseph. *Effeminate England: Homoerotic Writing after 1885.* Columbia, 1995. Paper: $15.00. (NF)

Bukowski, Charles. *Living on Luck: Selected Letters 1960s-1970s, vol. 2.* Ed. Seamus Cooney. Black Sparrow, 1995. Paper: $15.00. (NF)

Bumpus, Jerry. *The Civilized Tribes: New and Selected Stories.* Akron, 1995. Paper: no price given. (F)

Calvino, Italo. *Numbers in the Dark and Other Stories.* Trans. Tim Parks. Pantheon, 1995. $24.00. (F)

Carr, A. A. *Eye Killers.* Oklahoma, 1996. Paper: $12.95. (F)

Castillo, Ana. *My Father Was a Toltec.* Norton, 1996. Paper: $12.00. (Poetry)

Castle, Frederick Ted. *Anticipation.* McPherson, 1996. Paper: $14.00. (F)

Chernoff, Maxine. *American Heaven.* Coffee House, 1996. $21.95. (F)

Cohen, Robert. *The Here and Now.* Scribner, 1996. $22.00. (F)

D., H. *Kora and Ka.* New Directions, 1996. Paper: $7.00. (F)

Daugherty, Tracy. *What Falls Away.* Norton, 1996. $22.50. (F)

Davison, Peter. *The Fading Smile: Poets in Boston from Robert Lowell to Sylvia Plath.* Norton, 1996. Paper: $14.00. (NF)

De Grave, Kathleen. *Company Woman.* See Sharp, 1995. Paper: $11.95. (F)

Delany, Samuel R. *Silent Interviews: On Language, Race, Sex, Science Fiction, and Some Comics.* Wesleyan/New England, 1994. Paper: $16.95. (NF)

Di Piero, W. S. *Shadows Burning.* TriQuarterly, 1995. Paper: $12.95. (Poetry)

Dixon, Melvin. *Love's Instruments.* Tia Chucha, 1995. Paper: $10.95. (Poetry)

Dixon, Robert. *Writing the Colonial Adventure: Race, Gender and Nation in Anglo-Australian Popular Fiction, 1875-1914.* Cambridge, 1995. $59.95. (NF)

Donoso, José. *The Obscene Bird of Night.* Trans. Hardie St. Martin and Leonard Mades. Godine, 1995. Paper: $15.95. (F)

Doyle, Roddy. *The Woman Who Walked into Doors.* Viking, 1996. $22.95. (F)

Easton, Alison. *The Making of the Hawthorne Subject.* Missouri, 1996. $49.95. (NF)

Edwards, Paul, ed. *Volcanic Heaven: Essays on Wyndham Lewis's Painting and Writing.* Black Sparrow, 1996. Paper: $17.50. (NF)

Erhart, Margaret. *Old Love.* Steerforth, 1996. $24.00. (F)

Espada, Martín. *Imagine the Angels of Bread.* Norton, 1996. $18.95. (Poetry)

Falco, Edward. *Acid.* Notre Dame, 1996. $14.95. (F)

Faqir, Fadia. *Pillars of Salt.* Quartet, 1996. £9.00. (F)

Faulks, Sebastian. *Birdsong.* Random, 1996. $25.00. (F)

Federman, Raymond. *The Supreme Indecision of the Writer: The 1994 Lectures in Turkey.* SUNY-Buffalo Poetry/Rare Books Collection, 1995. Paper: no price given. (NF)

Felber, Lynette. *Gender and Genre in Novels without End: The British Roman-Fleuve.* Univ. Press of Florida, 1995. $39.95. (NF)

Fokkema, Douwe, and Elrud Ibsch. *Theories of Literature in the Twentieth Century.* St. Martin's, 1986 [*sic*]. Paper: no price given. (NF)

Furman, Jan. *Toni Morrison's Fiction.* South Carolina, 1996. $19.95. (NF)

Galang, M. Evelina. *Her Wild American Self.* Coffee House, 1996. Paper: $12.95. (F)

Gascoigne, David. *Michel Tournier.* Berg, 1996. Paper: $22.95. (NF)

Gättens, Marie-Luise. *Women Writers and Fascism: Reconstructing History.* Univ. Press of Florida, 1995. $39.95. (NF)

Godbout, Jacques. *The Golden Galarneaus.* Trans. Patricia Claxton. Coach House, 1996. Paper: $11.95. (F)

Gold, Jerome. *The Prisoner's Son: Homage to Anthony Burgess.* Black Heron, 1996. Paper: $11.95. (F)

Grimes, Martha. *Hotel Paradise.* Knopf, 1996. $24.00. (F)

Gummerman, Jay. *Chez Chance.* Pantheon, 1995. $21.00. (F)

Hacker, Marilyn. *Selected Poems 1965-1990.* Norton, 1995. Paper: $13.00.

———. *Winter Numbers.* Norton, 1995. Paper: $10.00. (Poetry)

Hamsun, Knut. *Dreamers.* Trans. Tom Geddes. New Directions, 1996. Paper: $9.95. (F)

———. *The Women at the Pump.* Trans. Oliver Gunnvor Stallybrass. Sun & Moon, 1996. $14.95. (F)

Hearon, Shelby. *Footprints.* Knopf, 1996. $21.00. (F)

Higgins, Lynn A. *New Novel, New Wave, New Politics: Fiction and the Representation of History in Postwar France.* Nebraska, 1996. $40.00. (NF)

Horvath, Brooke. *Consolation at Ground Zero.* Eastern Washington, 1995. Paper: $14.00. (Poetry)

Howells, Coral Ann. *Margaret Atwood.* St. Martin's, 1996. $35.00. (NF)

Hughs, Alex, and Kate Ince, eds. *French Erotic Fiction: Women's Desiring Writing, 1880-1990.* Berg, 1996. Paper: $16.95. (NF)

Ibnlfassi, Laïla, and Nicki Hitchcott, eds. *African Francophone Writing: A Critical Introduction.* Berg, 1996. Paper: $16.95. (NF)

Irving, John. *Trying to Save Piggy Sneed.* Arcade, 1996. $21.95. (F)

Kennedy, Thomas E. *Unreal City.* Wordcraft of Oregon, 1996. Paper: $11.95. (F)

Kincaid, Jamaica. *The Autobiography of My Mother.* Farrar Straus Giroux, 1996. $20.00. (F)

Lanchester, John. *The Debt to Pleasure.* Holt, 1996. $20.00. (F)

Leary, Timothy. *Surfing the Conscious Nets.* Last Gasp, 1995. Paper: $16.95. (Graphic novel)

Lee, Gus. *Tiger's Tail.* Knopf, 1996. $24.00. (F)

Malanga, Gerard. *Mythologies of the Heart.* Black Sparrow, 1996. Paper: $13.50. (Poetry)

Marek, Jayne E. *Women Editing Modernism: "Little" Magazines and Literary History.* Kentucky, 1996. $34.95; paper: $14.95. (NF)

Mason, Bobbie Ann. *Shiloh and Other Stories.* Kentucky, 1995. $18.00. (F)

Mathews, Harry. *Selected Declarations of Independence.* Sun & Moon, 1996. Paper: $10.95. (F)

McCoy, Horace. *I Should Have Stayed Home.* Serpent's Tail/Midnight Classics, 1996. Paper: $11.99. (F)

McInerney, Jay. *The Last of the Savages.* Knopf, 1996. $24.00. (F)

Meyer, Stewart. *The Lotus Crew*. Serpent's Tail/Midnight Classics, 1996. Paper: $10.99. (F)

Miller, Henry, and James Laughlin. *Selected Letters*. Ed. George Wickes. Norton, 1995. $27.50. (NF)

Morot-Sir, Edouard. *The Imagination of Reference II: Perceiving, Indicating, Naming*. Univ. Press of Florida, 1995. $49.95. (NF)

Morris, Alan. *Patrick Modiano*. Berg, 1996. Paper: $19.95. (NF)

Morrow, Bradford. *Come Sunday*. Penguin, 1996. Paper: $12.95. (F)

———. *Trinity Fields*. Penguin, 1996. Paper: $12.95. (F)

Morrow, Bruce, and Charles H. Rowell, eds. *Shade: An Anthology of Fiction by Gay Men of African Descent*. Avon, 1996. Paper: $12.00.

Murdoch, Iris. *Jackson's Dilemma*. Viking, 1996. $22.95. (F)

Nash, Susan Smith. *Mind Noir & el Siglo de Oro*. Luna Bisonte, 1995. Paper: no price given. (F)

Newman, Judie. *The Ballistic Bard: Postcolonial Fictions*. Arnold, 1996. Paper: 16.95. (NF)

Oates, Joyce Carol. *Will You Always Love Me? and Other Stories*. Dutton, 1996. $23.95. (F)

Osborn, Karen. *Between Earth and Sky*. Morrow, 1996. $23.00. (F)

Parks, Suzan-Lori. *Imperceptible Mutabilities in the Third Kingdom*. Sun & Moon, 1995. Paper: $10.95. (Drama)

Peabody, Richard, and Lucinda Ebersole, eds. *Mondo James Dean*. St. Martin's, 1996. Paper: $13.95. (F/Poetry)

Pendleton, Robert. *Graham Greene's Conradian Masterplot*. St. Martin's, 1996. $49.95. (NF)

Perez, Rolando. *The Lining of Our Souls*. Stranger Books, 1995. Paper: $5.00. (F)

Petrushevskaya, Ludmilla. *Immortal Love*. Trans. Sally Laird. Pantheon, 1996. $25.00. (F)

Phillips, Max. *Snakebite Sonnet*. Little, Brown, 1996. $22.95. (F)

Piglia, Ricardo. *Assumed Name*. Trans. Sergio Gabriel Waisman. Latin American Literary Review, 1996. Paper: $15.95. (F)

Pinter, Harold. *Collected Poems and Prose*. Grove, 1996. Paper: $11.00.

Polkinhorn, Harry. *Mount Soledad*. Left Hand, 1996. Paper: $9.00. (F)

Pope, Randolph D. *Understanding Juan Goytisolo*. South Carolina, 1995. $39.95. (NF)

Powell, Pedgett. *Edisto Revisited*. Holt, 1996. $20.00. (F)

Pruul, Kajar, and Darlene Reddaway, eds. *Estonian Short Stories*. Trans. Ritva Poom. Northwestern, 1996. Paper: $15.95. (F)

Pye, Michael. *The Drowning Room*. Viking, 1996. $22.95. (F)

Richter, David H. *Narrative/Theory*. Longman, 1996. Paper: no price given. (NF)

Roberts, Shelly. *Roberts' Rules of Lesbian Living*. Spinsters Ink, 1996. Paper: $5.95. (NF)

Roth, Martha. *Goodness*. Spinsters Ink, 1996. Paper: $10.95. (F)

Salerno, Mark. *Hate*. 96 Tears, 1995. Paper: $8.95. (Poetry)

Schaeffer, Susan Fromberg. *The Golden Rope*. Knopf, 1996. $26.00. (F)

Selvadurai, Shyam. *Funny Boy*. Morrow, 1996. $23.00. (F)

Sención, Viriato. *They Forged the Signature of God.* Trans. Asa Zatz. Curbstone, 1996. Paper: $14.95. (F)

Shearer, Cynthia. *The Wonder Book of the Air.* Pantheon, 1996. $24.00. (F)

Shields, Carol. *Small Ceremonies.* Penguin, 1996. Paper: $10.95. (F)

Skvorecky, Josef. *The Bride of Texas.* Trans. Kaca Polackova Henley. Knopf, 1996. $27.00. (F)

Soitos, Stephen F. *The Blues Detective: A Study of African American Detective Fiction.* Massachusetts, 1996. Paper: $15.95. (NF)

Spark, Debra. *Coconuts for the Saint.* Avon, 1996. Paper: $11.00. (F)

Sparling, Ken. *Dad Says He Saw You at the Mall.* Knopf, 1996. $20.00. (F)

Spoerri, Daniel. *An Anecdoted Topography of Chance.* Trans. Emmet Williams. Atlas, 1995. Paper: $19.99. (F)

Stein, Gertrude. *How to Write.* Sun & Moon, 1995. Paper: $12.95. (NF)

Steinman, Michael. *The Happiness of Getting It Down Right: Letters of Frank O'Connor and William Maxwell, 1945-1966.* Knopf, 1996. $26.00. (NF)

Strauss, Botho. *The Young Man.* Trans. Roslyn Theobald. Northwestern, 1995. $24.95. (F)

Tate, Trudi, ed. *Women, Men and the Great War: An Anthology of Stories.* St. Martin's, 1996. Paper: $19.95.

Tawfiq, Sahar. *Points of the Compass.* Trans. Marilyn Booth. Arkansas, 1995. $18.00; paper: $12.00. (F)

Thody, Philip. *Twentieth-Century Literature: Critical Issues and Themes.* St. Martin's, 1996. $39.95. (NF)

Thompson, William. *The Contemporary Novel in France.* Univ. Press of Florida, 1995. $49.95. (NF)

Van Leer, David. *The Queening of America: Gay Culture in Straight Society.* Routledge, 1995. Paper: $16.95. (NF)

Vesaas, Tarjei. *The Birds.* Trans. Torbjørn Støverud and Michael Barnes. Peter Owen/Dufour, 1996. Paper: $24.00. (F)

Wales, Dirk. *The Secret Heart of Numbers.* Sourcebooks, 1996. $16.95. (F)

Watson, Wallace Steadman. *Understanding Rainer Werner Fassbinder.* South Carolina, 1996. $39.95. (NF)

Watson, Brad. *Last Days of the Dog-Men.* Norton, 1996. $19.00. (F)

Weldon, Fay. *Worst Fears.* Atlantic Monthly, 1996. $21.00. (F)

Welsh, Irvine. *Marabou Stork Nightmares.* Norton, 1996. $21.00. (F)

Wellman, Mac. *Annie Salem: An American Tale.* Sun & Moon, 1996. Paper: $12.99. (F)

———. *The Land Beyond the Forest: "Dracula" and "Swoop."* Sun & Moon, 1995. Paper: $12.95. (Drama)

Witt, Lana. *Slow Dancing on Dinosaur Bones.* Scribner, 1996. $22.00. (F)

Wolf, Christa. *The Author's Dimension: Selected Essays.* Trans. Jan van Heurck. Chicago, 1995. $14.95. (NF)

———. *What Remains and Other Stories.* Trans. Heike Schwarzbauer and Rick Takvorian. Chicago, 1995. Paper: $14.95. (F)

Woolf, Douglas. *Fade Out.* Black Sparrow, 1996. Paper: $14.00. (F)

Zola, Émile. *The Belly of Paris.* Trans. Ernest Alfred Vitzetelly; rev. by Tracy Biga and Guy Bennett. Sun & Moon, 1996. Paper: $14.98. (F)

VQR

The Virginia
Quarterly Review

*A National Journal of
Literature and Discussion*

SPRING 1996

Volume 72, Number 2

Five Dollars
**The Virginia Quarterly Review
One West Range
Charlottesville, VA   22903**

Studies in 20th Century Literature

A journal devoted to literary theory and practical criticism

Volume 20, No. 2 (Summer, 1996)
Special Issue: The Object in France Today
Guest Editor: Martine Antle

Maryse Fauvel—Transparency and Pluralism
Dominique Fisher—From Object-images to Meta-objects
Jean-François Fourny—Fashion, Bodies, and Objects
Lawrence Schehr—Body/Antibody
Peter Shofer—What's Behind the Billboard
Monique Yaari—The Figure and the Great Divide

Essays also by:

Laurel Cummins—Reading in Colette
Barbara Klaw—On Beauvoir's *Tous les hommes sont mortels*
Elizabeth Mazza—On Redonnet's *Splendid Hôtel*
Juliette Rogers—On Colette's *La Naissance du jour*

Special Issues in preparation:
Special Issue on Contemporary German Poetry
Guest Editor: James L. Rolleston

Illness and Disease in 20th Century Literature
Guest Editor: Sander L. Gilman

Silvia Sauter, Editor
Eisenhower 104
Kansas State University
Manhattan, KS 66506-1003
  Submissions in:
    German and Russian

Marshall Olds, Editor
1111 Oldfather
University of Nebraska
Lincoln, NE 68588-0318
  Submissions in:
    French and Spanish

Subscriptions—add $5 for Air Mail
Institutions—$20 for one year ($35 for two years)
Individuals—$15 for one year ($28 for two years)

THE AMERICA AWARDS FOR LITERATURE 1995

(The "Ferns")
Instituted through a gift in memory of Anna Fahrni

INTERNATIONAL
awarded to a living writer of international stature for a body of literary writing
Harold Pinter
[England]

FICTION
awarded to the most outstanding book of fiction published in 1995
by a living American writer
Swanny's Ways, by Steve Katz
[Sun & Moon Press]
JUDGES: Will Alexander, David Bromige, Raymond Federman

POETRY
awarded to the most outstanding book of poetry published in 1995
by a living American writer
At Passages, by Michael Palmer
[New Directions]
JUDGES: Clark Coolidge, Tina Darragh, Leslie Scalapino

DRAMA
awarded to the most outstanding new play of 1995 by a living American writer
I've Got the Shakes, by Richard Foreman
[The Ontological Theater at St. Mark's Chruch, New York]
JUDGES: Shelley Berc, David Greenspan, Suzan-Lori Parks

BELLES-LETTRES AND COLLECTIONS
awarded to the most outstanding work of belles-lettres or collected or selected work
of fiction or poetry published in 1995 by an American writer
Selected Poems, by Barbara Guest
[Sun & Moon Press]
JUDGES: Lydia Davis, Jackson Mac Low, Rosmarie Waldrop

THE AMERICA AWARDS • P.O. BOX 481170 • Los Angeles, CA 90036

EPOCH

FICTION, POETRY, ESSAYS SINCE 1947

Zebra Mike gallops into Dutch rail station

ROTTERDAM, Netherlands (AP) Mar 7, 1991 -- Dutch rail commuters couldn't believe their eyes when a zebra galloped into the station instead of their morning train, a zoo spokesman says.

Vandals broke into Zebra Mike's stables at Blijdorp Zoo Tuesday and frightened the 2-year-old animal so badly that it jumped a 6-foot-high fence, spokesman Kuno Blijenberg said Wednesday.

Mike ran onto a nearby railway line and "galloped a kilometer (mile) or so along the tracks, straight into (Rotterdam) Central Station," Blijenberg said.

"You can't say he wasn't noticed," he said.

"You Can't Say He Wasn't Noticed" (from *The Annunciation Series*)
1992, 5 $^{3}/_{8}$" x 5 $^{3}/_{8}$" x $^{7}/_{8}$", mixed media, by Emoretta Yang Morris

the

Denver Quarterly

30 YEARS
of poetry, fiction,
& commentary
continuing

one year $15 ◆ 2 years $28 ◆ 3 years $35

DENVER QUARTERLY
Department of English
UNIVERSITY of DENVER
Denver CO 80208

sighted in some unexpected places

The
LITERARY
REVIEW

AN INTERNATIONAL JOURNAL OF CONTEMPORARY WRITING
285 Madison Avenue, Madison, NJ 07940

Subscriptions: $18 yearly   U.S./$21 elsewhere
Single issues: $5/$6

INTERTEXTS
IN BECKETT'S WORK et/ou
INTERTEXTES
DE L'OEUVRE DE BECKETT

Ed. by Marius Buning, Sjef Houppermans

Amsterdam/Atlanta, GA 1994. 135 pp.
(Samuel Beckett Today / Aujourd'hui 3)
ISBN: 90-5183-796-8   Hfl. 40,-/US-$ 25.-

Contents: KEIR ELAM: CATASTROPHIC MISTAKES: Beckett, Havel, the end. WOUTER OUDEMANS: EN ATTENDANT. MARY BRYDEN: BALZAC TO BECKETT VIA GOD(EAU/OT). CATHARINA WULF: AT THE CROSSROADS OF DESIRE AND CREATIVITY: A Critical Approach of Samuel Beckett's Television Plays "Ghost Trio", "...but the Clouds..." and "Nacht und Träume". ROD SHARKEY: SINGING IN THE LAST DITCH: Beckett's Irish Rebel Songs. RALPH HEYNDELS: TENACE TRACE TOUJOURS TROP DE SENS DEJA LA: Beckett, Adorno et la modernité. GIUSEPPINA RESTIVO: THE GENESIS OF BECKETT'S *ENDGAME* TRACED IN A 1950 HOLOGRAPH. SERGE MEITINGER: LA SPIRALE DE LECRITURE, D'*IGITUR* AU DERNIER BECKETT. LANCE ST. JOHN BUTLER: TWO DARKS: A Solution to the problem of Beckett's Bilingualism.

USA/Canada: Editions Rodopi, 233 Peachtree Street, N.E., Suite 404, Atlanta, GA 30303-1504, Telephone (404) 523-1964, Call toll-free 1-800-225-3998 (U.S. only), Fax (404) 522-7116
And Others: Editions Rodopi B.V., Keizersgracht 302-304, 1016 EX Amsterdam, The Netherlands. Telephone ++ (0) 20 622 75 07, Fax ++ (0) 20 638 09 48

The Literature of Politics, The Politics of Literature
Proceedings of the Leiden IASAIL Conference
General Editors: C.C. Barfoot, Theo D'haen and Tjebbe A. Westendorp

Volume 3: Tumult of Images
Essays on W.B. Yeats and Politics

Eds.: Peter Liebregts and Peter van de Kamp
Amsterdam/Atlanta, GA 1995. 249 pp.
(Costerus NS 100)

ISBN: 90-5183-779-8   Bound Hfl. 125,-/US-$ 83.-
ISBN: 90-5183-   Paper Hfl. 40,-/US-$ 27.-

By showing that the meaning of the word *politics* can be interpreted in various ways, the scope of the articles in *Tumult of Images: Essays on W.B. Yeats and Politics* is extensive. Rather than explicitly analysing W.B. Yeats's political views and opinions about social order, several of the authors demonstrate how these ideas have determined the textual strategy behind Yeats's works. Thus we find, for instance, how Yeats's politics of myth subsume the myth of politics, or how his play *The Player Queen* is an expression of sexual and textual politics. Other essays revaluate Yeats's role in Ireland's Literary Renaissance or argue that his recruitment of Homer throughout his work was politically motivated. The volume also offers an ero-political reading of Yeats's ballads next to an analysis of the strategy behind that apocalyptic idea of gyring history. *Tumult of Images* also deals with the politics of reception of Yeats's works by showing how the Irish poet has influenced South African poetry of the period of Apartheid, or by presenting the various ways in which the Japanese and the Dutch have become acquainted with the work of Yeats. The title of this volume thus reflects not only the many-sidedness of the discussions offered here but also their common contribution to an analysis of a fascinating aspect of Yeats's life and work.

USA/Canada: Editions Rodopi B.V., 2015 South Park Place, Atlanta, GA 30339, Telephone (770) 933-0027, *Call toll-free* (U.S. only) 1-800-225-3998, Fax (770) 933-9644, Internet *e-mail:* F.van.der.Zee@rodopi.nl

All Other Countries: Editions Rodopi B.V., Keizersgracht 302-304, 1016 EX Amsterdam, The Netherlands. Tel. + + 31 (0)20-622-75-07, Fax + + 31 (0)0-638-09-48, Internet *e-mail:* F.van.der.Zee@rodopi.nl

AMERICAN LITERARY TRANSLATORS ASSOCIATION

TriQuarterly

Fiction ❖ Poetry ❖ Art ❖ Criticism

THE BEST IN CONTEMPORARY LITERATURE FROM
NORTHWESTERN UNIVERSITY PRESS

A Little Hungarian Pornography
Peter Esterhazy
A kaleidoscopic digression on perversion and politics: satire and critique, trifle and tract, further support for Esterhazy's status as one of the best writers in Europe today.

THIS IS THE FRONTLINE OF HUNGARIAN LITERATURE. —TIBOR FISCHER, *THE TIMES*

The Historian: Six Fantasies of the American Experience
Eugene K. Garber

EUGENE GARBER, CASTING HIMSELF AS BOTH HERODOTUS AND NED BUNTLINE, HAS ELEVATED AMERICAN HISTORY IN THE SECOND HALF OF THE NINETEENTH CENTURY TO THE GRANDEUR OF A LEGEND ABOUT A MIGHTY CIVILIZATION OF THOUSANDS OF YEARS AGO. —KURT VONNEGUT

SPELLBINDING. —*BOOKLIST*

The Lost Scrapbook
FROM FC2 (DISTRIBUTED BY NORTHWESTERN UNIVERSITY PRESS)

Evan Dara
An experimental novel about the fragility of the environment and the delicate relationships that sustain and betray it. The Lost Scrapbook is the winner of the twelfth annual FC2/Illinois State University National Fiction Competition; this year's judge was William Vollman.

DARA SHOWS HOW A NOVEL CAN BE EXPERIMENTAL YET MORAL, RULE BREAKING BUT EMOTIONAL, AND POST-HUMANIST WHILE STILL REMAINING DEEPLY HUMAN. —RICHARD POWERS

At better bookstores everywhere, or call 1-800-621-2736

Finally available:

The Letters of Wanda Tinasky

Edited by T R Factor
Foreword by Steven Moore. Introduction by Bruce Anderson
Illustrations by Fred Sternkopf

"For Pynchon scholars, *The Letters of Wanda Tinasky* is a tantalizing document, one that should keep them busy and entertained for years."
—*Review of Contemporary Fiction*

Available only via mail order: send a check or money order
for $25.00 (which includes postage and handling) to:

VERS LIBRE PRESS
P.O. Box 2911
Portland, OR   97208-2911

NEW RELEASES

DALKEY ARCHIVE PRESS

NICHOLAS MOSLEY

Natalie Natalia

Natalie Natalia is Nicholas Mosley's brilliant examination of political life. It revolves around Anthony Greville, a conservative MP who is tormented by his ambivalence toward his career, by his religious doubts, and by his adulterous affair with Natalia Jones, the enigmatic wife of a colleague. The course of their affair dramatizes love in its most creative and perilously destructive aspects, the two facets symbolized in his lover's two names. Ranging in setting from England to Central Africa, the novel is a remarkable investigation of ethics and of fiction itself as an ethical activity. The author has revised the novel (first published in 1971) for this new edition.

"As a political parable the book is remarkable, divining and channelling some of the deepest undercurrents of our time." —Clive Jordan, *New Statesman*

"The finest novel of his career . . . a powerful and disturbing book as well as an amusing one." —*Sunday Times*

278 pages
$12.95, paper
ISBN 1-56478-086-4

FERNANDO DEL PASO

Palinuro of Mexico

This massive, encyclopedic novel is one of the most astonishing books to come out of Mexico in recent years. The original Spanish edition won the Romulo Gallegos Prize in 1977, the French translation was awarded the Prix au Meilleur Livre Etranger in 1985, and its U.S. debut is sure to draw comparisons not only to Latin American writers like Fuentes and Borges but to Joyce, O'Brien, Sterne, and Rabelais. Like these writers, del Paso draws upon myth, science, and world literature to expand his particular story to universal proportions.

Set in Mexico in the years after World War II as bureaucracy and corruption strangle its citizens, the novel satirizes advertising, politics, pornography, and mythology with Swiftian glee; at the same time, it celebrates the body with a thoroughness that only a student of medicine could manage and in language only a word-drunk novelist could command.

"Grotesque, macabre and Dionysiac . . . del Paso is a great and unorthodox writer." —*Le Monde*

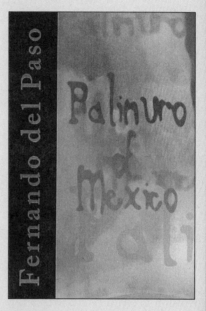

557 pp.
$14.95, paper
ISBN 1-56478-095-3

STANLEY CRAWFORD

Some Instructions to My Wife

From "Putting Things Away" to "The Marriage Almanac," Stanley Crawford gives the married, the unmarried, and the formerly married a classic satire on all the sanctimonious marriage manuals ever produced. Starting with the complete title, *Some Instructions to My Wife Concerning the Upkeep of the House and Marriage, and to My Son and Daughter Concerning the Conduct of Their Childhood,* a boorish narrator sets down some seventy-three pieces of advice to his wife, young son, and two-year-old daughter, intended to foster and maintain domestic tranquility in an age of anxiety.

"Stanley Crawford's satire on Victorian marriage manuals cheerfully lampoons male domination fantasies." —*Newsday*

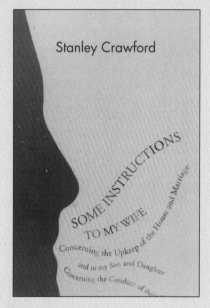

177 pages
$11.95, paper
ISBN 0-916583-15-5

JOHN BARTH

Sabbatical

Sabbatical is quintessential Barth: it
involves sailing, twinship, the joy
of love and literature, the sorrow of
death and disaster, and a playfully
complex narrative (by two narrators: perhaps the only novel ever
delivered in first-person plural).
Subtitled "a romance," the novel
combines the mysterious and mar-
velous (unexplained disappear-
ances, a fabled sea monster in
Chesapeake Bay) with romantic
love and daring adventure.

First published in 1982, *Sabbatical* is one of Barth's most accessible and affirmative novels. The
author has written a foreword for
this new edition.

"Unquestionably America's preemi-
nent practitioner of postmodernist
fiction." —*Houston Chronicle*

"The best writer of fiction in
America." —*New York Times*

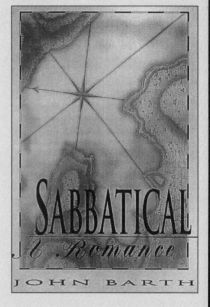

366 pages
$12.95, paper
ISBN 1-56478-096-1

DALKEY ARCHIVE PRESS

DALKEY ARCHIVE PRESS

COLEMAN DOWELL

Too Much Flesh and Jabez

This is a new edition of Coleman Dowell's "Southern Gothic," an innovative novel about sexual repression. Miss Ethel, a spinster schoolteacher, decides to write what she calls a "perverse tale" about one of her former students, a Kentucky farmer named Jim Cummins. Endowing him with unnaturally large genitals, she spins a tawdry tale of his frustrated relationship with his petite wife, which takes an unexpected turn with the appearance of a randy young teenager named Jabez, who is as intrigued by Jim's "too much flesh" as his wife is repelled.

Expressing all the bitterness of "an old woman's revenge," Miss Ethel's tale is nonetheless a surprisingly sensitive depiction of rural life in the early years of World War II. But it is Dowell's masterful use of the tale-within-a-tale convention to explore psychological states and the impulse to write that makes *Too Much Flesh and Jabez* a remarkable achievement.

"An intelligent and highly-charged erotic tale that is near impossible to put down." —*Gay Times*

160 pages
$9.95, paper
ISBN 0-916583-21-X

COLEMAN DOWELL

Island People

Considered by many to be Dowell's finest achievement, *Island People* explores John Donne's assertion "No man is an island" to find that a great many people are indeed islands. The fragmentation that results from prolonged isolation is conveyed in this complex novel by a variety of points of view, all of which originate from the nameless narrator, a gay man who has fled the city for an island retreat, his only companion a dachshund, his only occupation keeping a journal and writing stories.

"Coleman Dowell's new novel *Island People* attains a level of prose writing which is hardly distinguishable from a long, marvelously sustained narrative poem," Tennessee Williams said upon the novel's original publication in 1976. It is "the real thing," Ned Rorem said: "each page is stamped with novelty, spark, and a vague sense of grandeur, even tragedy."

309 pages
$12.95, paper
ISBN 1-56478-093-7

DALKEY ARCHIVE PRESS

STEVEN MOORE

Ronald Firbank: An Annotated Bibliography of Secondary Materials, 1905-1995

This latest volume in the Dalkey
Archive Bibliography Series gathers
and annotates virtually everything
written about this pioneering British
modernist, from his first book review in 1905 to essays that appeared
in late 1995. The bibliography also
includes a section listing other writers who have been influenced by
Firbank's work. A separate section
is devoted to materials written on
Firbank in foreign languages, giving
a well-rounded view of the critical
reception of this daring, outrageous
novelist.

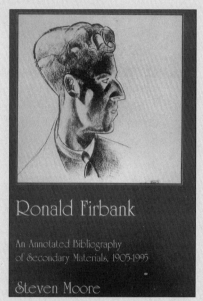

Ronald Firbank

An Annotated Bibliography
of Secondary Materials, 1905-1995

Steven Moore

xii + 154 pages
$30.00, paper
ISBN 1-56478-133-X

ALF Mac LOCHLAINN

The Corpus in the Library

An Irish cousin of Barthelme and
Borges, Alf Mac Lochlainn writes
comically erudite fictions (sometimes ludicrously illustrated) with
serious themes. *The Corpus in the
Library* is his first work of fiction
since *Out of Focus* (1977) and consists of two novellas and seven short
stories. The title novella reflects,
with a hint of revenge, the years
spent by the author consulting reference works in the learned libraries
in which it has been his duty and
privilege to serve and conceals a
mystery in its comic text. The eight
stories convey senses as different as
imprisonment and release, but they
sustain Mac Lochlainn's view of the
bicycle as the ultimate paradigm of
the triumph of humanity. Conclud-
ing the volume is another novella,
"A Narrative of the Proceedings of
the *Bounty of Nature Enterprise*,"
which retells the story of the *Bounty*
mutiny in space-travel terms in the
manner of an 18th-century travel-
ogue with overtones of the biblical
creation myth and Milton's *Paradise
Lost*. Taken as a whole, *The Corpus
in the Library* is a quirky fictional
treatment of reality, self-consciousness, perception, and time.

160 pages
$11.95, paper
ISBN 1-56478-068-6

Order Form

Individuals may deduct a 10% discount on orders of one book, or a 20% discount on orders of two books or more. Postage and handling for domestic orders is $3.50 for the first book, $.75 for each additional book; for foreign orders, $4.50 for the first, $1.00 for each additional.

Title	Quantity	Price

Subtotal_____

Less Discount_____

Subtotal_____

Postage_____

Total_____

☐ Check enclosed (payable to University of Chicago Press)

☐ Visa ☐ MasterCard

Acct no _____

Expiration date _____

Name_____

Address_____

Send orders to:
University of Chicago Press Distribution Center, 11030 S. Langley Ave.,
Chicago, IL 60628
Phone: (312) 568-1550   FAX: (312) 660-2235